News Cameras in the Courtroom:

A Free Press–Fair Trial Debate

SUSANNA BARBER

Emerson College, Boston

with
Preface by Judge Alfred T. Goodwin
and
Introduction by George Gerbner

A Volume in the Series
COMMUNICATION AND INFORMATION SCIENCE
Melvin J. Voigt, Series Editor

ABLEX PUBLISHING CORPORATION
NORWOOD, NEW JERSEY

Library of Congress Cataloging-in-Publication Data

Barber, Susanna R.
    News cameras in the courtroom.

    (Communication and information science)
    Bibliography: p.
    Includes index.
    1. Conduct of court proceedings—United States.
2. Video tapes in courtroom proceedings—United States.
3. Free press and fair trial—United States.
4. Television broadcasting of news—United States.
I. Title. II. Series.
KF8725.B37 1986   345.73′056   86–10858
ISBN 0–89391–349–9   347.30556

Ablex Publishing Corporation
355 Chestnut Street
Norwood, New Jersey 07648

CONTENTS

Acknowledgements   *viii*
Preface, *by Judge Alfred T. Goodwin*   *ix*
Introduction: Televised Trials—Historic Juncture for Our Courts?, *by George Gerbner*   *xii*

PART ONE   BACKGROUND TO THE COURTROOM CAMERAS DEBATE   *1*
1. The Hauptmann Trial   *3*
   A. Newspaper Reports   *4*
   B. Confusion in the Courtroom   *5*
   C. Crowds Outside the Courtroom   *6*
2. Oscar Hallam's Report and the Baker Committee Report   *8*
3. The American Bar Association and Canon 35   *9*
4. Early Coverage after the Passage of Canon 35   *10*
   A. Oklahoma and Kansas   *10*
   B. Waco Texas Murder Trial   *11*
   C. Colorado Sets the Example   *12*
5. A.B.A. Re-examination of Canon 35   *14*
   A. Canon 3A(7) and Proposed Revisions   *15*
   B. States Adopt New Camera Rules   *17*
   C. The A.B.A. Lifts the News Camera Ban   *19*
6. Florida's Experience with Courtroom Cameras   *20*
   A. The Ronny Zamora Trial   *20*
   B. The Noel Chandler and Robert Granger Trial   *21*
   C. The Mark Herman Trial   *22*
   D. The Theodore Bundy Trial   *24*
   E. The Arthur McDuffie Case   *24*
   F. The *Post-Newsweek* Opinion   *25*

PART TWO   CONSTITUTIONAL ISSUES AND POPULAR ARGUMENTS   *31*
1. The Presumption of Openness   *31*
2. A Public versus A Private Trial   *33*

3. The Courtroom Environment   *36*
    A. Physical Disruption   *36*
    B. Dignity and Decorum   *36*
    C. Psychological Dangers   *37*
4. Publicity and Juror Impartiality   *37*
    A. The U.S. Supreme Court's Views   *38*
    B. *Sheppard v. Maxwell*   *39*
    C. The Warren Commission and the Reardon Report   *40*
    D. The Sheppard Mandate   *41*
    E. Stemming Prejudicial Publicity   *43*
5. Access to Judicial Proceedings   *44*
6. The Right to Broadcast Audio-taped Evidence   *46*
7. Camera Access to Courtrooms   *46*
    A. *Estes v. Texas*   *47*
    B. *Chandler v. Florida*   *51*
8. Other Interpretations of Estes and Chandler   *52*
    A. The Image of the Judiciary   *53*
    B. Benefits Outweigh Risks   *54*

**PART THREE   SUMMARY AND DISCUSSION
OF THE COURTROOM CAMERAS RESEARCH**   *61*
1. Courtrooms and Communication   *62*
    A. Pretrial Stage   *63*
    B. Trial Stage   *64*
    C. Deliberation Stage   *66*
2. Video for Court Administration   *67*
3. Preface to the Analysis   *68*
4. Dignity, Decorum, Disruption, and Fairness   *69*
    A. Judges   *69*
    B. Attorneys   *69*
    C. Jurors   *72*
    D. Witnesses   *72*
    E. Court Personnel   *72*
5. Impacts on Jurors   *72*
    A. Jurors   *72*
    B. Attorneys   *73*
    C. Judges, Witnesses, and Court Personnel   *73*
6. Impacts on Witnesses   *74*
    A. Witnesses   *74*
    B. Jurors   *74*
    C. Attorneys   *75*
    D. Judges   *75*

7. Impacts on Judges   *75*
   A. Judges   *75*
   B. Attorneys   *76*
   C. Jurors, Witnesses, Court Personnel, and Spectators   *76*
8. Impacts on Attorneys   *77*
   A. Attorneys   *77*
   B. Judges   *78*
   C. Jurors, Court Personnel, and Witnesses   *78*
9. Impacts on Defendants and Litigants   *78*
10. Impacts on Court Personnel   *79*
11. Types of Proceedings that Attracted Media Coverage   *80*
12. Conduct of Media Personnel   *81*
13. Judicial Discretion and Guidelines   *82*
14. Negative Attitudes of Attorneys and Judges   *83*
15. Still versus Video Cameras   *84*
16. Attitude Change due to Greater Experience   *85*
17. Transferral of Impacts   *86*
18. Discussion of the Courtroom Cameras Research   *86*
19. Limitations of the Courtroom Cameras Research   *88*
20. Some Mitigating Factors   *89*
21. Suggestions for New Research   *90*
22. Questions for Social Scientists and the Courts   *92*

**PART FOUR   FOCUS CHANGES FROM THE COURTROOM TO THE
AUDIENCE**   *95*
1. The Proposed Benefits of Televised Trials   *95*
   A. Education About Judicial Process   *95*
   B. A Deterrent to Criminals   *96*
   C. Restoring Confidence in the Courts   *97*
2. The Potential Risks   *98*
3. The Risks to Witnesses   *99*
   A. Privacy and Coverage of Sensitive Cases   *99*
   B. Disclosing Victim Identity: The Big Dan's Rape Case   *100*
   C. Witness Protection   *101*
4. The Risks to Viewers: The Wayne Williams Case   *110*
5. The Risks to Defendants   *112*
   A. A Form of "Pillory By Publicity"   *112*
   B. Hounding Defendants: The Claus von Bulow Case   *113*
   C. Publicity About Defendants   *114*
6. Weighing Proposed Benefits against Potential Risks   *116*
   A. Learning About Crime, Criminals and the Courts   *116*
   B. Potential for Increased Prejudice Against Defendants   *117*

7. Conclusions   *119*

Bibliography   *127*

Author Index   *151*
Subject Index   *157*

To B.B. who knows why . . .

ACKNOWLEDGMENTS

My work would not be complete without acknowledging the interest and kind support of the following people: Denise Trauth and John Huffman for encouraging me to pursue this topic of research; Mel Voigt for waiting so patiently for the final manuscript; Judge Alfred Goodwin for suggesting new sources and prefacing the book with his legal insight; Dr. George Gerbner for asking to review the manuscript and for providing his expert introductory comments; John Rockwell at the National Center for State Courts for keeping me updated on the latest courtroom camera rules; Rolf Kaltenborn at the Kaltenborn Foundation for funding portions of my research in 1981, 1984, and 1985; and J.G., R.M., and J.F. for lifting my spirits while I was writing the text.

Thanks also to the journals *Communications and the Law, Journalism Quarterly, Judicature,* and *Justice System Journal* for allowing previously published articles of mine to be adapted for use in this book.

PREFACE

Alfred T. Goodwin

Circuit Judge
United States Court of Appeals for the Ninth Circuit

For at least half a century, the idea of news cameras in courtrooms has been a program topic at countless meetings of lawyers, news professionals, and public interest groups. Perhaps, like the law of torts, the law of photography and broadcasting is still developing. This book sheds substantial light on the subject, and better yet, clears away some of the misinformation that abounds.

The traditional position of the bar is forthrightly proclaimed in the words of Federal Rule of Criminal Procedure 53:

> The taking of photographs in the court room during the progress of judicial proceedings or radio broadcasting of judicial proceedings from the court room shall not be permitted by the court.

This rule was adopted in 1946. Between 1937 and 1972, Canon 35 of the American Bar Association's standards of judicial conduct provided that all photography and broadcasts in courtrooms should be prohibited. In 1972 the wording was changed, but the substance was not materially altered. See Code of Judicial Conduct 3 A(7). The news media, and the television industry in particular, did not cease to challenge the ABA rule, and in 1978 the conference of State Chief Justices approved a resolution to allow the highest court of each state to promulgate standards and guidelines regulating radio, television, and other photographic coverage of court proceedings (see Part One). By 1981, when the Supreme Court considered, and rejected, a defense proposition that Florida's permissive television coverage of a criminal trial constituted a denial of due process, 19 states were permitting some form of television in their courtrooms. See *Chandler v. Florida*, 449 U.SD. 560, 565 (1981).

Following the *Chandler* decision, and somewhat emboldened by technical improvements that had reduced the size of cameras and the amount of supplemental light needed to transmit a picture, the television industry asked the Judicial Conference of the United States to reconsider Rule 53 and its flat denial of television entry into the courtrooms. A committee of judges made an extensive study of the matter in 1983. After viewing sample broadcast techniques and consulting among themselves, the committee recommended against a change. The federal courts, accoridngly, remain closed both to television and still photography, to the apparent satisfaction of a majority of the judges, a significant element of the trial bar, and some observers of television news performance when television attempts to cover courts.

Critics of television in the courts note that because of time constraints, "gavel to gavel" coverage is virtually unworkable. They suggest that, except for trials which possess extraordinary voyeuristic appeal, coverage is economicall uninviting. Whatever may be the reasons, it does appear that even in the states where cameras are permitted in the courtrooms, the public sees little of the product on the evening news. More often the viewer sees only a few seconds of a picture of a judge and a witness, or a lawyer, or a scan of a jury box, with a voice-over by an announcer, giving a brief summary of what allegedly happened during the day in court. Some law professionals remain unconvinced that this type of coverage of the courts provides enough public education to balance the perceived institutional costs of allowing the cameras in the courtroom. The costs most commonly mentioned include added administrative burdens on the judge and an extra ingredient of worry to the lawyers. Critics express the fear that selectivity of the few minutes chosen for broadcast will distort or conceal what the jurors saw and heard. This book deals with these and other perceived costs, and points the way toward useful further studies (see Part Three).

One of the concerns noted in various studies of extended television coverage of trials is that jurors may go home at night and see and hear once again the evidence that they saw and heard during the day. This kind of emphasis by repetition and its ad hoc selection, some observers fear, can distort the fact-finding function, or at least introduce into it a wild card that can be controlled only by sequestration. Sequestration is a word that rolls easily off the tongues of the media representatives, but it rings warning bells for judges and jurors.

Experienced judges tend to agree that jurors are almost painfully conscientious about paying attention to the judge's instructions. Jurors try to avoid talking about the case. Jurors try not to commit other errors about which they have been warned. But if jurors are to be routinely sequestered in long and complicated criminal trials (the kind television seems most avid to cover), then the surface has not yet been disturbed in the lengths to which potential jurors will go in order to avoid service. It is bad enough for jurors to give up family vacations and business trips with spouses and to more or less cheerfully pay the other personal costs of long trials, without being shut up in hotel rooms without television. Sequestration also may go hard on future defendants whose colorful lifestyle and even more colorful means of terrorizing their victims result in wholesale sequestration orders so that the public may be entertained.

This volume examines the available studies in the whole fascinating area of cameras in court, and finds many of them wanting. The published material relies heavily on opinions and perceptions (see Part Three). There is understandably little hard evidence about what television has done (or will do) either to explain the justice process or to skew it. For example, the book raises the intriguing question of whether televised trials might result in longer sentences than would follow untelevised trials (see Part Four). No one really knows.

Another imponderable is the effect upon race relations in urban television markets where the number of defendants of one race may appear to be disproportionate to their number in the viewing community. No one really knows.

The manipulation of television outside the courtroom has recently been devleoped into a subspecialty of the public relations industry. Some lawyers have become celebrities as the result of their daily press conferences on the courthouse steps during protracted criminal trials from which cameras were excluded. The 1985 DeLorean case in Los Angeles provides a notorious example. A useful field of inquiry might include some study of the role of counsel in utilizing the media in aid of their clients, whether the client is the prosecutor or the prosecuted. Some judges say that the full utilization of First Amendment privileges is a duty owed by the lawyer to the client. English judges, and some American judges, still think the courtroom is the proper place to bring out the evidence.

INTRODUCTION: TELEVISED TRIALS—HISTORIC JUNCTURE FOR OUR COURTS?

George Gerbner

When state courts admit cameras into the courtroom, they set out on a road whose course and destination no one really knows or can foresee. Some think it leads to enlightenment and needed reform. Others fear that it represents an historic turning point, making the administration of justice dependent on entertainment values and media power in ways that are very different from the constitutionally protected functions of journalistic reporting.

Until now, there has been no handbook of well-organized intelligence on the subject, no road map to sort out the opportunities and hazards ahead. This book is such a road map; it helps chart a journey that has already begun but has not yet been fully understood or assessed. Those alert to the twists and turns and crossroads that will mark that journey will be equipped to take advantage of its opportunities and avoid its hazards. My purpose in this introduction is to highlight the historic significance of these choices and to sketch some of the issues and choice points— many also expertly handled in later chapters of this book—from the perspective of our own research on the subject.

HISTORIC JUNCTURE

Proponents claim that television coverage is desirable because conveying real courtroom procedure to millions of homes will enhance public understanding and reduce misconceptions about the administration of justice without necessarily interfering with what goes on within the courtroom. They contend that the addition of cameras enriches conventional reporting. They point to intense public interest in certain trials, to dissatisfaction with courts, and to the need for exposure and reform as added reason for admitting cameras into the courtroom (see Parts Two and Four).

Opponents agree that new cameras and unobtrusive equipment need not overtly interfere with the conduct of trials. But they argue that transporting the sights and sounds of courtroom behavior into a pulbic arena is a qualitative change and not merely journalistic enrichment. They question whether televising selected trials of great audience appeal improves responsible reporting, enhances public understanding, or hastens needed court reform. They are concerned that the audio-visual element may only enhance dramatic appeal, override journalistic considerations, contribute to the pressures for popular rather than fair and dispassionate courtroom behavior, inhibit rather than assist the exposure of less visible needs and problems, and, in general, transform television reporting into a dramatic spectacle (see Parts Two and Four).

Although most state courts have admitted cameras on a temporary or permanent basis, the Judicial Conference of the federal courts has rejected a media petition to do so. Furthermore, after an initial period of experience, and the systematic assessment of long-range consequences, state courts may wish to review their stand. This book will help provide the basis for making that judgment.

What are my reasons for believing that the issue of television cameras in the courtroom (and especially in ongoing criminal trials) is one of historic significance? Let me start with the question of the public image of the courts and then go on to discuss the dynamics of television as the context in which the issue has to be seen.

The public's expectations of and assumptions about the legal system define the political climate in which judicial policies are developed and applied. A study on "The Public Image of Courts" conducted by Yankelovich, Skelley and White, Inc., for the National Center for State Courts, found that most people cite formal education and the media as their primary sources of information about courts. Direct experience with courts (whether as juror, witness, spectator, or defendent, and so on) is claimed by relatively few people. This study reveals that courts are the least known and understood branch of government. For example: 37 percent of the public believe that a person accused of a crime must prove his/her innocence; 30 percent believe that a district attorney's job is to defend criminals who are unable to afford a lawyer; and 72 percent believe that the U.S. Supreme Court can review and reverse any state court decision (see Part Four). Clearly, there is a need for better communication about the courts.

However, before we conclude that televised trials can best address that need, we should consider the nature of television and its dynamics.

THE DYNAMICS OF TELEVISION

Television is our nation's most common and constant learning environment, the mainstream of our culture. In the typical American home, the set is on for more than

7 hours each day, engaging its audience in a ritual most people perform with great regularity.

Though television is only one source of citizens' knowledge about courts and law, it may well be the single most common and pervasive source of *shared* information and imagery. Our own reserach at the University of Pennsylvania's Annenberg School of Communications has found that typical viewers of prime time dramatic network programs will see 43 law enforcers, 6 lawyers, and 3 judges every week—all ficitonal but realistically portrayed. They nearly all work on criminal cases, mostly murder, and succeed in bringing the criminal to justice. The legal process is practically invisible on crime programs and largely mythical on courtroom drama. Viewers rarely see arraignments, indictments, pre-trial hearings, plea-bargaining, jury selection, or jury deliberations. While crime programs generally support the idea of compliance and the ideology of law, there is also the message that illegal activities by the police (constitutional violations and police brutality) are justified.

Our research has found that the amount of time people spend with television makes an independent contribution to their conceptions of social reality. When other factors, such as education and socioeconomic status, are held constant, heavy viewers of television hold beliefs and assumptions that parallel television portrayals more closely than do those of light viewers. Viewing tends to cultivate beliefs that have serious implications for the administration of justice in general and defendents' rights to a fair trial in particular. These beliefs include relatively high levels of apprehension and mistrust (what we call the "mean world" syndrome) and a relatively "hard line" approach to personal rights.

The vastly inflated incidence of violence and crime coupled with the clean, swift, and unerring justice of the television world already build expectations that may contribute to frustration and impatience with the courts. Would cameras in the courtroom alleviate or amplify that trend (see Part Four)? Studies conducted so far indicate that those who rely on what television presents are more likely than others to blame the court system for crime and to approve harsher punishment, warrantless searches, use of illegally obtained evidence, and other violations of due process. These influences may have contributed to the Roper Poll findings (Report 81-3 and 82-3) that the proportion of those who believe that the courts have been "too easy" on criminals increased from 52 percent in 1967 to 83 percent in 1981, and that "permissiveness in the courts" was named as the leading "major cause of the country's problems" (by 53 percent in 1982 compared to 39 percent in 1973).

These trends take on added significance when we contemplate the appeal of "real life" trials using courtrooms as program origination locations, selected and edited to the specifications of already existing programming of proven audience and ratings drawing power. The stakes become very high indeed. How can (and why should) broadcasters resist the pressures of the marketplace and the rewards of higher ratings? These are some of the questions readers of this book will want to pose, and questions this book will help them consider.

POLICY ISSUES

A broad range of policy issues has also been raised in discussions of the impact of television technology on courtroom procedures and judicial processes, all fully explored in this volume. One early argument against broadcast coverage was that television equipment is bulky, distracting, and cumbersome. But today, the advances in broadcast technology are such that the required equipment can be light, compact, and unobtrusive (see Part Two).

A related concern of critics is that knowledge that a trial is being televised may be psychologically distracting to witnesses, jurors, attorneys, or even the presiding trial judge. The Supreme Court in *Chandler* reviewed the existing evidence and concluded that there was as yet not enough support for claims of psychological distraction due solely to television. The broader issue the Court did not address is that "psychological distraction" need not be confined to the courtroom. The knowledge that "the whole world is watching," including one's neighbors, peers, constituents, friends, and enemies may be sufficient "distraction" to overwhelm primary concern with what goes on in the courtoom (see Part Two). Judges and prosecutors are often elected (and may aspire to other offices), and defense attorneys may utilize the exposure to enhance their private practice. In short, television trials will offer courtroom participants a powerful medium for exposure and possible gain—or loss. How do jurors, witnesses, and all other participants adjust to their new roles as players in a real-life courtroom drama piped into millions of homes for viewers brought up on Perry Mason, anxious for morally satisfying instant solutions and fed up with what appear to be legal quibbling, obstruction, and delay?

At the next level of concern is the possibility that extensive television coverage may damage a defendant's ability to obtain a fair trial. Of course, this is potentially true of any form of publicity, whether printed or broadcast, and whether emanating from within the courtroom or outside of it. The critical issue is not the just *amount* of courtroom coverage, but whether television from within the courtroom might be qualitatively as well as quantitatively different from television coverage without cameras in the courtroom (see Parts Two and Three). Reporting can synthesize, summarize, go behind the scenes to the essence of things. Cameras record opaque appearances, arguably the least illuminating and potentially most prejudicial aspects of a trial, and, given time limitations, possibly at the expense of balanced analysis. Will we make defendents guinea pigs in an uncontrolled experiment, and at what cost to justice and future litigation?

Next we come to the issue of broadcaster performance. Do news directors and network programmers select and edit trials and scenes from trials with legal principles or audience appeal in mind? Have the sensational trials that have been televised resulted in fairer verdicts and better understanding of due process, besides the undeniable notoriety of the participants?

Finally, we reach the broadest level of concern. Beyond the pressures, opportunities, risks, and stakes involved in courtroom behavior and broadcaster performance is the issue of impact on public perceptions (see Part Four). How does broadcaster control of public perceptions relate, if at all, to the mission of the courts? Even with the best of intentions, does the addition of sights and sounds and the spectacular aspects of certain trials change the nature of the coverage, and, if so, does the difference tend to correct or confirm and legitimize the mythology of the courtroom and other public misconceptions?

The basic policy issue behind these questions is not the freedom of the media to report matters of interest to the public. Broadcast journalists can attend and report trials as can other reporters. The policy question concerns the compatibility of the mission of the courts and the uses of cameras in courtrooms.

The courts, unlike other branches of government, have a limited and sharply defined mission whose performance does not require a public showcase or arena. That mission is to try cases according to law. The mission of the broadcaster is to succeed as a business by catering to, and, if necessary, exploiting, popular tastes. The basic public issue is, therefore, whether linking courts to television will enhance or diminish the integrity and independence of our administration of justice. This book illuminates many facets of that basic issue. It is an indispensable guide to all those involved with the courts, with the media, and with a concern for justice, as we confront the difficult choices on the road that lies ahead.

PART ONE

BACKGROUND TO THE COURTROOM CAMERAS DEBATE

The question of whether news cameras should be allowed in courtrooms has been a controversial issue for nearly 70 years. As early as 1917, the Illinois Supreme Court advised state courts not to allow still or newsreel photography of trials in its opinion in *People v. Munday*.[1] Taking the issue a step further, in 1925, at the request of the Chicago Bar Association, 45 judges voted unanimously to ban cameras from inside and from the vicinity of courtrooms (Kielbowicz, 1979, p. 15). This decision, however, did not disturb Judge John T. Raulston, who presided at the Scopes "Monkey" trial in Dayton, Tennessee, that same year. Judge Raulston not only permitted camera coverage of the trial, but welcomed radio coverage as well.[2]

The trial of John T. Scopes, a Kentucky school teacher, began on July 10, 1925, and lasted nine days. The case was a challenge to the Butler Act, a Tennessee statute which prohibited the teaching of any evolution theory that denied the Biblical version of the Divine Creation. The penalty for the offense was a fine of $100 to $500. According to James Wesolowski (1975, p. 76), the Butler Act may never have been challenged were it not for the avaricious ideas of a group of Dayton businessmen and civic leaders:

> It was agreed among them that a courtcase testing the Butler Act would provide a number of benefits. Motivations varied, but the test case was planned at least partly as a type of public relations gimmick, which would tend to bring business to the small town and, in effect, put Dayton on the map.

Along with, or even in spite of, the maneuverings of publicity hungry businessmen and civic dignitaries, the case was bound to attract public and press interest once it was announced that the trial attorneys would be William Jennings Bryan, three-time Democratic presidential nominee, for the prosecution, and Clarence Darrow, a well-known Chicago lawyer, for the defense. Newspaper reporters and photographers were present inside and outside the courtroom, and several photographs were taken during the proceedings, including one of Clarence Darrow addressing the court on July 10, 1925; another of John Scopes standing before the judge as he was sentenced; and one of a courtroom scene with members of the jury in the foreground (Settle, 1972).

WGN, Chicago, was awarded broadcasting rights partly by historical accident. Wesolowski found the explanation for this in the memoirs of Quin Ryan, the only remote broadcast announcer at the Scopes trial:

> The courthouse was almost a hundred years old . . . and the city fathers were afriad it would collapse from the multitide that seemed to be interested in coming there. . . . The courtroom was on the second floor, and it was kind of shaky. It wasn't unsafe for daily routines, but it would be unsafe for the mob that would rush the thing.
>
> Station WGN received the broadcasting privilege . . . by agreeing to wire up five places in the town with loudspeakers to accommodate the vast throngs who might endanger the old building (Wesolowski, 1975, p. 77, citing Ryan).

Ryan's recollections also attested to the atmosphere of the proceedings, and apparently there were no radio theatrics on the part of the trial participants. In fact, there was an almost total lack of interest on the part of the famous participants to get on the air, mainly because they thought the proceedings were only being broadcast within a 20 mile radius of the courthouse (Wesolowski, 1975, p. 79, citing Ryan).

In contrast to Judge Raulston's attitude during the Scopes trial, Judge Eugene O'Dunne, presiding at a Maryland murder trial in 1927, explicitly prohibited photography in the courtroom and its precincts. When a photographer took seven pictures, two of which were published, Judge O'Dunne began contempt proceedings against five Baltimore newspapermen (Kielbowicz, 1979, p. 16). In *Ex Parte Sturm* (1927),[3] the Maryland Court of Appeals affirmed the contempt citations and held that prohibiting news cameras at trials was not a denial of First Amendment rights. Interestingly, though, the trial judge's contempt citations were prompted more out of resentment that his authority had been ignored by the photographers, than by the actual photographic coverage. The cameramen were apparently so noiseless that the judge was not even aware photographs had been taken until the pictures were published. The appeals court affirmed the paramount authority of the trial judge despite the lack of disruption from the cameras. *Sturm* thus confirmed judicial discretion as the sole reason necessary for the exclusion of cameras (Goldman and Larson, 1978, pp. 2007–2008, and fn. 41).

For the next 10 years, judicial feeling about courtroom cameras remained inconsistent. Some judges banned cameras entirely, others allowed cameras to cover trials on a case-by-case basis, and still others applied an open-door policy in their courtrooms. In 1931, a judge presiding at a murder trial dismissed a juror's complaint that photography was distracting, and told the court that publicity is the key to safe administration of justice. And the judge presiding at a 1933 Oklahoma City kidnapping trial emphasized the public's constitutional rights to see trials, in person and in pictures, as well as to read about them (Kielbowicz, 1979, pp. 16–17). It was not until the 1935 spectacular trial of Bruno Richard Hauptmann,[4] accused of kidnapping and murdering the infant son of world famous aviator Charles Lindbergh, that the American Bar Association decided to take sweeping action against cameras in the courtroom.

1. THE HAUPTMANN TRIAL

Judge Thomas W. Trenchard, who presided at the Flemington, New Jersey, trial, allowed four photographers to take still pictures three times a day—just before the court convened in the morning, during the noon recess, and after the court adjourned in the afternoon. The judge also applied these restrictions to newsreel cameramen, who were allowed to place a silent camera on the floor of the courtroom, and sound cameras in the courtroom balcony (see Kielbowicz, 1979, p. 18; Reed, 1967, p. 4; Hallam, 1940, p. 461).

In the aftermath of the trial, direct blame for the carnival atmosphere of the proceedings was placed on still photographers and newsreel cameramen who attended the courtroom sessions. Such an accusation, however, failed to make two important distinctions: first, between "camera" disruptions, if any, which took place *inside* the courtroom, *during the trial* sessions, rather than those which may have occurred *outside* the courtroom or *during recesses;* and second, between the carnival atmosphere created by a variety of disruptive elements both inside and outside the courtroom, but not specifically the photographers and cameramen. First-hand reports about the so-called media circus created at the trial have been conflicting. Malcolm C. Bauer, associate editor of the Portland *Oregonion,* told the Montana Bar Association in 1958 that the courtroom scene was a "Roman Holiday" at which "photographers clambered on counsel's table and shoved their flashbulbs into the faces of witnesses" (see Kielbowicz, 1979, p. 19; Hoyt, 1978, p. 29; Reed, 1967, p. 17).[5] Joseph Costa, a founder and past president of the National Press Photographers Association, has a very different recollection. He was at the Hauptmann trial taking pictures for the New York *Daily News,* and lived in Flemington for the duration of the trial. His description of events clearly differentiates between the role played by photographers and other elements in generating the circus-like atmosphere:

> it was not the action of photographers, *per se,* but the very nature of the entire story that created the conditions that prompted such a characterization ["Roman Holiday"] and which was unfairly blamed on photographers (Reed, 1967, p. 5; see also Platte, 1981, p. 14).

Walter Lister, managing editor of the Philadelphia *Evening Bulletin,* was also present throughout the trial and has said that "no pictures (with one exception) were taken during the sessions and that in no way did photographers interrupt the proceedings" (Reed, 1967, p. 1). In fact, there was only one confirmed violation of Judge Trenchard's rules perpetrated by the newsreel cameramen, and only one violation perpetrated by a still photographer (another photographer took a picture while the court was in session, but was unaware of the Judge's rules). Furthermore, the sound movie camera was so unobtrusive and quiet that neither the judge nor the trial participants and observers were aware that it had been rolling for several days, until some of the footage was released. The still photography violation took place on the last day of the trial, and involved a picture of the jury announcing its verdict. Again, though, the photographer did not disturb the proceedings, since it was not known that the photograph had been taken until it was published the next day (see Kielbowicz, 1979, p. 19; Hoyt, 1978, p. 29; Reed, 1967, pp. 4–5).

Further testifying to the lack of disruption caused specifically by cameras *inside* the courtroom, Margaret Marshall (1935, p. 94) noted:

> there are now four cameramen stationed in court who are allowed to take pictures when the judge is off the bench. These "inside" men take their plates to a photograph pool in a former bakery shop where they are developed in an improvised dark room. Each newspaper or press service gets a full set of all successful pictures.

Marshall later described the hundred or so photographers *outside* the courthouse who did not pool their pictures, but she clearly indicates that since there was a pooling arrangement for photographs of the trial participants, there was no need for hoards of cameramen to be *inside* the courtroom. An article published in the *Christian Century,* February 27, 1935, adds credence to Marshall's and others' reports that photographers attending the trial were not obstreperous:

> There were no photographers ordering witnesses how to pose while on the stand. . . . When the news-reels disobeyed the judge's instructions and made public films of the actual trial the judge disciplined the offending cameramen quickly (Flemington Aftermath, 1935, p. 265).

But while Judge Trenchard was quick to admonish the photographers who violated his orders, he did nothing to prevent highly inflammatory newspaper reports about the case, and nothing to silence the attorneys and other trial participants who made numerous out-of-court statements to the press. As Hallam (1940, p. 462) noted: "Long before and during the trial there was a perfect riot of lurid publicity."

A. Newspaper Reports

There were nearly 700 newspapermen, including 129 cameramen, in Flemington during the trial, and over one million words a day were transmitted over 45 internationally connected telegraph, telephone, and teletype wires (Hallam, 1940, p. 454). The newspaper publicity was often stacked heavily against the defendant. Before the trial, headlines were damning: "Clues build an iron-clad case against Bruno, police claim;" "Bruno guilty but has aids, verdict of man in street." During the trial, pictures helped to illustrate the carnival atmosphere of the proceedings with headlines like: "Bruno witness blasts link to ladder wood"; "Wilentz traps witness in her own testimony"; "Hauptmann shows signs of cracking"; "Bruno alibi pierced"; "Hauptmann's case crumbles." On January 29, 1935, the *New York Post* sunk to the lowest depths of all when it described Hauptmann on the stand as "a thing lacking in human characteristics" (Hallam, 1940, p. 486).[6]

The attorneys offered their own highly charged analyses of the trial's progress to the press. Counsel for both sides held regular press conferences, hinting at testimony yet to come and commenting on what had already been heard (Hallam, 1940, p. 460). Highly prejudicial interviews were also granted by key witnesses, and even the defendant, in a state of panic and confusion, gave statements to the press (Hallam, 1940, p. 500). In January 1935, a writer for *Literary Digest* noted:

> Beginning weeks before the trial opened they [counsel] yielded to the pressure for publicity by disclosing the witnesses and the evidence to be presented, criticizing one another's tactics, and in general fulminating on the guilt or innocence of the accused. During the progress of the trial they have discussed with reporters after each session the value of the testimony given, even issuing statements on the subject (At the Observation Post, 1935, p. 11).

During his summation, Prosecutor David T. Wilentz branded Hauptmann as "an animal" and "Public Enemy No. 1 of the world," in front of the jury, the press, and the public in the courtroom (Appeal at Trenton, 1935). Even members of the press, who stood to gain readers by printing such inflammatory remarks, were shocked by the trial's degradation of justice.[7] The *Christian Century* commented:

> In this case it is probably true that the press overplayed its part. . . . But the real protection against a whipping up of the mob spirit lies far more in the hands of the courts than elsewhere.
> It is well within the range of possibility that half a dozen judges, presiding over important criminal trials, could by a wise and determined use of their powers to speed action, hold for perjury charges, and punish for contempt of court, change the entire atmosphere of American criminal proceedings in a few brief months (Flemington Aftermath, 1935, pp. 265–266).

None of these suggestions had been utilized by Judge Trenchard. In fact, as became more and more apparent after the close of the trial, the judge's lack of control over his courtroom had nothing to do with the (legendary) abuses of photographers. Almost a year after the trial ended, Richard Knight commented scathingly in *The Forum* that the trial took place "in the midst of a mob of peanut eaters in an atmosphere suggestive of a cockfight rather than a court" (Knight, 1936, p. 8; see also Martin, 1978, p. 853).

B. Confusion in the Courtroom

The trial began on January 2, 1935, and the verdict was returned on February 14, 1935. Two days after the trial began, the record showed that the courtroom was filled with laughter on several occasions, prompting the judge to warn: "Unless it is stopped, I shall have to have the courtroom cleared" (Hallam, 1940, p. 456). In fact, the courtroom was so noisy that the judge could not hear the counsel, and had to ask for questions to be repeated. But again, on January 7, 9, 18, 21, 24, and 28, the trial record showed that the courtroom was filled with laughter, and even applause. On January 18, for example, the judge announced: "There seems to be a coterie of ladies . . . who spend a very considerable part of the time in giggling and laughing" (Hallam, 1940, p. 456). On January 21, with laughter still persisting, the judge warned the court officers that they were being negligent in their duties to restrain such behavior among the spectators. He noted that, instead of sitting in the back of the court, they should move into the main throng of the room "where this confusion and laughter arises about every fifteen minutes" (Hallam, 1940, p. 457). On January 28, the court clerk announced that he could not poll the jury because they could not hear him (Hallam, 1940, p. 457). This type of rowdy atmosphere reigned throughout the trial.

The courtroom, with a maximum seating capacity of 260, was packed with some 275 spectators and witnesses, 135 newspaper and wire reporters, the attorneys and court bailiffs and, for part of the time, a panel of 150 jurors (Hallam, 1940, p. 478):

> The crowd was swelled by the use of subpoenas issued ostensibly to witnesses but in reality to friends seeking a place in the little courtroom, which was barely large enough to accommodate the newspaper reporters present in addition to the necessary functionaries in the room. *More than a hundred subpoenas were issued in one day"* (Hallam, 1940, pp. 458–459 emphasis added).

People stood on tables, in the aisles, at the back of the courtroom, and in the entrance to the courtroom gallery; they leaned against walls, perched on window sills, craned over balcony rails, and peered through doorways (Hallam, 1940, pp. 457–459). On January 28, 1935, the New York *Daily Mirror* reported that the fourth courtroom window had been broken by the spectators crammed onto the window sills (cited by Hallam, 1940, p. 481).

C.   Crowds Outside The Courtroom

Outside the courtroom things were equally chaotic. Eye witness reports estimated the crowds in the town of Flemington to be 20,000 strong each day (Hallam, 1940, p. 459). Throngs of over 300 people deluged the courthouse daily, congesting its hallways, and even breaking its glass entrance doors in an effort to get a glimpse of the trial in progress (Hallam, 1940, pp. 459, 482). Newspaper headlines reflected the atmosphere all too well: "The Flemington Circus—This Way to the Big Tent"; "It's a Sideshow, a Jamboree . . ."; "It's a Holiday, a Freak Show, For Thousands Laughingly Gathered to See a Man Fight Desparately for His Life" (Hallam, 1940, pp. 485–486).

Charles Lindbergh was a hero of international acclaim, so it is hardly surprising that a case involving him and his family would be such a highly sensational event. As with the Scopes trial in Dayton, Tennessee, townsfolk in Flemington, New Jersey were delighted with the increased business that the trial attracted. Hotels were packed; restaurants did a roaring trade with "Lindberg steaks" and "Hauptmann beans"; souvenir vendors sold miniature wooden ladders (a reminder of the ladder used to gain access to the Lindberg house); and, on Sundays, 4,000 sightseers flowed through the courtroom, escorted by tour guides (see At the Observation Post, 1935, p. 11; Both Guilty, 1935, p. 62; Flemington Aftermath, 1935, p. 264; Marshall, 1935, p. 93). In February 1935, *The New Republic* made the following assessment of the trial turned public spectacle:

> In the Hauptmann trial both the defendant and society were found guilty. The best thing one can say of it is that it is over. It was a microcosm showing us many of the faults of our system of justice—and indeed, of our society as a whole—in one vivid and humiliating example (Both Guilty, 1935, p. 62).

But as outrageous as the theatricality of the trial became, one thing is clear: the presence of cameras and news photographers inside the courtroom were not, in and of themselves, responsible for the undecorous tone of the trial proceedings. As several reports corroborate, both the still and newsreel photographers complied closely with Judge Trenchard's prohibitions of picture-taking during the trial. There is little evidence to substantiate the myth of a media circus *while the trial was in session*. The only violations of the judge's ruling were the operation of a sound-movie camera on one occasion and the taking of a still photograph on another, and in both instances the operation of equipment was so quiet and unobtrusive that no one in the court-room knew the film or photograph was being shot.

The so-called "Roman holiday" that existed during the trial was perpetrated, instead, by the prejudicial and notorious nature of the publicity accompanying the case, including statements made by the attorneys, witnesses, and police; the rowdy behavior of over 200 spectators crammed into the courtroom; the 700 or so reporters who descended on the town; and by neglectful court officials who allowed "intui-tions of the mob" to create a "judicial lynching" (Knight, 1936, p. 10). As Reed (1967, p. 5) has pointed out, "photographers at the Hauptmann trial were guilty *by association*" only (emphasis added), and in view of this observation, the ABA's rationale for banning courtroom cameras appears somewhat spurious, as Kielbowicz (1979, p. 23) had noted:

> [Canon 35] may have sprung from a desire to insulate the profession's status in society. Some occupational sociologists have pointed out that established professions resist full public scrutiny of their work; it tends to demystify their realm of expertise, reduce public respect for the profession and diminish their occupational status. Cameras threatened to open the judicial process to public scrutiny. Canon 35, however, helped keep the public largely ignorant of the judicial process.

2. OSCAR HALLAM'S REPORT AND THE BAKER COMMITTEE REPORT

In the aftermath of the Hauptmann trial in 1935, the ABA appointed a Special Committee on Publicity in Criminal Trials headed by former Minnesota Supreme Court Justice Oscar Hallam. Hallam conducted an exhaustive analysis of press and other activities surrounding the Hauptmann case, including a scrupulous review of the court transcript; a visit to the Flemington courthouse; an interview with the trial judge; correspondence with the attorneys from both sides; solicitation of signed statements from people present at the trial; and a reading of hundreds of newspaper and magazine articles dealing with the trial (Hallam, 1940, p. 455).

Hallam's report certainly did not underestimate the theatricality or the inherent notoriety of the Hauptmann case: "There never was a case that lent itself to greater temptation to lurid or excessive publicity, never a case more provocative of trial out of court, never a case beset with greater menace of disorderly procedure" (Hallam, 1940, p. 454). Nor can the importance of Hallam's investigation be overestimated—its major findings have been excerpted in detail in the preceding pages. His report, which culminated in 16 recommendations, included several items relating to media coverage of courts, but of equal importance were items expressly designed to curtail comments made to the press by law enforcement officers, legal officials, and other trial participants. In July 1935, Hallam submitted a preliminary draft of his report to the New Jersey Court of Appeals. Because the Court thought that the report should not be made public while Hauptmann's appeal was still pending, it was not submitted to the ABA's Executive Committee until January 1936.

Upon receipt of Hallam's document, the Executive Committee voted to establish a special panel made up of members of the bar and press (by some oversight, radio representatives were not included in the first sessions, but they were added later) to work out standards governing publicity in criminal trials. Newton D. Baker was named Chairman of the Joint Committee. In his subsequent report, Baker described the Hauptmann case as "perhaps the most spectacular and depressing example of improper publicity and professional misconduct ever presented to the people of the United States in a criminal trial" (cited by Hallam, 1940, p. 454). The Baker Committee reviewed Hallam's Hauptmann report and used its 16 recommendations as the basis of its own seven recommendations. The main point on which the two reports differed was the one concerning the use of cameras in courtrooms: while Hallam's report clearly advised against any use of courtroom photography, the Baker report suggested that cameras should be allowed only with the express knowledge and approval of the presiding judge, and possibly with the additional approval of counsel for both sides. This "cameras" clause was a point of strong disagreement between members of the bar and press.

On September 27, 1937, the ABA's House of Delegates heard the Baker Committee report and passed a resolution giving its approval to all portions of the document which had found agreement among members of the committee.[8] The House of Delegates then recommended that the Baker Committee continue meeting until the remaining proposals could be agreed upon by all its members. In the meantime, the ABA's Committee on Professional Ethics and Grievances had been considering amendments to its Canons of Professional and Judicial Ethics, and had constructed its own policy concerning courtroom photography and broadcasting, to be issued as a new version of Canon 35. With complete disregard for its earlier resolution regarding the Baker Committee recommendations passed on September 27, 1937, the House of Delegates passed the Professional Ethics and Grievances Committee revised Canon 35 on September 30, 1937 (Hallam, 1940, pp. 464–465).

3. THE AMERICAN BAR ASSOCIATION AND CANON 35

Canon 35, calling for a blanket ban on courtroom photography and radio broadcasting, was passed without discussion and with a unanimous vote (Blashfield, 1962, p. 430; see also Carter, 1981b; Witt, 1981; Broholm, 1979; White, 1979; Goldman and Larson, 1978; Hanscom, 1978; Martin, 1978; Whisenand, 1978a; and Roberts and Goodman, 1976). The 1937 version of Canon 35, entitled "Improper Publicizing of Court Proceedings," read as follows:

> Proceedings in court should be conducted with fitting dignity and decorum. The taking of photographs in the courtroom during sessions of the court or recesses between sessions, and the broadcasting of court proceedings are calculated to detract from the essential dignity of the proceedings, degrade the court and create misconceptions with respect thereto in the mind of the public and should not be permitted (see Gillmor and Barron, 1974, p. 452; see also Report of the Special Committee on Cooperation Between Press, Radio and Bar . . . , 1937, pp. 1134–1135).

Although the Committee on Cooperation Between Press, Radio and Bar continued to meet after the adoption of Canon 35, and even registered its views about the impropriety of the canon at the ABA's 1938 convention, it was finally disbanded in 1941. In 1952, Canon 35 was amended to specifically prohibit television cameras,[9] and in April 1961 the ABA extended its disapproval of cameras in the courtroom to a ban on the appearance of judges on courtroom programs, such as simulated courtroom broadcasts (see Figure 1).

At the federal court level, Rule 53 of the Federal Rules of Criminal Procedure, enacted by Congress in 1946, forbade any form of radio or photographic coverage of criminal cases in federal courts.[10] And in 1962, the Judicial Conference of the United States adopted a resolution adding television as a proscribed medium, and extending the Rule 53 prohibition to the environs of the courtroom (see Justices to Decide TV Trial Coverage, 1980, p. 2; Kielbowicz, 1979, p. 22).

Figure 1.   *Appearance of Attorneys and Judges on Broadcast Programs Opinion 298,*
Committee on Professional Ethics American Bar Association, April 15, 1961

1. Appearance of judges on commercial programs simulating or recreating judicial proceedings in courts
    or other tribunals, even though they be not identified as judges or by name, is a violation of the
    Canons of Judicial Ethics.
2. Where lawyers appear on commercial programs as actors or performers, whether in the roles of judges
    or lawyers or otherwise, but are not identified as lawyers either generally or individually, such
    participation is not improper. Their names may also properly appear as members of the cast under
    such circumstances.
3. In the case of programs produced, sponsored, or supported and assisted by Bar Associations, simulat-
    ing or creating judicial proceedings in courts or other tribunals, designed and used as public
    information programs, lawyers or judges may properly appear in the roles of judges or lawyers, and
    may be identified as such and by name.
4. No lawyer or judge should appear in any program, commercial or otherwise, unless it is made clear
    that such program is not an actual trial or proceeding but is a dramatization, unless such program
    conforms to the proper standards of the Bench and Bar in their participating in judicial or other
    proceedings.
5. In the case of continuing educational or public information programs, such as the panel or interview
    type, sponsored or supported or assisted by Bar Associations or affiliated groups, or those non-
    commercial programs of this type produced by the television and broadcasting companies, designed
    and used as public information programs, lawyers and judges may properly appear and be identified
    as such, either generally or individually, provided always that such programs conform to the proper
    standards of the Bench and Bar.

4.   *EARLY COVERAGE AFTER THE PASSAGE OF CANON 35*

Despite the anti-cameras climate created by the ABA in 1937, many judges did not
move swiftly or decisively to enforce Canon 35 for several years after its adoption.
While the higher courts in some jurisdictions observed the canon, the lower courts
allowed photographers to work unhampered, and in many cases quiet, cautious
cameramen could take courtroom pictures without being detected. During the
1950s, three states at least—Oklahoma, Kansas, and Texas—allowed limited coverage of courtrooms by cameras and radio microphones (White, 1979, p. 5).

A.   *Oklahoma and Kansas*

The first *television* coverage of a court case probably took place in Oklahoma City on
December 13, 1953, at the trial of Billy Eugene Manley. Cameras and personnel
from WKY-TV recorded the case from a specially constructed booth at the back of
the courtroom; a hidden microphone placed at the front of the courtroom picked up
sound, and additional lighting was attached to the courtroom's existing chandeliers.
The trial judge was able to push a small button attached to his bench if he wished to
halt the operation of the cameras at any point during the proceedings. Footage of the
trial, broadcast on WKY TV news, included edited versions of the swearing in of

the jury, witness testimony, and the sentencing of the defendant (Geis, 1957, p. 420). Although cameras were banned from Oklahoma courtrooms in the late 1950s, the Oklahoma Supreme Court temporarily lifted this prohibition during the pretrial hearing of Gene Leroy Hart, accused of murdering three Girl Scouts. Coverage was permitted in part because public interest in the trial was high and the courtroom could not accommodate large numbers of spectators. A closed circuit broadcast of the proceedings was transmitted from the coutroom to an auditorium across the street. Three restrictions were placed on the coverage: the single camera had to be in a fixed location and operated by one cameraman, no rebroadcast of the proceedings was allowed, and the trial judge had the authority to terminate or restrict the coverage at any time (Martin, 1978, p. 862).

Albert Blashfield (1962, pp. 431–432) briefly refers to "complete photographic coverage of a criminal trial" as part of an experiment with courtroom cameras in Pratt, Kansas, in the fall of 1955. He cites the Pratt *Daily Tribune* as noting after the experiment that "a good working relationship between the press and the Bar is highly desirable in the public interest," and that courtroom photography "would do much to benefit judicial administration if it is properly handled and is not abused."

B.   *Waco Texas Murder Trial*

Waco, Texas, is generally agreed to be the site of the first *"live"* television broadcast of a trial. On December 6, 1955, Harry L. Washburn was tried for murder while a single television camera from KWTX-TV recorded the proceedings from a balcony behind the jury. Judge D. W. Bartlett was apparently unopposed to television coverage of the case because of a successful experiment he had run the previous summer involving still camera coverage of a trial (see White, 1979, p. 5; Geis, 1957, p. 420, citing McCall, 1956).

Writing about the Waco experience in some detail, Gilbert Geis (1957) referred to the comments of several of the trial's participants. The defendant reported he had no objections to the television coverage and, as a gesture of approval, said he would not care even if the case were broadcast "all over the world." Letters received by Geis from two of the jurors indicated they felt televised trials could be educationally valuable to the public, and Judge Bartlett responded to a colleague on the Georgia bench, who said camera coverage turned the Waco trial into a "bull fight," as follows: "That's water off my back, just like a duck's . . . . They just don't understand—if they understood how this is being handled they wouldn't object" (Geis, 1957, p. 420).

A study conducted soon after the trial showed that the television coverage was well received by the viewing public. McCall (1956) examined 1,400 letters and cards, and several hundred phone call reactions to the program received by the airing station, KWTX-TV. Apart from a few calls from people who objected to their favorite programs being pre-empted, only four of the written comments were opposed to the idea of televised trials. The Waco-McLennon County Bar Association also conducted a small study on the Washburn coverage. Fifty-nine of the 61 association members who responded to a questionnaire said they had watched at least part of the trial on television and had few objections to such coverage. In fact, these lawyers perceived television as the least disturbing form of media covering the trial, followed by newspaper reporting, still photography, and film (Geis, 1957, p. 421, citing study by McCall, 1956). An excerpt from the bar association's 1956 report reads as follows:

> the fact that the trial was being televised seemed to dignify the proceedings . . . Judge Bartlett stated that there was no "grandstanding" by the witnesses or the attorneys and the television camera was no more distracting than a court reporter taking notes, or an electric light burning in the court room. . . . From their experience in the Washburn trial, none of the participants expressed any objection to televising future trials in the same manner . . . the response was . . . they would favor it (cited by Blashfield, 1962, p. 432).

C.   Colorado Sets the Example

On February 27, 1956, Colorado became the first state to permit cameras in its courtrooms on a *permanent* basis with the provisions that: (a) final consent for coverage should rest with the trial judge, and should be decided on a case by case basis; and (b) there could be no camera coverage of an objecting witness or juror. The build-up to the passage of a revised code of judicial conduct, and hence the rejection of Canon 35 in Colorado, involved television coverage of one of the most sensational cases ever to receive media attention.

In November 1955, John Gilbert Graham was arraigned in Denver District Court charged with the murder of 44 people resulting from a mid-air time bomb explosion. Graham had apparently planted the time bomb in his mother's luggage and placed her on a flight to Portland, having taken out several insurance policies on her life totalling $37,500.

Although cameras were allowed to cover the arraignment, District Court supervisor Judge E. V. Holland reimposed a ban on cameras at the subsequent hearing. Media representatives, led by Hugh B. Terry of WKLZ-AM-TV in Denver, objected to the ban and managed to get the trial postponed until a hearing could be held to determine whether cameras should be permitted to cover the case. On January 30, 1956, a hearing began, presided over by Justice O. Otto Moore. During the week-long hearing, attorneys and several witnesses, predominantly representing media organizations, spoke before the judge. Their arguments focused on three main points: (a) that Canon 35 was an unconstitutional restriction of free speech rights of the press, (b) that the public has a right of access to trials, and (c) that a person involved in a public trial has no privacy rights.

The media representqtives also set out to convince Judge Moore that photographic and broadcast coverage of courtrooms could be conducted quietly, unobtrusively, and without detracting from the dignity or decorum of the proceedings. To further bolster their case, the media agreed to impose some self-regulation, such as pooling arrangements (to limit the amount of equipment and personnel needed to cover a case), and even the installation of "cutoff" buttons so that judges could stop trial recordings at any time they might wish.

After 3 weeks of consideration, Justice Moore recommended to the Colorado Supreme Court that Canon 35 be rejected and a new code of judicial conduct, simply titled Colorado Rule 35, be established in its place.[11] One of the most interesting outcomes of the hearing was that Judge Moore changed his own mind about courtroom cameras after the extensive presentation of evidence and practical demonstrations. At the end of the hearing he wrote: "the vast majority of those supporting continuance of Canon 35 have failed to, neglected or refused to expose themselves to information, evidence, and demonstrations of progress which are available in this field" (Geis, 1957, pp. 421–422).

In light of the Colorado Supreme Court ruling, District Judge Joseph M. McDonald, who presided at the Graham murder trial, allowed radio and television stations to record the proceedings for later broadcasts, though no "live" coverage was allowed. At a judicial conference some 6 months after the Graham trial, Charles S. Vigil, one of Graham's attorneys, told the audience:

> As far as I'm concerned, I had no objection to it, as long as the picture taking did not interfere with the trial itself. So far as I could tell in the Graham case it did not interfere. . . . I feel as long as the judge was able to set his own rules, as he did there, the picture taking offered no conflict to the conduct of the court (cited by Geis, 1957, p. 422).

The John Gilbert Graham case has been the focus of important discussion here, partly because it was a test case for the change in Colorado's rules, and partly because it is a vigorous example of how blame may be placed on *camera* coverage when, in reality, a variety of media transgressions often surround sensational cases. In 1960, some 4 years after the Graham case was in the public eye, attorney Marshall Quiat, a former Colorado District Judge and County Judge, responded to popular charges that courtroom broadcasting is detrimental to a fair trial (Quiat, 1960).[12] He emphasized that the accused is deprived of a fair trial, not by the mere fact of allowing cameras to cover a case, but by the ways in which *all* media (print and broadcast) report crimes, and deal with suspects and defendants. To make his point, Quiat outlined a dozen instances which made the Graham case a nightmare for those concerned with fairness, and all but two examples involved prejudicial newspaper reporting rather than broadcast coverage (Quait, 1960, pp. 11–13). Compounding the injury caused by the inflammatory media reports was the fact that they were published before the suspect was even arraigned; the only suggestion so obviously lacking was any mention of the suspect's right to a presumption of innocence until tried and found guilty.

The ultimate importance of Quiat's argument rests on two lessons he draws from the Graham case. The first emphasizes that publicity surrounding a case should not be confused with actual broadcast trial coverage:

> The broadcasts did not inflame the passions of the public. Any inflammation had taken place long before the trial began. The search for truth was no more difficult, nor had truth become more elusive because of the broadcasts. Editing and selecting of portions of the trial to be broadcast had been done carefully with the active participation of a concerned committee and the available advice of the judge (Quiat, 1960, p. 12).

The second explains that broadcast and photographic coverage which takes place *inside* a courtroom has at least the *potential* to be more accurate and tasteful than out-of-court reporting, because it takes place under the strict purview of the trial judge. Reports of cases that are not subject to the discretion of the court (as cameras are) can afford to be less careful and restrained than broadcast coverage, since future camera access largely depends on that restraint (Quiat, 1960, p. 15).

Similar views have been expressed by former Colorado Chief Justice Frank H. Hall. In 1961, referring to the performance of broadcasters in Colorado's courts over a 6-year period (since the passage of Rule 35), Justice Hall noted that they "have been scrupulous in conforming to the judge's wishes. . . . If they were to transgress, the judges have ample remedies available" (Hall, 1962, p. 1122). Justice Hall's point is well taken, though it does not account for what might happen to trial footage between the time it is recorded and the time it is broadcast. Still, it further highlights another significant aspect of the courtroom cameras debate: the crucial role that trial judges play in monitoring (and, if necessary, restricting) the activities of broadcasters inside their courtrooms.

5. A.B.A. RE-EXAMINATION OF CANON 35

Although ABA canons do not have the force of law, by 1965 48 states had banned cameras from their courtrooms—the exceptions were Colorado and Texas (Texas followed the majority movement in 1976). The proverbial nail in the coffin for courtroom cameras arrived with the U.S. Supreme Court decision in *Estes v. Texas* (1965). The Court held that businessman and convicted swindler Billie Sol Estes had been denied his constitutional rights to a fair and impartial trial because the presence of television cameras disrupted the proceedings and prejudiced the jury. A year later, the celebrated trial of doctor Sam Sheppard reached the U.S. Supreme Court and generated heated discussion over the related issue of pretrial publicity and its potentially prejudicial effects on the local community and jurors (*Sheppard v. Maxwell*, 1966).

The difference, however, between pretrial prejudice and the potential for prejudice associated with cameras inside the courtroom during a trial has not been distinguished in the minds of those who regard cameras as a nuisance on all fronts.

Debate generated first by the Hauptmann and Graham trials, and later by the Estes and Sheppard cases, all points to some consistent conclusions: members of the bench and bar have sometimes been reluctant to admit that heightened and often highly prejudicial information which reaches the public about a case has been spread by newspapers with the aid of court personnel and through the absence of judicial control. "Cameras" appear to be a convenient scapegoat when judicial authority is in question.

A. Canon 3A(7) and Proposed Revisions

The dampening effects of *Estes* and *Sheppard* took their toll for nearly 10 years. Although, on August 16, 1972, the ABA's House of Delegates approved a new Code of Professional Responsibility, the revision still prohibited camera coverage of trials for news purposes. Included in the 1972 code was Canon 3A(7), really a revised version of Canon 35. The new canon allowed cameras in courtrooms for specific and restricted purposes only, such as making a court record or presenting evidence, and televised materials could only be viewed for educational purposes by students and for administrative purposes by court personnel (see Figure 2). It was not until the mid-1970s that media representatives began to voice objections against the prohibition of cameras for news purposes. Although there is no clear historical catalyst which marks this turn of events, it might be attributed to the general trend promoting freedom of information and access to government proceedings that flourished in the aftermath of the Watergate "cleansing" and the Nixon presidency.

Figure 2. *Canon 3A(7) of the American Bar Association Code of Judicial Conduct* (as amended in 1972)

A judge should prohibit broadcasting, televising, or taking photographs in the courtroom and areas immediately adjacent thereto during sessions of court or recesses between sessions, except that a judge may authorize:

(a) the use of electronic or photographic means for the presentation of evidence, for the perpetuation of a record, or for the purposes of judicial administration;

(b) the broadcasting, televising, recording, or photographing of investitive, ceremonial, or naturalization proceedings;

(c) the photographic or electronic recording and reproduction of appropriate court proceedings under the following conditions:

(i) the means of recording will not distract participants or impair the dignity of the proceedings;

(ii) the parties have consented, and the consent to being depicted or recorded has been obtained from each witness appearing in the recording and reproduction;

(iii) the reproduction will not be exhibited until after the proceeding has been concluded and all direct appeals have been exhausted; and

(iv) the reproduction will be exhibited only for instructional purposes in educational institutions.

Commentary: Temperate conduct of judicial proceedings is essential to the fair administration of justice. The recording and reproduction of a proceeding should not distort or dramatize the proceedings.

In February 1978, the ABA Committee on Fair Trial and Free Press issued a report asking that the camera ban be lifted. About 4 months later, Attorney General Griffin Bell, acting Deputy Attorney General Benjamin Civiletti, and ABA President-Elect Leonard Janofsky expressed support of camera coverage of appellate courts. They saw no compelling reasons for refusing camera coverage, and felt that the public would be afforded a more realistic view of judicial administration if appellate proceedings were televised (see Bar Group Moves for TV in Courts, 1978, p. 22; Lawyers Defer Action on TV Trial Proposal, 1978, p. 29; Television in the Courts, 1978, p. C6). In August 1978, the ABA's Standing Committee on Standards for Criminal Justice presented its proposal for a revision of the ban on courtroom cameras. The key clause of the proposed resolution stated:

> Television, radio and photographic coverage of judicial proceedings is not per se inconsistent with the right to a fair trial. *Subject to conditions and restrictions established by local rule or by agreement with representatives of the news media, such coverage should be permitted if the court in the exercise of sound discretion concludes that it can be conducted unobtrusively and without distracting the attention of trial participants* (Goodwin, 1979, p. 75, emphasis added).

The House of Delegates voted to defer implementing the proposal, pending revision to its wording. The revised version of the proposal, presented before the ABA at its meeting in Atlanta, Georgia, in February 1979, read:

> Television, radio and photographic coverage of judicial proceedings is not per se inconsistent with the right to a fair trial. *Subject to rule(s) established under the supervisory authority of the highest appellate court in the jurisdiction, such coverage may be permitted if it would be unobtrusive and would not distract the attention of the trial participants, demean the dignity of the proceedings, or otherwise interfere with the fair administration of justice* (Goodwin, 1979, p. 75, emphasis added).

However, the revised language of the proposal made no difference. The resolution was defeated by a vote of 146-153, leaving the 1972 Canon 3A(7) as the official position of the ABA (see ABA Tests Cameras in "Court," 1979, p. 5; Goodwin, 1979, p. 76; Graves, 1979, p. 25).[13] In refusing to lift the ban on cameras, the ABA's House of Delegates appears to have acted emotionally rather than on the basis of a studied evaluation of the arguments concerning courtroom cameras. The delegates ignored the fact that 23 states, at the time of their vote, were permitting television coverage of trial and/or appellate courts on a permanent or experimental basis. They also ignored a letter from former Colorado Chief Justice Edward E. Pringle applauding the use of cameras in Colorado's courts since 1956 (see ABA Keeps Courtroom TV Ban, 1979, p. 22), and they disregarded the opinion of the Conference of Chief Justices which, 1 week prior to the ABA decision, had voted 44-1 to allow television cameras in courtrooms (Douglass, 1982, p. 367; Lawyers Defer Action on TV Trial Proposal, 1978, p. 29).

In a March 1979 editorial, the *American Bar Association Journal* recognized the delegates' decision as one based on long-held suspicion of courtroom cameras, rather than on existing facts:

> The vote of the House of Delegates, in the face of this wide and apparently not disastrous experimentation, seems to indicate the existence of a majority position that favors the retention of the ban as a matter of principle, not necessarily practice. There remains a mistrust of the "carnival effect" of electronic coverage . . . [and the] vote also must be taken as a distrust of how effectively judges will be able to administer electronic coverage rules (Cameras Out of Courtrooms? Editorial, 1979, p. 304).

And in August of that year, U.S. Appeals Court Judge Alfred T. Goodwin, Chairman of the ABA's Fair Trial and Free Press Committee, expressed concern about the continued ban's effect on the public's right to know: "The cost of a per se rule shielding the courts from the administrative problems caused by the broadcast media is the denial of public information to the growing number of citizens who rely on television and radio for their news" (Goodwin, 1979, pp. 76–77).

B.   States Adopt New Camera Rules

Despite the ABA's resistance to a modification of Canon 3A(7), pressure from media representatives mounted during the 1970s and many state Supreme Courts agreed to review proposals for electronic coverage of trial and/or appellate proceedings. For example, although Texas banned cameras from its courtrooms in 1976 (for a while leaving Colorado as the only state which permitted news cameras in the courtroom), two other states, Alabama and Washington, adopted *permanent* rules *allowing* camera coverage of judicial proceedings that same year. Changing attitudes of members of the bench and bar are also reflected in the number of other states that lifted bans on news camera coverage of their courtrooms, on a permanent or experimental basis, between 1976 and January 1981, when *Chandler v. Florida* was handed down by the U.S. Supreme Court. [14]

Table 1 shows that, by the time *Chandler* was decided, 29 states were allowing some form of electronic or photographic news coverage of their courtrooms: 13 states had adopted *permanent* rules allowing camera coverage of trial and/or appellate courts, and 16 states were allowing coverage on an *experimental* basis (14 permitted television coverage; Texas allowed audio recording only, and Utah allowed still photography only). After *Chandler* was handed down, 11 of the 16 states which had already adopted experimental rules changed them to permanent ones; 10 states which had not allowed coverage at all adopted *experimental* rules permitting electronic and photographic coverage (two of these states, Kansas and Maine, later changed these to permanent rules); and Oregon and Kentucky adopted permanent rules allowing coverage of courts without going through an interim experimental stage.

Table 1   Camera Coverage of State Courts (Effective January, 1985)

State	Type of Court	Level of Court	Effective Date Experimental	Effective Date Permanent
Alabama***	Trial, Appellate	Civil, Criminal*		Feb. 1, 1976
Alaska***	Trial, Appellate	Civil, Criminal*	Sept. 18, 1979	Nov. 1, 1979
Arizona	Trial, Appellate	Civil, Criminal	May 31, 1979	July 1, 1983
Arkansas***	Trial, Appellate	Civil, Criminal	Jan. 1, 1981	Mar. 8, 1982
California	Trial, Appellate	Civil, Criminal	June 1, 1980	July 1, 1984
Colorado	Trial, Appellate	Civil, Criminal*		Feb. 27, 1956
Connecticut	Trial, Appellate	Civil, Criminal	Apr. 12, 1982	
Delaware	Supreme Court	Civil	May 1, 1982	—Ext. indef.
D.C.	Trial		Pending	Pending
Florida	Trial, Appellate	Civil, Criminal	July 5, 1977	May 1, 1979
Georgia	Trial, Appellate	Civil, Criminal*		May 12, 1977
Hawaii	Trial, Appellate	Civil, Criminal	Jan. 1, 1984	—For 2 years
Idaho	Supreme Court (Boise)		Dec. 4, 1978	Aug. 27, 1979
	Supreme Court (on circuit)		Oct. 9, 1979	Oct. 1, 1980
	Court of Appeals		Jan. 4, 1982	—Ext. indef.
Illinois	Appellate	N.S.	Jan. 1, 1984	—For 1 year
Indiana	None			
Iowa	Trial, Appellate	Civil, Criminal	Jan. 1, 1980	Jan. 1, 1982
Kansas	Appellate	Civil, Criminal	Sept. 14, 1981	Sept. 1, 1982
	Trial, 13 districts	Civil, Criminal	Jan 1, 1984	—For 2 years
Kentucky	Trial, Appellate	Civil, Criminal		July 1, 1981
Louisiana	Trial, Appellate	Civil, Criminal	July 13, 1979	Pending
Maine	Supreme Court		Apr. 4, 1982	Mar. 13, 1984
Maryland**	Trial, Appellate	Civil	Jan. 1, 1981	July 1, 1984
Massachusetts	Trial, Appellate	Civil, Criminal	June 1, 1980	Jan. 1, 1983
Michigan	None			
Minnesota**	Trial, Appellate	Civil, Criminal	Apr. 18, 1983	
Mississippi	None			
Missouri	None			
Montana	Trial, Appellate	Civil, Criminal	Apr. 1, 1978	Apr. 18, 1980
Nebraska	Supreme Court		Oct. 1, 1982	—Ext. indef.
Nevada	Trial, Appellate	Civil, Criminal	Apr. 1, 1980	
New Hampshire	Trial, Appellate	Civil, Criminal		Jan. 1, 1978
New Jersey	Trial,	Civil, Criminal	May 1, 1979	June 9, 1981
	Appellate	N.S.	May 1, 1979	Oct. 8, 1980
	Municipal Courts	Civil, Criminal	Jan. 3, 1984	—Ext. indef.
New Mexico	Trial, Appellate	Civil, Criminal	July 1, 1980	Jan. 1, 1983
New York	Appellate			Jan. 1, 1981
Nth. Carolina	Trial, Appellate	Civil, Criminal	Oct. 18, 1982	—Ext. to 12/85
North Dakota	Appellate	Civil	Feb. , 1979	July 1, 1980
Ohio***	Trial, Appellate	Civil, Criminal	June 1, 1979	Jan. 1, 1982
Oklahoma***	Trial, Appellate	Civil, Criminal*	Jan. 1, 1979	Feb. 22, 1982
Oregon	Appellate	Civil, Criminal	June 1, 1983	—Ext. indef.
Pennsylvania	Non-jury civil trial		Oct. 1, 1979	—Ext. indef.

Table 1   *(Continued)*

State	Type of Court	Level of Court	Effective Date Experimental	Permanent
Rhode Island	Trial, Appellate	Civil, Criminal	Oct. 1, 1981	—Ext. to 9/85
Sth. Carolina	None			
South Dakota	Pending			
Tennessee***	Trial, Appellate	Civil, Criminal*		Feb. 22, 1979
Texas	Appellate		Audio recording only	
Utah	Trial, Appellate	Civil, Criminal	Still photography only	
Vermont	Supreme Court		July 1, 1984	—For 2 years
Virginia	None			
Washington***	Trial, Appellate	Civil, Criminal		Sept. 20, 1976
West Virginia	Trial, Appellate	Civil, Criminal	Jan. 1, 1979	May 28, 1981
Wisconsin	Trial, Appellate	Civil, Criminal		July 1, 1979
Wyoming	Supreme Court		Aug. 14, 1981	—Ext. indef.

Table Compiled from Data in: "Summary of Cameras in the State Courts" (Williamsburg, VA: National Center for State Courts, January 15, 1985); "News Media Coverage of Judicial Proceedings With Cameras and Microphones: A Survey of the States" (Washington DC: Radio-Television News Directors Association, July 1, 1984).

  *Consent of accused required in criminal trials
 **Consent of parties and witnesses required
***No coverage of individuals who object
N.S.   Not Specified
Notes: 1.   In Maryland, coverage in trial courts is experimental; in appellate courts it is permanent. Permission needed unless defendant is a government official.
    2.   Colorado, New York, Pennsylvania, Vermont, and Wyoming are considering liberalization of existing rules.
    3.   Louisiana's statute allows coverage only if all parties consent. In paractice no coverage exists.

C.   The A.B.A. Lifts the News Camera Ban

In August 1982, at the ABA's annual convention in San Francisco, the Committee on Standards for Criminal Justice and the Committee on Ethics and Professional Responsibility submitted Resolution 107 to the House of Delegates. The resolution outlined a new Canon 3A(7) to replace the canon approved by the House of Delegates in 1972, and recommended that camera coverage for news purposes be allowed under the supervision and discretion of a state's highest appellate court. The House of Delegates approved Resolution 107 on August 11, 1982 by a vote of 162 to 112 (see ABA Ends Opposition to Cameras, 1982, p. 45; Appleson, 1982, p. 256; Douglass, 1982, p. 367; Middleton, 1982, p. 1199; Owles, 1982, p. 985). While the new canon in no way endorses the use of cameras, its passage marks a milestone in the ABA's long history of opposition to electronic media in courtrooms. Canon 3A(7) of the ABA Code of Judicial Conduct now reads:

   A judge should prohibit broadcasting, televising, recording or photographing in courtrooms and areas immediately adjacent thereto during sessions of court, or recesses between sessions, except that under rules prescribed by a supervising appellate court or other appropriate authority, a judge may authorize broadcasting, televising, recording and photographing of judicial proceedings in courtrooms and areas immediately adjacent thereto consistent with the right of the parties to a fair trial and subject to express conditions, limitations, and guidelines which allow such coverage in a manner that will be unobtrusive, will not distract the trial participants, and will not otherwise interfere with the administration of justice (ABA Adopts New Cameras Rule, 1983, p. 250).

By July 1, 1984, a total of 43 states had adopted either experimental or permanent rules permitting some form of electronic or photographic coverage of their trial or appellate courts—the exceptions were the District of Columbia, Indiana, Michigan, Mississippi, Missouri, South Carolina, South Dakota, and Virginia.

6. FLORIDA'S EXPERIENCE WITH COURTROOM CAMERAS

One of the forerunners in the fight to gain electronic access to courtrooms was Florida. On May 1, 1979, it became the first state to permit coverage of trial courts on a permanent basis, *without the need for prior consent of witnesses, jurors, or defendants.* [15] The fight for access began in January 1977, when Post-Newsweek Stations, Florida, Inc., filed a petition with the Florida Supreme Court for a change in the state's Code of Judicial Conduct, Canon 3A(7). The petition sought to substitute Canon 3A(7) with a new code which would permit camera coverage of all Florida courtrooms for broadcast or print media publication.

Although the Court denied the request for a new canon, it did agree to re-examine the existing rules and said that ". . . a test period during which trials would be conducted with electronic media coverage was essential to a reasoned decision in the petition for modification of Canon 3A(7)."[16] In June 1977, the Court ordered a 1-year pilot program to begin on July 5, 1977, and end on June 30, 1978, and the Court's opinion described a series of rules that would govern the use of cameras during the experiment. Paragraph nine of the guidelines requested that parties in a case, media representatives, and participating judges file reports with the Florida Supreme Court describing their experiences during the pilot program.[17]

A. The Ronny Zamora Trial

The first trial to be televised during the experimental year took place in October 1977 and involved Ronny Zamora, a so-called television addict and victim of television violence intoxication. Fifteen-year-old Zamora was accused of shooting to death his 85-year-old neighbor, Elinor Haggart, while he was in the act of robbing her home in Miami Beach. Gavel-to-gavel coverage of the trial proceedings was broadcast in Florida by public television station WPBT, and excerpts of the trial were broadcast across the United States and abroad.

In all, 27 hours of the trial were aired by the station. Television ratings, reported later, indicated that the trial averaged 100,000 viewers per night in the Miami area, with a peak of 124,000 (Craig, 1979, p. 706; see also Did TV Make Him Do It?, 1977, p. 87; *TV On Trial,* 1978).

Only one still photographer and one television camera person were allowed in the courtroom, and pooling arrangements were coordinated by Steve Tello (at that time of WPLG-TV, Florida), who was appointed media liaison officer by the presiding judge, Paul Baker. At the end of the trial, Judge Baker said: "I think we have found a common ground to protect the First Amendment rights of the press to be in the courtroom and not to give up the defendant's right to a fair trial" (Tello, 1977, p. 11). Prosecutor Tom Headley "saw no distraction from the television and still cameras," and defense counsel Ellis Rubin told reporters that "the televising of the Zamora trial is the greatest educational tool this country will ever have as to what goes on in a court of law . . . I think it is a wonderful thing!" (Tello, 1977, p. 12).

According to Judge Baker's report, submitted to the Florida Supreme Court in *Petition of Post-Newsweek Stations* (1979), the presence of television and audio equipment at Zamora's trial did not cause any physical disruptions. After privately interviewing jurors, he found that, while the cameras were slightly distracting, they did not interfere with the jurors' ability to consider testimony or concentrate on the arguments of counsel or the Court's instructions. Interestingly, the slight distraction experienced by the jurors stemmed from their concern about the impact of television coverage on the defendant and his family, not from any noise or movement of the media equipment (Baker, 1977). Judge Baker praised the cooperation of media personnel, and concluded that coverage of Zamora's trial must be viewed as a success, a conclusion he elaborated upon during a subsequent television interview:

> I define success as not having an impact on the witnesses to the extent that they were given to overstatement or that they were intimidated. I define it as having little or no impact on the jurors' ability to consider the testimony, the argument of counsel, and be attentive to the charge of the law. I believe that the success can also be shown by the self-policing of the entire press corps, not just the one television cameraman or the one still cameraperson who was in the courtroom. I think that as an educational tool and as news, it was successful, since it gave the public an opportunity to see what goes on in a courtroom. And most of them have not had that experience (*TV On Trial,* 1978, p. 48).

B. *The Noel Chandler and Robert Granger Trial*

However, not everyone who participated in one of Florida's televised trials had such a positive view of the situation as Judge Baker. Miami attorney Joel Hirschhorn presented a totally negative view of courtroom cameras when he argued before the U.S. Supreme Court for reversal of his client's burglary convictions on the grounds that their trial had been prejudiced by the presence of a television camera. Hirschhorn's clients were Noel Chandler and Robert Granger, two Miami Beach policemen accused of attempting to rob a restaurant. The occupation of the two defendants, coupled with their crime, understandably attracted a great deal of media attention to the case (see Witt, 1981, pp. 24–25; Fox, 1980, p. 1; Olson, 1980, pp. 1, 4; Trial Coverage Before Court, 1980, pp. 8–10; Voboril, 1980, p. 9).

The trial was televised in December 1977 as part of Florida's 1-year pilot program with courtroom cameras. In a pretrial motion, Hirschhorn asked that the state's experimental Canon 3A(7) be declared unconstitutional, but the trial judge rejected the motion and referred the matter to the Florida Supreme Court. The Florida Supreme Court refused to rule on the matter which it deemed irrelevant to the charges against the appellants. Writing for the majority in *Chandler*, Chief Justice Burger described the television coverage as follows:

> A television camera was in place for one entire afternoon, during which the state presented the testimony of Sion, its chief witness. No camera was present for the presentation of any part of the case for the defense. The camera returned to cover closing arguments. Only two minutes and fifty-five seconds on the trial were broadcast—and those depicted only the prosecution's side of the case.[18]

While it could certainly be argued that news coverage of the trial was biased, portraying as it did only the prosecution's side of the case, Hirschhorn's argument that the *mere presence* of a television camera prejudiced his client's trial is a weak one. The appellants claimed that the atmosphere of the trial was psychologically distorted by the presence of a camera—that the jurors and witnesses were distracted and inhibited by knowledge of the coverage. But since a camera was only present during the prosecution's side of the case, then, by Hirschhorn's own reasoning, it was the prosecution's case that suffered, not the defense's. Chandler's and Granger's convictions were affirmed by the Florida District Court of Appeals; review was denied by the Florida Supreme Court,[19] and the U.S. Supreme Court concluded that there was no evidence of specific prejudice during the trial.

C. The Mark Herman Trial

The televised trial of Mark Herman, accused of killing Palm Beach oil executive Richard Kreusler, took place in February 1978. While national interest in the trial was low, there was a great deal of local interest.

> WPBT trial coverage attracted 29% of the West Palm Beach viewing market on the evening of Feb. 17, running dead even with two of its commercial competitors, which were ironically "Rockford Files" and "Quincy," both murder mystery series (Craig, 1979, p. 706).

Judge Thomas Sholts, presiding at the Herman trial, filed his report with the Florida Supreme Court in *Petition of Post-Newsweek Stations* (1979). He noted that media coverage did not interfere with the defendant's due process rights, and he mentioned the cooperative attitudes of the media representatives who covered the proceedings. Indeed, Judge Sholts said that camera coverage worked out much better than he believed possible, and he rejected the notion that cameras create a theatrical atmosphere in the courtroom (Sholts, 1978, p. 10). However, several severe problems were reported as being directly related to television coverage: a witness refused to testify for fear of her safety (though the court rejected the witness's position and held her in contempt), and an objection was raised by the prosecutor about the safety of prison inmate witnesses who testified for the state, and who feared possible reprisals if recognized by fellow inmates. Judge Sholts also noted that the presence of electronic media added to his administrative duties. Examples of this were the need to meet with media representatives, the monitoring of cameras and personnel in the courtroom, the need to sequester jurors, and the lengthier *voir dire* or the use of pre-qualifying *voir dire* to examine potential jurors on matters of pretrial publicity and attitudes toward television and other media coverage of trials.

Another administrative problem encountered in the Herman trial involved bomb threats. Six bomb threats were telephoned anonymously to the courthouse, and courthouse staff also received three or four telephone messages regarding so-called leads in the case. The bomb threats, it seems, were hoaxes and did not affect the process of the trial or its outcome. Judge Sholts was particularly worried about the added financial burden ($11,500) placed on the court in having to sequester the jury, and he suggested that in future the cost of jury sequestration should be paid by the media organizations wishing to cover trials, not by the taxpayers.

Despite these administrative and financial burdens, the majority of participants in the Herman trial had neutral or favorable reactions to the camera coverage. Attached to the judicial report were copies of questionnaire responses gathered at the end of the trial. Questionnaires were completed by the judge, two spectators, one prosecuting attorney, one court reporter, two bailiffs and eleven jurors. Respondents did not generally find cameras distracting, although still cameras were perceived as more of a distraction than television cameras. Still cameras were regarded as a little more fair than television cameras to the defendant, but a little less fair to witnesses, and while some respondents said camera presence inhibited witness testimony, most participants did not feel tense during camera coverage. Overall, between half and over three quarters of all respondents had positive reactions to camera coverage of the trial.

Five months after the Herman trial, the experimental use of courtroom cameras ended and the Florida Supreme Court began its evaluation of the pilot-program. After reading several judicial reports (see Mounts, 1978; Sholts, 1978; Baker, 1977), and having examined the results of three surveys carried out during the experimental period (see Florida Conference of Circuit Judges, 1978; Judicial Planning and Coordination Unit, 1978; Strawn, Buchanan, Meeske, and Pryor, 1978), the Court granted Post-Newsweek's petition on April 12, 1979. The Court's decision introduced a new canon allowing electronic coverage of all trials on a permanent basis, without the need for prior consent of trial participants. The rules expressed in the canon can only be limited if the presiding judge believes special injury may result from photographing particular participants, such as victims of sex crimes, undercover informants, witnesses with new identities, and children involved in custody proceedings.

D.   The Theodore Bundy Trial

In July 1979, the first trial to be televised under the new canon was that of Theodore Bundy, accused of murdering two students at a Florida State University sorority house, and suspected of murdering about 36 women in different states. The scope of Bundy's crimes attracted a great deal of public attention to his trial. However, cameras in the courtroom were not intrusive. As *Time* magazine (covering the proceedings) pointed out, "people have become accustomed to the pervasiveness of TV"; so much so that at Bundy's trial "two jurors were blasé enough to fall asleep— on-camera" (Cameras in the Courtroom: Florida's Bundy Case Tests the Fairness of Televising Trials, 1979, p. 76).

Even the presiding judge, Edward Cowart, who had been skeptical of camera coverage prior to the trial, priased the media personnel and noted the lack of disruption caused by the cameras:

> I felt strongly when the experiment began . . . that we were going to lose all of those things we consider sacrosanct . . . it just isn't so. Modern minicameras don't interfere with the proceedings at all . . . I will assure you that the sketch artists we used to have in the courtroom created more distraction than any television camera off in the back of the courtroom has ever created. Once the trial gets under way, you really can truly forget the presence of the camera. . . . We haven't found any bad effects from it. (Bass, 1981, p. 44; see also Hoyt, 1980, p. 293).

E.   The Arthur McDuffie Case

Nearly a year later, however, in May 1980, an incident sparked a furor of accusations about the dangers of broadcasting trial footage on nightly newscasts. The case involved five white policemen who were acquitted of beating to death a black businessman, Arthur McDuffie. The trial was not covered gavel-to-gavel, and anti-cameras forces were quick to imply that media coverage was biased, leaving the public with an inaccurate and incomplete picture of the case, particularly weaknesses in the state's case against the policemen. Word about the acquittals spread quickly through Dade County, and, by the evening of the trial's close, Miami was the scene of rioting involving loss of life and property.

Miami officials attributed the rioting in large part to "underlying social and economic factors including a long string of episodes of alleged police brutality against blacks" (Davis, 1981, p. 20; see also Bass, 1981; Witt, 1981; Justices to

Decide TV Trial Coverage, 1980; and Weingarten, 1980). Others, like Miami broadcaster Norman Davis, have pointed out that it is unrealistic to accuse broadcasters, alone, of triggering riots; newspaper reports as well as television coverage had the potential to aggravate an already explosive situation. Perhaps if news stories about the case had been longer, if more in-depth coverage had been given to the 6-week trial prior to the verdict announcement, there might have been greater awareness of the facts presented to the jury (see Davis, 1981). Resentment on the part of the black community about the acquittals stemmed at least in part from doubts that the all-white jury reached its verdict solely on the evidence. Speculation on both sides could have merit, but clearly the public would have drawn its own conclusions about the verdict whether or not trial footage had been televised.

F.   The Post-Newsweek Opinion

Florida has probably televised more trials than any other state: one report estimates the number as several "hundreds," maybe even "thousands" (Davis, 1980, pp. 85–86). Many of these trials dealt with highly notorious murder cases, and yet the consensus of opinion from the state's judiciary and public officials seems to be that televised trials are worthwhile sources of public information, and that camera coverage does not detract from the smooth operation of justice. In short, the "marriage" between free press and fair trial has been, and continues to be, a positive experience throughout the state.

Several other factors place Florida in the forefront of any discussion of courtroom cameras. It was the first state to permit televised trials over the objections of defendants; it was from Florida that the U.S. Supreme Court heard the landmark *Chandler* appeal on the courtroom cameras issue, and it is a state which has thoroughly documented its experience with televised trials in the form of survey research and judicial reports.

For these reasons, the Florida Supreme Court's *Post-Newsweek* decision, which opened the state's courts to cameras on a permanent basis, deserves careful attention in any discussion of the camera access movement. The Court's opinion, written by Chief Justice Alan Sundberg, is a well researched and perceptive analysis of the courtroom cameras issue, and the guidelines which it laid down for televised trials were cited in *Chandler* as the model to be followed by other states wishing to adopt camera access rules. Justice Sundberg's opinion summarized the evidence on courtroom cameras that was gathered during Florida's pilot-program, and it also answered several complaints which have generally been made against electronic coverage of trials, including those expressed in the *Estes* plurality opinion.

1. PHYSICAL DISRUPTION	Technological advancements have so reduced size, noise, and light levels of the electronic equipment available that cameras can be employed in courtrooms unobtrusively.

2. PSYCHOLOGICAL
    EFFECT:
    ★ "grandstanding"
      lawyers
    ★ "posturing"
      judges
    ★ intimidated
      witnesses
    ★ distracted
      jurors
    ★ camera presence
      will turn the
      case into a
      cause celebre

3. EXPLOITATION OF
    THE COURTS FOR
    COMMERCIAL
    PURPOSES AS
    OPPOSED TO THE
    PERFORMANCE OF
    AN EDUCATIONAL
    FUNCTION

4. PREJUDICIAL
    PUBLICITY

    ★ witnesses will
      watch other
      witnesses'
      testimony
    ★ jurors will
      watch excerpts
      from the trial
    ★ it will be
      impossible to
      find impartial
      jurors in the
      event of a new
      trial or a
      retrial

No respondent has been able to point to any instance during the pilot program period where these fears were substantiated. Such evidence as exists would appear to refute the assumptions. . . . [A]ssumed influences upon participants were perceived to vary in degree from not at all to slightly. More importantly, there was no significant difference in the presence or degree of these influences as between the electronic and print media.

. . . it must be recognized that newsworthy trials are newsworthy trials, and that they will be extensively covered by the media both within and without the courtroom whether Canon 3A(7) is modified or not.

As to the lack of serious content on the part of the electronic media, we must concede that much of its broadcast time is devoted to entertainment. However, so too is substantial space in newspapers and magazines devoted to cartoons, comics, sports, entertainment, advertising, and the like.[20]

. . . we discern no appreciable difference in this regard between willful exposure to electronic media as opposed to the print media. A witness or juror disposed to disregard an oath or direction from the court is just as apt to read about the trial in the newspaper as to view a film of it on television or listen to it on a radio broadcast.

Just as electronic media broadcast may contaminate a prospective venire, so may extensive newspaper coverage. Furthermore, it is unrealistic to equate the presence of electronic media in the courtroom with the amount of publicity which will be generated about any trial. Newsworthy trials will be covered by the electronic media whether from within or without the courtroom. . . . Who can assess whether this type of coverage will be any less sensational or have any less impact on the community than an accurate, direct broadcast of the events occuring in the courtroom.[21]

The only problems encountered during Florida's experimental use of courtroom cameras involved coverage of particular types of witnesses, such as those under federal protection. Other categories of witnesses who may be adversely affected by trial broadcasts include children, confidential informants, and sexual abuse or rape victims. Justice Sundberg stressed that such problems are not insurmountable. It is the duty of the presiding judge to weigh the possible dangers against the principle of open justice, and if necessary to use discretionary authority to bar electronic media coverage of certain witnesses. In conclusion he wrote, "there is more to be gained than lost in permitting electronic media coverage of judicial proceedings subject to standards for such coverage."[22]

FOOTNOTES

1. Cited by Kielbowicz (1979, p. 15).
2. It is interesting to note that the ABA did not question radio broadcasting of trials until about 1932: see *Estes v. Texas*, 381 U.S. at 597 footnote 3, Justice Harlan concurring (Appendix). See also Cedarquist (1961, p. 147), who notes that, although the Canons of Judicial Ethics were originally adopted in 1924, no canon dealing with broadcasting from courtrooms was even proposed until 1932. In 1932 a complaint was filed with the ABA about a Los Angeles judge who had permitted a radio broadcast of a murder trial. Shortly after, the ABA Committee on Professional Ethics proposed Canon 35, but it was not adopted until 1937.
3. For further discussion of this case, see Douglass (1982, p. 366).
4. *State v. Hauptmann*, 115 N.J.L. 412, 180 A. 809 (1935); *Hauptmann v. New Jersey, Cert. denied*, 296 U.S. 649 (1935).
5. Reed (1967, p. 1) also notes that Bauer later said he and his sources "had been confused in general statements on the photography at recess and in the corridors at the Hauptmann trial."
6. See also Goldman and Larson (1978, footnote 49), citing an article from the *Los Angeles Times*, February 2, 1977, which stated:
   The police and press, playing on public fear of Hitler's Germany, emphasized Hauptmann's national origin, repeatedly referring to him as "Bruno," a name he had never used in all his 11 years in the United States, and "the German machine-gunner," even though his only contact with the weapon was as a draftee during World War I. Outside the courtroom, crowds chanted "Burn Hauptmann!"
   For other details about events which exacerbated the inflammatory nature of the case, see Prosser (1961).
7. Marshall (1935, p. 94) reported that the circulation of one New York newspaper jumped by 50,000 during the first week of its coverage of the Hauptmann trial.
8. Newton Baker's report was actually presented to the Committee by Hallam, because Baker was seriously ill at the time and died soon afterward (Blashfield, 1962, p. 430).
9. The 1952 amendment to Canon 35, describing specific rules relating to television coverage, read as follows:

Proceedings in court should be conducted with fitting dignity and decorum. The taking of photographs in the courtroom, during sessions of the court or recesses between sessions, and the broadcasting or televising of court proceedings are calculated to detract from the essential dignity of the proceedings, distract the witness in giving his testimony, degrade the court and create misconceptions with respect thereto, in the mind of the public, and should not be permitted.

10. The 1946 version of Rule 53 of the Federal Rules of Criminal Procedure states: "The taking of photographs in the courtroom during the progress of judicial proceedings or radio broadcasting of judicial proceedings from the courtroom shall not be permitted by the court."

11. Colorado Rule 35, adopted by the Colorado Supreme Court, February 27, 1956, reads:
     Proceedings in court should be conducted with fitting dignity and decorum.
     Until further order of this Court, if the trial judge in any court shall believe
     from the particular circumstances of a given case, or any portion thereof, that the
     taking of photographs in the courtroom, or the broadcasting by radio or television
     of court proceedings would detract from the dignity thereof, distract the witness in
     giving his testimony, degrade the court, or otherwise materially interfere with the
     achievement of a fair trial, it should not be permitted; provided, however, that no
     witness or juror in attendance under subpoena or order of the court shall be
     photographed or have his testimony broadcast over his expressed objection; and
     provided further that under no circumstances shall any court proceeding be pho-
     tographed or broadcast by any person without first having obtained permission
     from the trial judge to do so, and then only under such regulations as shall be
     prescribed by him.
     In 1983, the Colorado Supreme Court approved a 2-year experiment under which a
     judge can allow camera coverage of a trial over the objections of either party in the case.
     See Reaves (1983, p. 1213).

12. In large part, Quiat was responding to comments made by Justice William O. Douglas addressing an audience at the University of Colorado Law School in 1960 (see Douglas, 1960).

13. It is very possible that the presence of Chief Justice Warren Berger at the Atlanta meeting helped to harden opposition to the proposed resolution. Burger, who is "a steadfast foe of cameras in court" (ABA Keeps Courtroom T.V. Ban, 1979, p. 22), was quick to express his vehement opposition to broadcast journalists both inside and outside courtrooms:
     when Chief Justice Burger encountered NBC's Carl Stern and his crew at a break-
     fast at which the chief justice was to receive an award, he walked up to Mr. Stern
     and said, "You leave or I'll leave" (ABA Makes it Perfectly Clear on Cameras in the
     Courtroom, 1979, p. 58).

14. For general roundup of information on the changing numbers and attitudes of states permitting cameras in their courts see: Braverman (1984); Cameras Allowed in 37 States' Courts (1983); Cameras in Court: Justices' Prejudice Caps Lenses (1983); Krasno (1983); Television Coverage in the State Courts: An Update (1983); Carter and Ito (1982); TV Trial Coverage (1982); Appleson (1981); Camera Ban Pleases Judges, Keeps Journalists Plugging (1981); Driver (1981); Merry (1981); Spain, Fuqua, Shobe, and Venters (1981); Cameras and Mikes Allowed in Massachusetts Courts (1980); Freedman (1980); Maryland Experiment Begins Jan. 1 (1980); Morrow (1980); Mundt (1980);

Owles (1980); Pressman (1980); Court TV in 14 States (1978); Jersey's High Court Admits Cameras and TV as a Test (1978); Jersey to Test TV in a Courtroom (1978); Ohio Court Nears Decision to Permit TV Coverage of Trials (1978); Alabama News Photographer Records Courtroom "First" (1976).

15. Other states allowed news cameras in their courtrooms by May 1, 1979, but they imposed one or more of the following restrictions: (a) permitted coverage only of appellate courts, (b) required the consent of trial participants, or (c) allowed coverage only on an experimental basis.

16. *Petition of Post-Newsweek Stations, Florida, Inc.,* Fla. 370 So. 2d 764 at 766 (1979).

17. See *Petition of Post-Newsweek Stations, Florida, Inc.,* Fla. 347 So. 2d 404 (1977) for full guidelines outlined by the Florida Supreme Court governing electronic coverage during Florida's one-year experiment. For the permanent guidelines see Fla. 370 So. 2d 764 at 792 (1979). The permanent guidelines are identical to the experimental ones with the exceptions of paragraphs eight and nine. For detailed discussion of the background to Florida's experiment with courtroom cameras see: Boyd (1978, pp. 815–818) and Whisenand (1978b, pp. 1860–1864). For views opposing the change in Florida's canon, see Hirschhorn (1978).

18. *Chandler v. Florida,* 449 U.S. 560 at 568 (1981). See also Giving Cameras a Day in Court (1981, p. 102).

19. See *Chandler v. State,* 366 So. 2d 64 (D.C.A. Fla. 1978) and *Chandler v. State,* 376 So. 2d 1157 (Fla. 1979).

20. *Petition of Post-Newsweek Stations, Florida,* Fla., 370 So. 2d 764 at 776 (April 12, 1979).

21. *Petition of Post-Newsweek Stations, Florida,* Fla., 370 So. 2d 764 at 775–778 (April 12, 1979).

22. *Petition of Post-Newsweek Stations, Florida,* Fla., 370 So. 2d 764 at 780 (April 12, 1979).

PART TWO

CONSTITUTIONAL ISSUES AND POPULAR ARGUMENTS

The question of whether trials should be televised for news purposes involves what appears to many to be a conflict of constitutional rights: those guaranteed by the First, Sixth, and Fourteenth Amendments. The free speech rights of broadcast journalists are perceived as competing against the rights of defendants to receive fair and impartial trials.[1] The controversy also questions whether television journalists can enjoy the same freedoms as their newspaper counterparts if cameras are barred from courtrooms.

At the heart of the courtroom cameras controversy are two Supreme Court decisions: *Estes v. Texas* (1965), in effect banning cameras; and *Chandler v. Florida* (1981), in essence granting limited camera access under judicial discretion and over the objections of defendants. But the debate cannot be viewed from the limited perspective of these two decisions. In 1976, the Supreme Court noted that the free press fair trial controversy is "almost as old as the Republic."[2] The debate digs both deep and wide, encompassing an array of legal views on a broad spectrum of free press fair trial considerations, including prejudicial publicity, juror impartiality, prior restraint, contempt, and privacy.

These issues and more have played a significant role in coloring judicial interpretation of the two landmark "cameras" cases, and they have helped to create a complex web of judicial opinion which serves to emphasize the highly explosive and sensitive nature of the courtroom cameras issue. In 1941, Justice Hugo Black acknowledged that "free speech and fair trials are two of the most cherished policies of our civilization, and it would be a trying task to choose between them."[3] Just over 30 years later, he summarized the ongoing debate as a "civil libertarian's nightmare."[4]

1. THE PRESUMPTION OF OPENNESS

The traditional view within a democracy is that government and its executive branches should be open to public scrutiny. Within this framework of a presumption of openness, citizens have access to places and institutions supported by public funds,[5] and business that is conducted by publicly elected or appointed officials is also open to scrutiny; hence the passage of "Sunshine" (open meeting) laws, various state public records acts, and the Freedom of Information Act, which grants limited access to federal records (see Paul and Kamp, 1982, pp. 233–238; Weinstein and Zimmerman, 1977, pp. 157–158).

Today, television cameras record the activities of the U.S. House of Representatives (see House Begins TV Coverage, 1979; TV to Start in Congress, But Probably With House Control of News Content, 1977), and cameras will soon be allowed in the U.S. Senate (see Radio, TV Coverage of Senate Floor Proceedings Begins Soon, 1986; Baker, 1984; TV in Senate Debated, 1983; The Greatest Show on Earth?, 1982; Senate's Turn for "TV or Not TV," 1981). In the past, television has played an important role in delivering information to the public about the workings of several government committees, most notably the hearings of the House Committee on Un-American Activities in the late 1940s, the Senate Crime Committee (better known as the Kefauver Committee) Hearings investigating organized crime in 1951, and the Army–McCarthy Hearings in 1954 (see Garay, 1978). Many believe that it was 36 days of television exposure to the American public which severely damaged Senator Joseph McCarthy's reputation and led to his demise (see Weinstein and Zimmerman, 1977, p. 165).

The courts, as a branch of government, are also presumptively open to the public—judges, public defenders, and public prosecutors are public servants. Many judges are elected, and even those who are appointed must be willing to face public inspection and comment. Several members of the bench and bar (as well as the press) have commented on the need for greater public awareness of judicial administration, and have argued that the press should take on the role of surrogate informer.

Chief Administrative Judge of New York, Herbert B. Evans, has said on several occasions that he favors cameras in courtrooms in part because "public scrutiny keeps the court system efficient" (Evans, 1982, p. 27; for similar views, see Cooke, 1982, p. 25; Hanscom, 1978, p. 226; Stone and Edlin, 1978, p. 1132). First Amendment advocate Floyd Abrams believes cameras in the courtroom "will lead to a better judiciary . . . [and] will help us deal with the problems of corrupt prosecutors, of defendants who are too close to judges, or judges who have a tendency to doze off" (quoted by Bass, 1981, pp. 37–38. Judge Jack Weinstein and law professor Diane Zimmerman have emphasized that "in our complex society which fragments our time and limits our ability to observe in depth jobs and professions other than our own, the press is more than ever the interpreter to the people of their public institutions. It is also a catalyst for public interest in those institutions" (Weinstein and Zimmerman, 1977, p. 161). Carl Stern, NBC's legal correspondent, has explained that the job of the media "is not only a quest for actual information; it is the job of calling attention to standards and describing as intelligently as possible when there is deviation from those standards" (Stern, 1976, p. 351). Newspaper editorials, too, have argued that televised trials could help the public to better understand the judicial issues and personnel it votes for (Mirror of Opinion: Courtroom Cameras, 1979, p. 19).

Although the First Amendment says nothing about the public's right to be informed, nor for that matter the press' right to inform the public, the Supreme Court has held that free speech implies the right to gather and disseminate information, and the right to receive information.[6] The First Amendment, then, has yielded to a fairly broad interpretation of where, when, and how the press should be allowed to act as public surrogate, public informer, and the distributor of information.

2. A PUBLIC VERSUS A PRIVATE TRIAL

Allied to the notion of public scrutiny of the courts is the defendant's right to receive a trial held in public. Indeed, the Sixth Amendment right to a public trial was introduced as a safeguard for the accused, reasoning that the public's presence at trials would help to ensure fairness. Although, today, the public's interest in attending trials is motivated more out of curiosity than any notion of protecting the defendant's right to due process, the presumption is still valid and has been emphasized by several Supreme Court decisions.[7]

Those opposed to camera access contend that the right to choose a public trial should rest with the accused, not the public or the press. They emphasize that both First and Sixth Amendment rights are being met, not only because people can visit courtrooms, but also because the press can send reporters to cover trials. They also argue that privacy rights of defendants and witnesses are violated when cameras enter courtrooms: these participants, they say, are subjected to humiliation in an atmosphere resembling a public pillory rather than a dignified judicial arena. Those who support camera access to courtrooms claim that defendants and witnesses take on "public figure" and "public interest" status, and thereby surrender a right to privacy.[8] They also argue that, since the public's interests are involved in every criminal trial, the public should have access to those trials, whether in person or through a surrogate in the form of a camera.[9]

While the privacy question has prompted some strongly polarized arguments (see Linsdey, 1984, pp. 393–397; Kuriyama, 1982, pp. 116–130; Ares, 1981, pp. 180–182; Television in the Courtroom—Limited Benefits, Vital Risks? 1981; Kulwin, 1978, pp. 913–919; Roberts and Goodman, 1976, pp. 331–332), the courts have rarely accepted a right to privacy in the context of judicial proceedings. Although the Supreme Court has noted an *implicit* constitutional guarantee to privacy,[10] and has at times limited public and press access to courtrooms, privacy has yet to be used as the *single* criterion for excluding the press (or television cameras) from criminal courtrooms. If applied at all, it has been done so only when coupled with due process arguments focusing on the dangers of pretrial publicity and juror prejudice.[11] More often, the Court has upheld public and press access to trials, emphasizing that "what transpires in the courtroom is public property";[12] that a public trial is a "safeguard against any attempt to employ the courts as instruments of persecution,"[13] and that public scrutiny helps to ensure the defendant a fair trial.

In *Cox Broadcasting Corp. v. Cohn* (1975), a case involving a suit filed against an Atlanta, Georgia, television station for broadcasting the name of a young woman who was raped and murdered, the Court held that the press is not liable for invasion of privacy for reporting information which is already part of the public record, i.e., part of a criminal prosecution.[14] In *Waller v. Georgia* (1984), a case involving racketeering charges, the Court held that a defendant's Sixth Amendment right to a public trial must extend to pretrial suppression hearings. Writing for a unanimous Court, Justice Powell dismissed prosecution claims that privacy interests of not yet indicted persons might be infringed if such a hearing were open to the public.[15] In an earlier case, *People v. Jelke* (1954), the New York Court of Appeals held that exclusion of press and spectators from a trial for compulsory prostitution violated the defendant's Sixth Amendment rights. The case is particularly interesting in view of the trial judge's reasons for closure, which included safeguarding public morals against disclosure of "obscene and sordid details."[16] The Appeals Court noted: (a) though the statute in question authorized closure in cases of divorce, seduction, abortion, rape, sexual assault, sodomy, bastardy, or filiation, it did not apply to a case involving charges of compulsory prostitution; (b) anticipation of evidence "of an indecent or filthy nature" (describing a sodomous act) was not sufficient to trigger imposition of the statute; (c) "demands of public morality do not . . . justify nullification of the right of public trial, even in cases of an obscene or indecent nature. . . ."[17]

The Florida Supreme Court first discussed the privacy issue with specific regard to camera access in *Petition of Post-Newsweek Stations, Florida, Inc.* (1979), the case which opened Florida courts to cameras on an experimental basis without the need for defendant consent. In his opinion, Justice Alan Sundberg noted: "First, a judicial proceeding . . . is a public event which by its very nature denies certain aspects of privacy. Second . . . there is no constitutionally recognized right to privacy in the context of judicial proceedings."[18] Applying this philosophy some four years later, the Florida Supreme Court held, in *Doe v. Sarasota-Bradenton Television* (1983), that a rape victim who is identified, and whose testimony is videotaped in open court and then broadcast, cannot sue the television station for invasion of privacy. However, the Court severely criticized the prosecution for making no effort to keep the victim's name out of the records, and for not recommending that the judge bar cameras while the victim was on the witness stand, although it had promised anonymity. The Court also criticized the television station for being insensitive to the distress it caused the woman, saying that broadcasting her name and footage of her testimony added little to the story about the trial.[19]

In a similar case, *Globe Newspaper Co. v. Superior Court* (1982), the press applied a First Amendment challenge to a Massachusetts statute requiring closure of rape and sexual assault trials during the testimony of victims who are minors. The Court held that, even though the statute was applied with the good intentions of protecting the well-being of such victims, *mandatory* closure was unjustified. Justice Brennan, writing for the majority, explained that: (a) minors who are victims of sex crimes could be protected from "further trauma and embarrassment" by allowing judges to close trials on a case-by-case basis;[20] (b) it is both speculative and illogical to close a trial in the interests of protecting a victim's identity, and thereby "encouraging [other] such victims to come forward and testify," since (1) the press could obtain an account of a victim's testimony from the trial transcript, court personnel, or other sources, and (2) the statute did not prevent publication of a victim's identity or the testimony's substance.[21]

In reading Chief Justice Warren Burger's dissenting opinion in *Globe Newspaper,* in which he was joined by Justice Rehnquist, it appears that there were two very different views about the issues involved in this case. The Chief Justice understood the purpose of the closure statute as follows:

[It] is intended not to preserve confidentiality, but to prevent the risk of severe psychological damage caused by having to relate the details of the crime in front of a crowd which inevitably will include voyeuristic strangers. In most states, that crowd may be expanded to include a wide television audience, with reruns on the evening news.[22]

However, in a footnote to his opinion, Chief Justice Burger included a portion of the prosecutor's report about interviews she conducted with the three victims regarding their privacy concerns. From a reading of this note, it is clear that the victims were not so much afraid to testify in front of members of the press (print or broadcast) *inside the courtroom,* as they were extremely worried about any resultant publicity. In essence, they would agree to press attendance at the trial only if the press would guarantee "not to print their names or where they go to school or any personal data or take pictures of them or attempt to interview them . . . ."[23] The "severe psychological" trauma, according to the two witnesses themselves, would have occurred because of a lack of confidentiality, e.g., disclosure of their identities among friends and family, not because of the actual process of testifying in front of reporters and spectators inside the courtroom. The two young witnesses were prepared to testify in front of the press as well as strangers, but only with the assurance that personal details and identities would not go beyond the courtroom walls. Presumably, the witnesses would even have been willing to accept camera presence at the trial, so long as their faces or any other pictorial or verbal information clueing viewers to their identities would not have been broadcast. This type of plea for privacy calls for tremendous sensitivity and self-restraint on the part of the press (print and broadcast).

As compelling as such witness fears of publicity may be, the prevailing stance of the Supreme Court appears to rest on the side of First Amendment freedoms and the view that public trial means both spectators and the press must be allowed to attend.[24] Only very carefully tailored restraints, or specific time, place, and manner restrictions can be applied, and then only in the event that the information disclosed would have harmful or dangerous results on government interests.[25]

3. THE COURTROOM ENVIRONMENT

Those opposed to televised trials, however, have adopted the stance that any First Amendment claims of the news media should always be regarded as subordinate to the rights of a defendant to receive a fair trial. They emphasize that cameras in the courtroom present particular hazards which make their presence inconsistent with due process (see Fuoco, 1982, pp. 874–882; Tongue and Lintott, 1980, pp. 782–800; Doubles, 1965, pp. 13–16).

A. Physical Disruption

One of the earliest arguments proposed against cameras in courtrooms rests on the assumption that they disturb judicial serenity and calm—they are disruptive and physically distracting—and therefore hamper the search for truth. In the early days of televised trials, this was undoubtedly a valid charge, but not today. Even Justice Clark, writing for the Court in *Estes,* realized that television equipment which was so disruptive and obtrusive in the *Estes* pretrial hearings was unsophisticated, and that, when camera and recording technology advanced, the U.S. Supreme Court would have another case. That case, in effect, was *Chandler.* In the years between these two "cameras" decisions, the technological advances in electronic recording equipment were dramatic, and they continue to improve almost daily. Video machinery is no longer cumbersome, requiring a multitude of cables, distracting lighting, or numerous technicians. Today's cameras are noiseless, often hidden at the back of the courtroom, sometimes built-in to the courtroom wall, and require no additional lighting. In most courtrooms, television and radio stations have pooling arrangements, so that a single camera and microphone feed all stations wanting coverage. Often, a single cable links video and audio signals to a media room outside the courtroom where media personnel can gather to watch and record the footage they want for the day's news broadcasts.

B. Dignity and Decorum

But while physical disruption from camera equipment may no longer be a problem in today's televised trials, perhaps the issue is a lack of dignity and decorum in the courtroom as participants vie for media attention. Not according to former Colorado Chief Justice Edward Pringle. In 1979, after the state had gathered some 23 years of experience with televised trials, he wrote a letter to John C. Shepherd, then chairman of the ABA's House of Delegates, supporting proposed changes in Canon 3A(7). In part the letter read:

I was the presiding trial judge in one of the first extensively televised cases. Both as a trial judge and a member of the Colorado Supreme Court, I have found that these matters have been handled with dignity and no less decorum in the courtroom. . . . It is my opinion that photography tends to provide more dignity rather than less in judicial proceedings (ABA Keeps Courtroom TV Ban, 1979, p. 22).

Attorney Jerome Wilson also believes that camera presence might actually promote decorum: "It would serve as a restraint to breaches in dignity, be they judicial bullying, antics of counsel, or unfair treatment of the accused and witnesses. Even the possibility that there might be television coverage would serve as a restraint" (Wilson, 1974, p. 295; see also D'Alemberte, 1980, p. 8; Graham, 1978, p. 546; Stone and Edlin, 1978, p. 1130).

C. Psychological Dangers

However, the most serious claims against cameras in courtrooms have nothing to do with physical disruption or a lack of courtroom dignity and decorum. They have to do with psychological impacts, or what California Superior Court Judge Donald Fretz has called "the human part of the problem" (Fretz, 1978b, p. 550). The psychological effects of televising trials are often thought to be so subtle as to be imperceptible (see Hirschhorn, 1978, 1980a,b). Psychological dangers include witness fright and intimidation; juror fears of a lack of anonymity; community pressure on jury verdicts or witness testimony; fears of physical, financial, or reputational harm as a consequence of being identified during a broadcast; the grandstanding or flamboyant performance of judges and attorneys; and the "mental harassment" of defendants (see Boone, 1981, pp. 24–27; Block, 1978, pp. 454–455; Doubles, 1965, p. 14).

4. PUBLICITY AND JUROR IMPARTIALITY

Another serious hazard associated with televised trials is the possibility that added publicity will turn the trial into a "cause celebre," and that this will prejudice potential jurors. Members of the local community who may be called to serve as jurors will undoubtedly have made up their minds about the case before the trial begins, and those who have not will tend to place added importance on the case simply because it has been earmarked for television coverage. Witnesses, too, may have a tendency to regard the trial as more important if they know it will receive broacast coverage, and may embellish their testimony accordingly (see, for example, Block, 1978, pp. 454–455).

Although the courts have measures at their disposal to ensure juror impartiality, including change of venue, *voir dire* examination, juror (and witness) sequestration, and judicial admonition to jurors and witnesses not to read about, watch, or discuss the case, courtroom-cameras skeptics point out that these types of safeguards offer only post facto solution to the problem of prejudice. They emphasize, too, that televised coverage of trials (and pretrial hearings) exacerbates an already volatile situation, and that extra precautions are necessary to ensure fairness which add significant financial and administrative burdens to the courts. Moreover, the press (both print and broadcast) have shown little willingness to adhere to voluntary codes of conduct regarding the selection of cases for coverage and crime news reporting in general.

Juror impartiality is, of course, a problem in any trial, not just in sensational cases and not just in cases which may be televised. A notorious case is not only covered by the electronic media but is inevitably covered by newspapers as well, and several highly publicized cases have shown that printed stories can be equally, if not more, prejudicial than broadcast reports.[26] Members of the bench and bar, as well as media representatives, have emphasized these very points. Attorney Talbot D'Alemberte, for example, has explained that "the presence of a camera renders a case no more newsworthy than that of sketch artists, newspaper and television reporters, cameramen on courthouse steps, or a full courtroom of people. The circumstances give rise to cases of great public interest, not whether a reporter or cameraman happens to be in the courtroom" (D'Alemberte, 1982, p. 22; see also Brigner, 1982, pp. 12–16; Broholm, 1979, pp. 291–297; Wright, 1964, p. 1127, for similar views).

A.   The U.S. Supreme Court's Views

Even the Supreme Court has historically shown a reluctance to recognize prejudicial publicity and the possibility of juror contamination as sufficient reason to reverse convictions. The Court's first review of a defendant's challenge to his conviction on the basis of jury prejudice was *Reynolds v. U.S.* (1878).[27] Here, the Court refused to reverse the lower court's ruling saying that the defendant bears the burden of proof in showing that a juror was actually prejudiced. Later, in *Spies v. Illinois* (1887) and *Holt v. U.S.* (1910), the Court held that jurors need not be totally ignorant of circumstances surrounding a case, as long as they can lay aside their impressions of the defendant and render a verdict based on the evidence.

Although attitudes changed briefly in *Tumey v. Ohio* (1927),[28] where the Court indicated that failure to provide a fair and impartial hearing violates even minimal standards of due process, in *Stroble v. California* (1952)[29] the Court adopted a contrary stance and refused to overturn a murder conviction, even though the case was smothered with publicity. The defendant was convicted of murdering a 6-year-old girl and complained that sensational and prejudicial reporting had deprived him of a fair trial. The Court disagreed, noting that Stroble had failed to show "actual prejudice."

The conflict between free press and fair trial continued during the 1950s and 1960s. In 1955, Justice Black wrote that "our system of law has always endeavored to prevent even the probability of unfairness."[30] Similar thinking prevailed when the Court modified *Stroble* in *Irvin v. Dowd* (1961)[31] by vacating a defendant's murder conviction because the trial court had not ensured an impartial jury. The Court emphasized that it was not enough that jurors *said* they could render an impartial verdict despite exposure to prejudicial publicity. And the same tone continued in *Rideau v. Louisiana* (1963),[32] where the Court reversed a defendant's murder conviction on the basis that the jury was prejudiced by three television broadcasts of a confession, and the trial court had refused to change venue. This "probability" of prejudice argument was later implicitly affirmed in *Estes v. Texas* (1965), *Turner v. Louisiana* (1965),[33] *Sheppard v. Maxwell* (1966), and *Estelle v. Williams* (1976).

B. *Sheppard v. Maxwell*

In the years between *Estes* and *Chandler,* one case dominated the free press-fair trial issue from the standpoint of prejudicial publicity. But while *Sheppard* helped to bolster the arguments of anti-cameras commentators—because the appeal made reference to, among other things, pretrial television coverage—it was, perhaps, the most notorious appeal concerning prejudicial *newspaper* publicity ever to reach the U.S. Supreme Court.

In 1954, Dr. Sam Sheppard was convicted in the Cuyahoga County Court, Ohio, of murdering his wife. He appealed the conviction on the grounds that his right to a fair trial had been tainted by pervasive prejudicial media coverage. The Supreme Court found ample grounds for reversal: first, because the trial judge failed to stem the prejudicial publicity which saturated the community; and, second, because the judge failed to control disruptive influences in the courtroom during the trial. Justice Clark, writing for the majority, described numerous examples of flagrant unfairness that surrounded the trial and prejudiced the proceedings:

> From the outset officials focused suspicion on Sheppard. After a search of the house and premises on the morning of the tragedy, Dr. Gerber, the Coroner, is reported—and it is undenied—to have told his men, "Well, it is evident the doctor did this, so let's go get the confession out of him." He proceeded to interrogate and examine Sheppard while the latter was under sedation in his hospital room.[34]

After a barrage of highly inflammatory newspaper stories and editorials, including a front-page charge that Sheppard was "getting away with murder," the Coroner subpoenaed Sheppard and held the inquest in a school gymnasium. Crowds of reporters and photographers attended the hearing, which was also televised live, and Sheppard was brought into the room and searched by police in front of hundreds of spectators. Other activities during the hearings were reminiscent of the Hauptmann trial spectacle: "When Sheppard's chief counsel attempted to place some documents in the record, he was forcibly ejected from the room by the Coroner, who received cheers, hugs, and kisses from the ladies in the audience."[35]

However, what particularly disturbed the Supreme Court were, not simply the incriminating newspaper stories and undignified courtroom atmosphere, but Judge Blythin's (the trial judge) retort to defense counsel's complaints that he could do nothing to prevent the trial prejudice:

> The court's fundamental error is compounded by the holding that it lacked power to control the publicity about the trial. From the very inception of the proceedings the judge announced that neither he nor anyone else could restrict prejudicial news accounts. And he reiterated this view on many occasions. Since he viewed the news media as his target, the judge never considered other means that are often utilized to reduce the appearance of prejudicial material and to protect the jury from outside influence.[36]

Because blame for the unfair trial was seen to lay predominantly with its judge, the Supreme Court saw no reason to consider sanctions that might have been available against the press. Instead, Justice Clark described how Judge Blythin could have prevented the trial prejudice:

> The number of reporters in the courtroom itself could have been limited at the first sign that their presence would disrupt the trial. They certainly should not have been placed inside the bar. Furthermore, the judge should have more closely regulated the conduct of newsmen in the courtroom.
>
> Secondly, the court should have insulated the witnesses. All of the newspapers and radio stations apparently interviewed prospective witnesses at will, and in many instances disclosed their testimony.
>
> Thirdly, the court should have made some effort to control the release of leads, information, and gossip to the press by police officers, witnesses, and the counsel for both sides. Much of the information thus disclosed was inaccurate, leading to groundless rumors and confusion.[37]

There is little doubt, after reading the Court's opinion, that Sam Sheppard's trial was a mockery of justice. From the outset, law enforcement officials focused suspicion on Sheppard, and the news media picked up their cue from there. Four pages of the Court's 16-page opinion are replete with the headlines of newspaper articles written about the trial, the evidence, witness testimony, the defendant, the jurors, the judge, and other contemptuous material, all of which implied Sheppard was guilty. Even the trial judge incriminated Sheppard by remarking that this was "an open and shut case . . . he is guilty as hell."[38]

C. *The Warren Commission and The Reardon Report*

Detailed analysis of the impacts of prejudicial publicity on trial fairness began in earnest in 1964, when the Warren Commission released its report on press coverage surrounding the trial of Jack Ruby (Report of the President's Commission on the Assassination of President John F. Kennedy, 1964). The report noted the press had made numerous inflammatory statements surrounding the investigation, arrest, and trial of Ruby, aided in large part by law enforcement, bar, and bench officials.

The American Bar Association responded to the Warren report by forming a committee to study the free press fair trial issue further. The committee was headed by Justice Paul C. Reardon of the Massachusetts Supreme Judicial Court. Soon after *Sheppard* was handed down, the Reardon committee published its findings and recommendations, which were adopted with minor changes as part of the ABA's Standards of Criminal Justice (see Schmidt, 1977, p. 452; Gillmor and Barron, 1974, p. 418). Like the Warren Commission, Reardon's committee concluded that the principal offenders in the dissemination of prejudicial pretrial and trial information are often attorneys and law enforcement officials, and the committee's major recommendations were to restrict these people in their communications with news reporters (see Figure 3).[39] Canon 20 of the ABA's Canons of Professional Ethics, issued in 1964, 4 years *before* the *Reardon Report,* also advised that lawyers be prohibited from releasing prejudicial information to the press. But, as Wright (1964, p. 1126) has pointed out, the canon has largely been ignored: "At present Canon 20 is more honored in breach than in observance. The press may well wonder why Canon 20 is so hard to enforce while judicial Canon 35, which prohibits cameras in courtrooms, is so effective."

D. The Sheppard Mandate

Although the Supreme Court has charged trial judges with the responsibility to prevent prejudicial publicity, judges have emphasized that they often lack the power to enforce the guidelines espoused in *Sheppard,* and reinforced in the Warren and Reardon reports. As Younger (1977, p. 1) explains, "It's easier to criticize than to explain the legal system's handling of the crises that arise in highly publicized cases." The average trial judge, he notes, has little experience in handling highly notorious cases and so lacks proficiency in dealing with them when they do arise. Also, short of initiating contempt proceedings against members of the bar or the press—which many are reluctant to do because they use up valuable court time and money—trial judges lack practical powers to deal with publicity problems. If anything, explains Younger, the *Sheppard* mandate has been confusing. It has used strong language to admonish judges for not preventing prejudicial publicity, but it has offered them paltry means to apply stringent restrictive measures. Post facto measures such as contempt proceedings, continuances, changes of venue, jury sequestration, and new trials are merely "palliatives" (Younger, 1977, p. 8), and when attempts, such as gag orders, are made to stem prejudicial publicity at its sources, judges are often not backed in higher courts and their orders are reversed on appeal.

Attitudes of the press about the "absolute" rights of the media vis-a-vis criminal proceedings have frequently seemed inflexible and lacking in sensitivity for both the needs of the courts and the defendant (Landau, 1976). Much of the bitterness between press and courts stems from a lack of sympathy for the trial judge who is bound by appellate rulings. Yet even members of the bar, such as public prosecutors, have argued that, if the media are prevented from obtaining information

Figure 3.   *The Reardon Report* (Summarized by Gillmor and Barron, 1974, p. 418)

1. Lawyers must be restrained from making extrajudicial comments before or during a grand jury investigation or trial or, after a trial, before imposition of a sentence. Similar rules would apply to law enforcement officers and all judicial employees.
2. Prohibited extrajudicial comment would include:
   (a) The prior criminal record or the character or reputation of the accused;
   (b) The existence or contents of any confession, admission, or statement given by the accused, or the refusal of the accused to make any statement;
   (c) The performance of any examination or tests or the accused's refusal to submit to an examination or test;
   (d) The identity, testimony, or credibility of prospective witnesses;
   (e) The possibility of a plea of guilty to the offense charged or a lesser offense;
   (f) Any opinion as to the accused's guilt or innocence or as to the merits of the case or the evidence in the case.
3. It would be appropriate for a lawyer or law enforcement officer:
   (a) To announce the fact and circumstances of arrest;
   (b) To announce the identity of the investigating and arresting officer or agency;
   (c) To make an announcement of any physical evidence, other than a confession, that is seized;
   (d) To disclose the nature, substance, or text of the charge;
   (e) To quote from or refer without comment to public records of the court in the case;
   (f) To announce the scheduling or result of any stage in the judicial process;
   (g) To request assistance in obtaining evidence.
4. Judges should refrain from any conduct or the making of any statements that may tend to interfere with the right of the defendant to a fair trial.
5. The public and press should be excluded from all pretrial hearings on motion of the defendant unless the presiding officer determines that there would be no interference with a fair trial.
6. Where there is a threatened interference with the right to a fair trial, motions should be granted for a change in venue, . . . sequestration of the jury, or a new trial.
7. Prospective jurors should be examined outside the presence of other jurors and if they have been exposed to and remember reports of highly significant informantion, . . . they should be subject to challenge for cause without regard to their state of mind.
8. If the jury is not sequestered, the defendant should be permitted to move that the public and the press be excluded from any portion of the trial that takes place outside the presence of the jury.
9. The court should supervise the use to be made of the courtroom by newsmen.
10. The contempt power should be used against any person who, knowing that a criminal trial by jury is in progress or that a jury is being selected, disseminates by any means of public communication an extrajudicial statement relating to the defendant or to the issues in the case, that is willfully designed by that person to affect the outcome of the trial, and that seriously threatens to have an effect.

about criminal proceedings from direct sources (attorneys and the proceedings themselves), they will turn to less reliable sources (Younger, 1970). In an effort to repair relations between the bench and press, the ABA's Legal Advisory Committee has recommended that judges provide notice and a hearing to all parties, including the news media, when considering restrictive orders against the press (Roney, 1976). Judges themselves have emphasized that any efforts to restrict prejudicial publicity can only work if there is some recognition by both sides that neither fair trials nor a free press are absolute in nature (Burger, 1975; Finley, 1969).

E. Stemming Prejudicial Publicity

In an effort to stem prejudicial news reporting, the U.S. Supreme Court has traditionally sought measures to prevent publication of information about cases and courts. One measure has been the adoption of summary contempt proceedings. In *Toledo Newspaper Company, v. U.S.* (1918),[40] the Court explained that any reporting which had an impact on judicial administration could be punished summarily (in this case, the newspaper articles criticized the trial judge). However, 23 years later, in *Nye v. U.S.* (1941), the Court in essence reversed *Toledo Newspaper* and held that a federal court had no summary contempt power and could not prevent the press from publishing information about federal court procedures. In the same year, the Court decided *Bridges v. California* (1941)[41] and applied the First Amendment as a barrier to contempt proceedings, holding that state courts could not penalize the news media unless the publication created a "clear and present danger" to the fair administration of justice.

The First Amendment and the "clear and present danger" test were applied soon after to decisions in *Pennekamp v. Florida* (1946),[42] *Craig v. Harney* (1947),[43] and, later, in *Wood v. Georgia* (1962)[44] (note, however, that these were all nonjury civil cases). In *Dorfman v. Meiszner* (1974), the Seventh Circuit reviewed a district court order prohibiting photography and broadcasting both inside and in the environs of the courtroom.[45] The circuit court held that, while cameras could be restricted or excluded from the courtroom itself, it was too broad a rule to prohibit cameras from the environs. And in *United States v. CBS* (1974), the Fifth Circuit held that in-court artist sketching could not be banned unless it could be shown that sketching was disruptive to the proceedings.[46]

In 1976, the Supreme Court handed down another positive ruling for the press, applying First Amendment restrictions to strike down a gag order issued by a Nebraska judge. Writing for the Court in *Nebraska Press Association v. Stuart* (1976),[47] Chief Justice Burger made it clear that a judge may only place a prior restraint on reports of a trial if: (a) the publicity will be so pervasive as to affect jurors, (b) there are no alternative methods of dealing with the problems of prejudice; and (c) the prior restraint will prove effective. In fact the Court admonished the trial judge for placing a gag order on the press, saying his decision about the impact of publicity on prospective jurors was merely speculative. Moreover, it tones reminiscent of *Sheppard,* the Court recognized that, even in cases where pretrial publicity has been deemed prejudicial, prejudice arose not only because of press access and coverage but also because the trial judge neglected to control the inflammatory situation, and that sanctions against the press may not always be warranted.

In *Landmark Communications, Inc. v. Virginia* (1978),[48] a case involving the prosecution of two Virginia newspapers for identifying judges under investigation by a state ethics commission, the Court held 7-0 that the press could not be penalized for reporting about court proceedings, even if a local statute existed to the contrary. Writing for the Court, Chief Justice Burger noted that the First Amendment guaranteed the press the right to discuss and scrutinize the courts as well as judicial conduct.

5. ACCESS TO JUDICIAL PROCEEDINGS

Despite the Court's affirmative First Amendment stance in *Nebraska Press Association* and *Landmark Communications,* attitudes changed considerably a year later when the Court upheld the closure of pretrial hearings to the press and public in an effort to reduce pretrial prejudice. *Gannett v. DePasquale* (1979)[49] had sweeping and serious implications: no sooner was the decision handed down than courts around the country began to shut out reporters, not just from pretrial hearings, but from trials as well. A 6-page table, published in the November–December 1979 issue of *The News Media and The Law,* summarized a "Secret Court Watch" study and listed 109 efforts to close criminal proceedings between July and December that year. Several trends which emerged from the study were listed as follows:

> Judges are relying on *Gannett* to close pre-indictment, trial and post-trial proceedings—in addition to closing pretrial proceedings.
>
> Judges are closing proceedings for such reasons as embarrassment to witnesses, defendants and to lawyers—in addition to closing proceedings in order to protect juries from the effect of possible prejudicial publicity.
>
> Judges are issuing more prior restraint orders against publication by the press of court news—a trend which had stopped after the U.S. Supreme Court 1976 decision in the Nebraska Newspapers case.
>
> Prosecutors are not—as the *Gannett* opinion predicted they would—frequently opposing court secrecy. In fact, out of 109 reported cases, prosecutors supported or did not oppose closure motions in 67 instances and opposed them in 42 (Secret Court Watch, 1979, pp. 17–23; see also Court Watch Summary, 1980, pp. 4–5 for an update).

Newsweek, August 27, 1979, reported Chief Justice Burger's comment, tinged with a note of sarcasm, that the judges were misinterpreting the Court's opinion, perhaps because they were "reading newspaper reports of what we said" (Open and Shut Cases, p. 69). But as the magazine pointed out, much of the blame for any misunderstanding of the *Gannett* decision lay in the words of the justice's numerous and varied opinions.[50]

One chance to clarify the muddled *Gannett* opinion arrived the very next term, with the case of *Richmond Newspapers v. Virginia* (1980).[51] Ten media organizations filed friend of the court briefs on behalf of Richmond Newspapers, generally urging the Court to reverse its decision in *Gannett* and hold, instead, that criminal trials must remain open unless there is proof "of a direct, immediate and irreparable injury to the administration of justice" (News Media Hoping for Turnaround in Gannett Case, 1979, p. 72). Similar sentiments were expressed by media representatives attending a First Amendment Conference in Williamsburg, Virginia, in March 1980. The delegates were interested in informing the public about First Amendment issues, and wished to continue "dialogue with judges, prosecutors and lawyers to reduce bar-press conflict" (Fanfare for the First Amendment, 1980, p. 30).

The Supreme Court handed down its decision in *Richmond Newspapers* on July 2, 1980, holding that the public's (and the media's) right to attend trials is implicit in the guarantees of the First and Fourteenth Amendments, and that a Court could not be closed merely at the request of the defendant and the prosecution. The Court also emphasized the notion that, notwithstanding a defendant's fair trial rights, the media act as surrogates for the public and should therefore be allowed wide access to courtrooms:

> Instead of acquiring information about trials by firsthand observation or by word of mouth from those who attended, people now acquire it chiefly through the print and electronic media. In a sense this validates the media's claim of functioning as surrogates for the public.[52]

The *Richmond* holding was greeted with considerable relief by the media. Curtis Beckman, then president of the Radio-Television News Directors Association, read the decision as an affirmation of press rights to gather news in public places. Jack Landau, director of the Reporters Committee for Freedom of the Press, predicted it would guarantee the public's right to attend and be informed about criminal trials for years to come. And Vincent Wasilewski, then president of the National Association of Broadcasters, suggested the decision could help broadcasters in their efforts to gain approval for televised trials (High Court Bars Trial Held in Secret, 1980, p. 27). But legal experts were more cautious in their interpretations of the court's decision. As communications lawyer Bruce Sanford realized, footnotes accompanying the various opinions placed limitations on the sweep of the decision (Sanford, 1980, p. 47), and *Richmond* should not necessarily be regarded as a striking victory for the First Amendment, particularly where camera access is concerned.

In January 1984, the Court went a step further in upholding press freedoms when it said that jury selection proceedings must be held in public. In *Press Enterprise Co. v. Superior Court,*[53] the Court noted that the First Amendment guarantees the public's and the media's right to attend jury selections in nearly all criminal cases, and that in rare instances where *voir dire* might be closed, the trial judge must release transcripts of the proceedings as soon as possible. However, the Court acknowledged for the first time that, in certain circumstances, a juror's right to privacy overrides the public's right of access. For example, a prospective juror, questioned during *voir dire,* should not be forced to publicly disclose intimate personal details.

6.   THE RIGHT TO BROADCAST AUDIO-TAPED EVIDENCE

The presumption of openness in judicial proceedings also extends to the public's right to inspect judicial records. Questions arose, however, regarding a right to copy and broadcast audio and video tapes introduced in evidence in the Watergate hearings and the Abscam trials. In *United States v. Mitchell* (1976)[54] and *United States v. Haldeman* (1976), the D.C. Circuit Court reversed the trial judge's denial of a press application to copy audio tapes. However, in *Nixon v. Warner Communications* (1978),[55] the U.S. Supreme Court held that the electronic media have no First Amendment right to copy and broadcast audio tapes introduced in evidence and widely reported in newspapers. The 7-2 decision prohibited the three networks from copying the Nixon tapes that were played to the public and jury during the Watergate cover-up trial. The Court said that, while there is a general right to inspect a case record, this is not an absolute right, and cited Justice Harlan in *Estes* to support its claim that the rights of reporters are no greater than the rights of the public when attending trials.

In the Abscam federal prosecutions, videotapes of government officials discussing or taking bribes were introduced in evidence. While the district courts denied applications by the television networks to copy and broadcast the tapes, three federal appeals courts upheld a right of access to the tapes. In *United States v. Criden* (1980),[56] the Third Circuit said that the right to copy trial materials is the same consideration as supporting open trials. *In re Application of National Broadcasting Co., Inc.* (1980),[57] concerning Congressman Michael Myers, the Second Circuit said only the most compelling reasons can override access to materials in the trial record. And *In re Application of National Broadcasting Co., Inc.* (1981),[58] involving Congressman John Jenrette, the D.C. Circuit said the presumption should be in favor of public access to judicial records, though the decision is a matter of discretion for the trial judge. However, in *Belo Broadcasting Corp. v. Clark* (1981), the Fifth Circuit upheld a denial to copy and broadcast tapes because of potential prejudice to a defendant who had not yet been tried.

7.   CAMERA ACCESS TO COURTROOMS

Prior to the camera access movement of the 1970s and widespread state experimentation with televised trials, courts traditionally regarded in-court photography as an infringement of the defendant's right to a fair trial. In states where camera access was prohibited, courts often used contempt powers to punish cameramen who violated court orders. In *State v. Clifford* (1954), the trial judge held a photographer in contempt for taking pictures during the arraignment of a man indicted for embezzlement. The judge's order was upheld on appeal:

> A Judge is at all times during the sessions of the court empowered to maintain decorum and enforce reasonable rules to insure the orderly and judicious disposition of the

court's business. . . . It is therefore impossible for this court to hold that the trial court, in promulgating the rule against photographers . . . abused its descretion. . . . When the court is in session it is under the complete control of the judge, whose discretions, reasonably necessary to maintain order and prevent unnecessary disturbance and distraction must be obeyed. Deliberate disobedience of such orders constitutes a contempt of court punishable under statutes of this state.[59]

However, in states where cameras were permitted on a case-by-case basis, the judge's authority was still paramount, and defendants seeking to have convictions overturned because of camera presence met with little success. In *Lyles v. State* (1958), for example, the Oklahoma Criminal Court of Appeals dismissed the defendant's claim that his case was prejudiced by the presence and use of television cameras. The Court concluded that the defendant failed to demonstrate substantial prejudice and said: "there is no sound reason why photographers and television representatives should not be entitled to the same privileges of the courtroom as other members of the press."[60] The Court also rejected two arguments often used against courtroom cameras: that they violate privacy interests, and that they interfere with the orderly conduct of proceedings. Responding to the first argument, the Court said that a criminal defendant "becomes a public figure in which the public has more than an ordinary interest."[61] To the second argument, the Court said: "We are of the opinion that the presumption upon which Canon 35 has been constructed is fabricated out of sheer implication and not hammered out on the anvil of experience."[62] Ultimately, the Court concluded that the decision to allow courtroom broadcasting and photography rests with the trial judge. The same emphasis on judicial authority and discretion was evident 2 years later in another Oklahoma case, but involving contrasting circumstances. In *Cody v. Oklahoma* (1961),[63] the defendant said he was denied a fair and public trial because the judge refused to allow television cameras to cover his rape case. The appeals court said that the circumstances of this trial rendered it inappropriate for broadcast coverage.

A. *Estes v. Texas*

In 1965, any presumption on the part of broadcasters and photographers that camera access was gaining momentum was quickly and abruptly laid to rest. The U.S. Supreme Court handed down its decision in *Estes v. Texas*[64] and triggered a rally of anti-cameras sentiments that were to have long-lasting and pervasive impacts on the camera access movement. While many of the justices' concerns have merit and deserve thorough examination, the precise activities of the television crews and news photographers at the trial of Texas businessman Billie Sol Estes have often been grossly exaggerated by those supporting a ban on courtroom cameras. These commentators have focused on a series of arguments about the dangers of televising trials which were listed in Justice Thomas Clark's plurality opinion (Fuoco, 1982; Hirschhorn, 1980a,b; Tongue and Lintott, 1980; Block, 1978; Fretz, 1978a,b; Kulwin, 1978; Doubles, 1965). However, in concentrating on the unsubstantiated fears, the courtroom camera critics lost sight of what actually took place at the Estes trial—what, if any, were the prejudicial effects of media coverage of the proceedings.

Both Justice Clark's opinion for the Court and Justice Potter Stewart's dissenting opinion very clearly describe media activities at the trial. What becomes obvious from a reading of these opinions is that any instances of prejudice created by electronic coverage only took place during 2 days of pretrial hearings, not during the trial itself. As Justice Stewart noted, television cameras at the trial were "so controlled and concealed as to be hardly perceptible in the courtroom . . . ."[65] Justice Clark described how the case received a great deal of publicity and national notoriety before cameras even entered the courtroom, and how the trial judge was partly responsible for his court's lack of decorum, having allowed it to fill with spectators beyond capacity:

> Massive pretrial publicity totalling 11 volumes of press clippings . . . had given [the case] national notoriety. All available seats in the courtroom were taken and some 30 persons stood in the aisles. . . . The initial hearings were carried live by both radio and television, and news photography was permitted throughout. The videotapes of these hearings clearly illustrated that the picture was not one of that judicial serenity and calm to which petitioner was entitled.[66]

The physical presence of news photographers and television cameramen and their equipment was, indeed, obtrusive and disturbing during the pretrial hearings. However, at the trial, itself, there was no disruption on the part of media personnel or their equipment:

> When the case was called for trial . . . the scene had been altered. A booth had been constructed at the back of the courtroom which was painted to blend with the permanent structure of the room. It had an aperture to allow the lens of the camera an unrestricted view of the courtroom. All television cameras and news photographers were restricted to the area of the booth when shooting film or telecasting.[67]

Nevertheless, Justice Clark was adamant about the prejudicial nature of cameras in the courtroom, and was particularly disturbed by the psychological considerations of televising trials. He noted that, while empirical knowledge of television's effect on trial participants was limited: "experience teaches that there are numerous situations in which it might cause actual unfairness—some so subtle as to defy detection by the accused or control by the judge."[68] He then proceeded to list 20 ways in which television may jeopardize a fair trial by adversely affecting jurors, witnesses, judges and defendants. His arguments are paraphrased here:

Impacts on Jurors

1. Prospective jurors will become fascinated by the notorious details of a case once they know it will receive television coverage.

2. These jurors will enter a trial already prejudiced by publicity about the case.
3. Only sensational cases will be televised, because of the need for advertising revenue, and consciously or unconsciously the notoriety of a case will prejudice jurors.
4. If a trial is televised, juror anonymity will be lost and jury verdicts will be based on local community views.
5. Jurors will be distracted, not only by the physical presence of cameras in the courtroom, but also by the mere awareness that they are being televised.
6. Jurors will watch newscasts of the trial in which they are participating and will be subconsciously influened by the testimony given air time.
7. New trials will be jeopardized because television viewers may later be called to serve as jurors.

Impacts on Witnesses

1. The quality of testimony will be impaired: some witnesses will be inhibited and frightened by the presence of cameras; memories may falter due to embarrassment. Other witnesses will become flamboyant and exaggerate testimony.
2. Witnesses could view earlier testimony at home and then base their own testimony on that of others.
3. Witnesses may be reluctant to testify if a trial is to be televised.

Impacts on Trial Judges

1. Camera presence will place additional responsibilities on the judge.
2. The judge will have to supervise the conduct of media representatives.
3. Judges will constantly be distracted by the mere awareness of camera presence.
4. Televised trials will become "political weapons" for elected judges.
5. In states where judges are elected, if one judge permits the televising of a trial other judges will feel compelled to do the same in order to get equal media exposure.

Impacts on the Defendant

1. Television coverage of a trial is a form of mental, if not physical, harassment for the defendant.
2. Close-up shots of the defendant's gestures and expressions may compromise his dignity and ability to concentrate on the proceedings.
3. Heightened public interest in televised trials will inevitably prejudice the defendant's case.
4. The televising of trials may deprive the defendant of effective counsel. Cameras

may intrude into confidential client–attorney relationships, and attorneys may be tempted to play to the public audience.

5. Since television coverage will predominantly focus on notorious cases, only unpopular and infamous defendants will be televised.

In contrast, Justice Stewart (dissenting) explained that, while activities of the television crews and news photographers led to considerable disruption of the *pretrial hearings,* he could find nothing in the record to indicate that limited televising of the *trial* resulted in denial of any constitutional rights. The sequestration of jurors prevented any possibility of prejudice from trial publicity, and the presence of television cameras during the trial went unnoticed. What finally struck Justice Stewart about this case was not that Estes had been denied due process, but that press freedom and the public's right to know may be in jeopardy:

> there are intimations in the opinions filed by my Brethren in the majority which strike me as disturbingly alien to the First and Fourteenth Amendments' guarantees against federal or state interference with the free communication of information and ideas. The suggestion that there are limits upon the public's right to know what goes on in the courts causes me deep concern. The idea of imposing upon any medium of communications the burden of justifying its presence is contrary to where I had always thought the presumption must lie in the area of First Amendment freedoms . . . and the proposition that nonparticipants in a trial might get the "wrong impression" from unfettered reporting and commentary contains an invitation to censorship which I cannot accept.[69]

Although *Estes* served to bolster the arguments of states which already banned cameras from their courtrooms at the time of the decision, and while it stymied the spread of courtroom cameras into new states, Colorado continued to televise trials unabated, and even Texas was not deterred for another 10 years. Defendants in these states met with little success when appealing convictions on the grounds that cameras were present at their trials.[70]

Once states began to adopt revised versions of Canon 35 or Canon (3A(7) in the 1970s—permitting trials to be televised—new subtleties emerged in judicial interpretation of camera access rules, and in general the burden of proof was placed on the presiding judge to show why cameras should be barred. In *State ex rel. Grinnell Communications Corp. v. Love* (1980), for example, the Ohio Supreme Court held that, unless a judge can determine that broadcasting a trial would distract participants, impair dignity, or otherwise interfere with the defendant's fair trial rights, camera coverage must be allowed. A judge may, however, prohibit coverage of specific witnesses or victims who raise objections. In *State ex rel. Miami Valley Broadcasting Corp. v. Kessler* (1980), the Ohio Supreme Court held that television representatives must be given notice of any hearing on trial coverage, and have the right to offer evidence and cross examine witnesses when objections to cameras are raised. And in *King v. State* (1980), the Florida Supreme Court held that general allegations of prejudice were insufficient to deny camera access.

B. *Chandler v. Florida*

By the time the U.S. Supreme Court decided its second landmark "cameras" case, *Chandler v. Florida* (1981),[71] the atmosphere surrounding televised trials was very different from the situation which existed at the time *Estes* was handed down. Not only was no justice who voted with the majority in *Estes* still on the Court in *Chandler*, but the reasoning of the justices in the two cases was in sharp contrast. In *Estes*, the Court held that television coverage of a trial was inherently prejudicial and that a defendant could claim due process violation merely by referring to the *potential* prejudice associated with camera coverage. In *Chandler*, the Court said that a defendant must demonstrate *actual* prejudice.

Despite the sharp turnaround in attitude between *Estes* and *Chandler*, it seems that *Chandler* offers broadcasters and photographers mixed hopes. While the Court said that it is not unconstitutional for states to experiment with camera coverage of trials over defendants' objections, its holding was a narrow one, circumscribed by five major points. First, it emphasized that there is no constitutional right to broadcast or photograph trials, only the opportunity to do so if state trial court judges permit. Second, nothing was said about camera access to federal courts, including the U.S. Supreme Court.[72] Third, *Chandler* did not overrule *Estes*, but merely read *Estes* as not providing a constitutional ban on all broadcast coverage, only coverage of highly sensational trials to be dealt with on an individual basis. Fourth, the Court emphasized that stringent guidelines must be applied to monitor courtroom media activities. Finally, the Court said there is a need for more research on the psychological effects of televised trials, particularly effects on defendants, and it left the door open for future appeals on the same question by saying that cases must be decided on the merit of individual appeals.

Chief Justice Burger, writing for the majority, conceded that physical disruption of trials by media equipment is no longer a factor, because of sophisticated cameras and recording devices. He concentrated, instead, on the sensitive question of potential psychological prejudice associated with broadcast trial coverage. Having reviewed briefs for both sides of the issue, he noted that, while empirical data was not available on all aspects of the problem, no one has yet shown that "electronic coverage creates a significant adverse effect upon the participants in trials—at least not one uniquely associated with electronic coverage as opposed to more traditional forms of coverage."[73] But the Chief Justice hovered cautiously between positive and negative assessments of the research:

> While the data thus far assembled are cause for some optimism about the ability of states to minimize the problems that potentially inhere in electronic coverage of trials, even the Florida Supreme Court conceded that the data were "limited" . . . and "non-scientific" . . . .[74]
>
> Other courts that have been asked to examine the impact of television coverage on the participants in particular trials have concluded that such coverage did not have an adverse impact on the trial participants sufficient to constitute denial of due process. . . . On the other hand, even the *amici* supporting Florida's position concede that

further experimentation is necessary to evaluate the potential psychological prejudice associated with broadcast coverage of trials. Further developments and more data are required before this issue can finally be resolved.[75]

Given the Court's cautious reliance on the courtroom cameras research, what other reasons are presented in the majority opinion for allowing broadcast trial coverage? There appear to be three: (a) support of federalism—states' rights to experiment with camera coverage if they so choose, (b) the ability to protect due process by implementing guidelines and safeguards governing camera use, and (c) the notion of parity between print and broadcast media in courtrooms. Chief Justice Burger made substantial reference to the principle of federalism and the right of states to experiment with new ideas. He defined the limited jurisdiction of the U.S. Supreme Court, and observed that, unless the Court were to conclude that television coverage under *all* circumstances is prohibited by the Constitution, states must be free to experiment.[76] The Court also emphasized that safeguards against prejudice, such as the guidelines set down by the Florida Supreme Court, should be implemented by other states. *Chandler* suggested that states adopt canons which ensure that witnesses who have substantial reasons for not wishing to be televised or photographed will not be subjected to such coverage. Other suggestions emphasized the prominent role that must be played by trial judges in monitoring media activities in their courtrooms.[77]

Perhaps the most positive aspect of *Chandler* for broadcasters was its recognition that criminal cases may be intrinsically sensational, not made notorious only because they are televised, and its reference to the equal rights of print and broadcast media to cover trials. Chief Justice Burger noted that a double standard should not be applied to broadcast versus print media coverage: "The risk of juror prejudice in some cases does not justify an absolute ban on news coverage of trials by the printed media; so also the risk of such prejudice does not warrant an absolute constitutional ban on all broadcast coverage."[78]

8.   OTHER INTERPRETATIONS OF ESTES AND CHANDLER

Perhaps the most original and thought-provoking interpretations of the two landmark "cameras" cases have been offered by Charles Nesson and Andrew Koblenz (1981) and David Tajgman (1981). They focus, not on the behavioral consequences (to trial participants) of allowing cameras inside courtrooms, but on the image of the courts that is presented to the audience by allowing trials to be televised. This distinction is a crucial one, since even when assessing the impacts of camera coverage from a trial participant's perspective, the concern should not simply be that a television camera is *present* inside the courtroom, but how the *viewing audience* will perceive those who are being displayed on the screen. Presumably, few judges, attorneys, witnesses, or jurors would fear the literal process of being recorded on videotape if they could be assured that the footage would not be broadcast. Anxiety stems, instead, from knowing that thousands may watch and listen to them.

A. The Image of The Judiciary

Nesson and Koblenz (1981) explain the *Chandler* Court's departure from precedent (*Estes*) as a matter of "image." *Estes* was motivated by a desire to protect a "perfect" image of justice, and to keep the courts out of the public's living rooms. In *Chandler*, there was a belief that televising trials could help to improve the image of justice.

> The Supreme Court's long attention to the *appearance* of justice underscores a preoccupation with judicial image. The Court is concerned about the status of courts as institutions and the status of justice as an ideal. It recognizes that tension often exists between the legal merits of a case and the public's perception of its merits, a conflict between whether justice appeared to be done and whether justice actually was done (p. 405).

What differences existed between the two landmark cases to account for these contrasting views? First, the footage that was broadcast of the Estes pretrial hearings (though not the trial) was highly indecorous, and revealed "a scene more like a press conference than a trial" (Nesson and Koblenz, 1981, p. 406). In contrast, the few minutes of the Chandler and Granger trial that were broadcast could only have served to give the public a positive image of justice—in this case the fact that justice was served when policemen-turned-burglars were brought to trial.

> Burger is not asserting that the pretrial indecorum in the *Estes* case produced a distorted or unjust verdict. What was prejudiced was the appearance of judicial control, the image of the courts. . . . The focal point of *Estes*, then, according to Burger, was not the risk of distortion in the behavior of the trial participants . . . but rather the likelihood that the public would hold a lasting impression of the press-conference atmosphere of the *Estes* pretrial proceeding, and would not discriminate between the pretrial and trial proceedings (Nesson and Koblenz, 1981, p. 413).

Second, in the years between *Estes* and *Chandler* there was growing concern among the judiciary that the public lacked confidence in the courts to control crime and criminals, and that the courts were partly responsible for increasing crime rates.

> Televising trials looks to some judges like a possible counter to charges against the judiciary. Trials, after all, show the justice system at its best. The camera's eye will see impartial justice, fair procedure, conviction of the guilty, and the imposition of sentence. Though some may denigrate the trial process, it is impressive. By contrast, the seamy side of the criminal process—plea bargaining, the procedural inefficiency, the arbitrariness inherent in police and prosecutorial discretion—will go unseen. Televising trials, in other words, is unlikely to hurt and may help shore up the image of the judiciary (Nesson and Koblenz, 1981, pp. 408–409).

B. Benefits Outweigh Risks

Similar arguments have been expressed by Tajgman (1981). He emphasizes that the Court's change in attitude toward television between *Estes* and *Chandler* "is based on the court's assessment of objectives sought to be served through the power of the press at a particular time" (p. 509). In the case of *Chandler,* the Court regarded the electronic press as having multiple benefits for the courts: "promoting due process by protecting rights of the accused against unfair trial proceedings, and controlling criminal behavior while promoting respect for the criminal justice system" (p. 508). Tajgman also explains the different perceptions about printed versus electronic media which juxtapose the two landmark decisions:

> The United States Supreme Court in *Chandler v. Florida* has, essentially, updated *Estes* . . . the Court's 1981 perceptions of the "function and effect" of television, the rights of the accused, and the socializing, educating role of the "press" challenged *Estes'* sixteen-year-old concerns about, and impressions of, television. It was this conflict of modern values regarding media, i.e., the proper role and function of television cover-age of criminal trial proceedings *vis-a-vis* the traditional role of newspaper coverage, rather than century old ideals of free press and fair trial, that resulted in the *Chandler* court's granting freer access to the courtroom. (Tajgman, 1981, pp. 507–508)

Hence, according to Tajgman (pp. 519–526), the *Estes* Court perceived the risks of prejudicial behavioral and psychological impacts to be far more serious than any purported crime control or educational benefits. Newspapers were viewed as possess-ing high due process value, low due process detriment, and inconsequential crime control value; television, on the other hand, was viewed as possessing low due process value, high due process detriment, and high crome control value—but the Court rejected the crime control value argument as being outweighed by the due process risks.

In contrast, notes Tajgman (pp. 526–537), the *Chandler* Court said that: (a) television may no longer be regarded as possessing low due process value, i.e., it can serve to scrutinize the courts just as effectively as newspapers do; (b) television should no longer be regarded as possessing high due process detriment, since tech-nological changes have made video recording unobtrusive, and since state experi-mentation has found claims of behavioral and psychological prejudice to be unsub-stantiated (at least not any different from potential risks associated with newspaper coverage); and (c) television can serve a desirable crime control function.

In essence, then, *Estes* took the cautious approach that anything which does not promote better justice (fairer trials), and which is inherently suspicious (outcome unknown), presents a risk too great to balance against due process rights. *Chandler* took the opposite approach, showing a willingness to *experiment* with the proposi-tions that television coverage is not inherently prejudicial, and that it could have crime control value. In effect, the *Chandler* court was establishing its own experi-ment: Will televised trials improve public opinion of the justice system? Will televised trials serve a crime control purpose?

FOOTNOTES

1. The First Amendment, which guarantees press freedom, reads in part: "Congress shall make no law . . . abridging the freedom of speech, or of the press. . . ." The Sixth Amendment guarantees the right to a fair, impartial, public trial and reads in part: "In all criminal prosecutions, the accused shall enjoy the right to a speedy and public trial, by an impartial jury of the State and district wherein the crime shall have been committed . . . to be confronted with the witnesses against him . . . and to have Assistance of Counsel for defense." The Fourteenth Amendment makes both the First and Sixth Amendments binding upon state governments and says in part: "No state shall make or enforce any law which shall abridge the privileges or immunities of citizens of the United States; nor shall any state deprive any person of life, liberty, or property, without due process of law; not deny to any person within its jurisdiction the equal protection of the laws."

   Although commentators have described the free press fair trial debate as one of "conflicting constitutional rights," Oregon Supreme Court Justice Hans Linde has outlined the inherent fallacy of this argument by explaining the *Sheppard* legacy, as follows: "Its premise is the defendant's constitutional right to be tried by an impartial jury and only on evidence presented in court. But note that the constitution gives a defendant these guarantees against the state that tries him, not against the press. Irresponsible publicity may make it difficult or impossible to select an impartial jury, at least at the immediate time and place. Irresponsible publicity may cause a jury to act on information, or misinformation, that is not and could not be presented in court. If that happens, the state cannot constitutionally convict a defendant. But nothing in *Sheppard* said that the state could forbid a publication in order to assure itself of the ability to obtain a conviction. *Sheppard* was a decision protecting one constitutional right, under the sixth amendment, not infringing another one under the first amendment" (Linde, 1977, p. 213).

2. *Nebraska Press Association v. Stuart,* 427 U.S. 539, at 547 (1976).

3. *Bridges v. California,* 314 U.S. 252 at 260 (1941).

4. *U.S. v. Dickinson,* 465 F.2d 496 at 499 (5th Cir. 1972) *cert. denied,* 414 U.S. 797 (1973).

5. See, for example, *Houchins v. KQED, Inc.,* 483 U.S. 1 (1978). For further discussion of this case, see Kuriyama (1982), Fenner and Koley (1981), Pequignot (1981), Jacobs (1980), O'Brien (1980).

6. See *Branzburg v. Hayes,* 408 U.S. 665 (1972) where the Supreme Court recognized for the first time that the news media have at least a limited constitutional First Amendment right to gather information, though not the right to refuse to reveal sources to a grand jury. For further discussion of this case see: Kuriyama (1982), Fenner and Koley (1981), Jacobs (1980), O'Brien (1980).

7. See, for example, *Waller v. Georgia,* 10 Med.L.Rptr. 1714 (1984); *Richmond Newspapers, Inc., v. Virginia,* 448 U.S. 555 (1980); *Landmark Communications, Inc., v. Virginia,* 435 U.S. 829 (1978); and *Craig v. Harney,* 331 U.S. 367, 347 (1947).

8. See *Gertz v. Robert Welch, Inc.,* 481 U.S. 323 (1974), and *New York Times v. Sullivan,* 376 U.S. 254 (1964). See also: Gertz Wins $400,000 in Damages Following 14-Year Court Battle (1982).

9. See *Red Lion Broadcasting Co. v. FCC,* 395 U.S. 367 (1969), where Justice White, writing for a unanimous Court, emphasized the licensee's responsibility is to serve listeners and viewers for whom he acts in proxy; and *CBS v. Democratic National Committee,* 412 U.S. 94 (1973), where Chief Justice Warren Burger described the licensee as a "public trustee" whose duty is to fairly and impartially inform the listening and viewing public.

10. See *Eisenstadt v. Baird,* 405 U.S. 438 (1972), and *Griswold v. Connecticut,* 381 U.S. 479 (1965), where, in his separate concurring opinion, Justice Goldberg said that privacy had a place in the Ninth Amendment; cf. *Whalen v. Roe,* 429 U.S. 589 (1977).

11. Early clarification of this point appeared *In re: Oliver,* 333 U.S. 257 (1948) and *United Press Association v. Valente,* 308 N.Y. 71, 123 N.E.2d 777 (1954), and was implied in *Estes v. Texas,* 381 U.S. 532 (1965). More recently, a stronger declaration of this argument arrived in *Gannett Co. v. DePasquale,* 443 U.S. 368 (1979), upholding the right of a state court to close a pretrial hearing. In its holding, the Court emphasized that the press has no affirmative right of access to pretrial proceedings, and that the Sixth Amendment guarantee of a public trial is for the benefit of the defendant alone, not the public or the press.

12. *Craig v. Harney,* 331 U.S. 367, 347 (1947). See also, generally, Kuriyama (1982), Ares (1981), Schmidt (1977), Stanga (1971).

13. *In re: Oliver,* 333 U.S. 257, 270 (1948). See also generally Stanga (1971).

14. *Cox Broadcasting Corp. v. Cohn,* 420 U.S. 469 (1975). *Cox* was later implicitly affirmed in *Paul v. Davis,* 424 U.S. 693 (1976), where the Court held that publication and circulation of flyers containing the photograph of a shoplifter did not violate privacy concerns, and in *Landmark Communications, Inc. v. Virginia,* 435 U.S. 829 (1978), *Smith v. Daily Mail Publishing Co.,* 443 U.S. 97 (1979), and *Globe Newspaper Co. v. Superior Court,* 457 U.S. 596 (1982). For further discussion, see, generally, Lindsey (1984), Kuriyama (1982), Ares (1981), Fenner and Koley (1981), Kulwin (1978).

15. *Waller v. Georgia,* 10 Med.L.Rptr. 1714 at 1715 (1984).

16. *People v. Jelke,* 123 N.E.2d 769 at 770 (1954).

17. Id., at 771–773.

18. *Petition of Post-Newsweek Stations, Florida, Inc.,* 370 So.2d 764 at 799 (1979). For general discussion of this case see: Pequignot (1981), Boyd (1978).

19. *Doe v. Sarasota-Bradenton Television,* 436 So.2d 328 (Fla. App., 1983). For further discussion of this case, see Rape Trial Tape Privileged (1984, p. 43). Judges have also exercised the right to clear a courtroom of spectators when witnesses are to testify about unpleasant sexual experiences. See for example, *People v. Latimore,* 33 Ill. App. 3rd 812, 342 N.E. 2d 209 (1975); *United States ex rel. Latimore v. Sielaff,* 561 F.2d 691 (7th Cir. 1977); *United States ex rel. Latimore v. Sielaff, cert denied* 434 U.S. 1076 (February 21, 1978), where the U.S. Supreme Court let stand a lower court order affirming the rape conviction of two men who claimed that the public should not have been excluded during the testimony of the rape victim. The press, however, was not excluded.

20. *Globe Newspaper Co. v. Superior Court,* 457 U.S. 596 at 607–608 (1982). See also Lindsey (1984) for further discussion.

21. Id., at 609–610,

22. Id., at 618.

23. Id., at 612 footnote 1. For details of the earlier decision in this case by the Massachusetts Supreme Court, see Legality of Sex Trials Approved if Victim Under Eighteen (1980), and *Globe Newspaper Co. v. Superior Court,* 401 N.E. 2d 360 (Mass. 1980).

24. See, for example, *Press Enterprise Co. v. Superior Court*, 52 U.S.L.W. 4113 (1984), supporting qualified access to *voir dire* jury selection proceedings; *Globe Newspaper Co. v. Superior Court*, 457 U.S. 596 (1982); *Richmond Newspapers, Inc. v. Virginia*, 448 U.S. 555 (1980), announcing a qualified right to attend criminal proceedings; and *Landmark Communications, Inc., v. Virginia*, 435 U.S. 829 (1978), confirming a right to report about judicial conduct.
25. See *Nebraska Press Association v. Stuart*, 427 U.S. 539 (1976); *Clark v. Community For Creative Non-Violence et al.*, 104 S.Ct. 3065 (1984); and *Regan v. Time, Inc.*, 104 S.Ct. 3262 (1984).
26. See, for example, *Sheppard v. Maxwell*, 384 U.S. 333 (1966); *Hauptmann v. New Jersey*, *cert. denied*, 296 U.S. 649 (1935).
27. *Reynolds v. U.S.*, 98 U.S. 145 at 157 (1878). For further discussion of this case see Boyd (1978); Stanga (1971).
28. See also *In re Oliver*, 333 U.S. 257 (1948).
29. For further discussion of this case, see Ares (1981), Boyd (1978), Portman (1977), Stanga (1971).
30. *In re Murchison*, 349 U.S. 133 (1955).
31. See also, generally, Ares (1981), Boyd (1978), Portman (1977), Stanga (1971).
32. See also Ares (1981), Boyd (1978), Portman (1977), Schmidt (1977), Stanga (1971).
33. See also Portman (1977).
34. *Sheppard v. Maxwell*, 384 U.S. 333 at 337 (1966). Prejudicial publicity was the key argument in Sheppard's appeal to the Ohio Supreme Court: *Sheppard v. State*, 135 N.E. 2d 340, 342 (1955). For discussion of *Sheppard* and other cases surrounding the free press-fair trial issue, see Kuriyama (1982), Portman (1977), Schmidt (1977), Younger (1977), Stanga (1971).
35. Id., at 334. Other examples of pretrial prejudice are outlined in the majority opinion at 338–345; examples of trial prejudices are described at 345–349.
36. Id., at 357–358.
37. Id., at 358–359.
38. Id., at 358 footnote 11.
39. For discussion of recently proposed revisions to the Reardon Report, see American Bar Association Study Opposes Court Secrecy (1978, pp. 11–12). For discussion of the implications of the Reardon Report, see Revised Report of the Judicial Conference Committee on the Operation of the Jury System on the 'Free Press-Fail Trial' Issue, 87 F.R.D. 518 (approved by the U.S. Judicial Conference, September 25, 1980), and Free Press–Fair Trial Proposed Revised Guidelines of the Judicial Conference of the United States—1980: A Recommendation Relating to Information by Attorneys in Criminal Cases, 91 F.R.D. 289 (1981).
40. For further discussion, see Portman (1977).
41. For further discussion, see Ares (1981), Schmidt (1977), Stanga (1971).
42. See also Schmidt (1977), Stanga (1971).
43. See also Kuriyama (1982), Ares (1981), Schmidt (1977), Stanga (1971).
44. See also Schmidt (1977).
45. See also Kulwin (1978), Roberts and Goodman (1976).
46. See also Kulwin (1978), Roberts and Goodman (1976).
47. For further discussion of this case see Kuriyama (1982), Ares (1981), Fenner and Koley (1981), Pequignot (1981), Jacobs (1980), O'Brien (1980), Kulwin (1978), Portman (1977), Schmidt (1977), Younger (1977), Roberts and Goodman (1976).

48. For further comments on this case, see Fenner and Koley (1981); U.S. Supreme Court Rules that Courts and Judges are Public Issues (1979, p. 10). But see also *U.S. v. Dickinson*, 465 F.2d 496, (5th Cir. 1972) *cert. denied*, 414 U.S. 797 (1973) and discussion by Pember (1984, pp. 321–325).

49. See also Cedarquist (1961, p. 150–151), who cites an earlier and similar ruling, *Maryland v. Baltimore Radio Show*, 338 U.S. 912 at 919 (1950), where denying *cert*. Justice Frankfurter said that broadcasters do not have an automatic or guaranteed right to cover court proceedings, and the rights of the accused to a fair trial take precedence over broadcasters' First Amendment rights. For further comments on the *Gannett* decision, see Ares (1981), Fenner and Koley (1981), First Amendment Guards Public, Press Access (1981), Pequignot (1981), O'Brien (1980), U.S. Supreme Court Upholds Broad Pretrial Secrecy (1980), Goodale (1979), Secret Pretrial Proceedings Upheld (1979), High Court to Review Pretrial Secrecy (1978).

50. Justice Stewart delivered the opinion of the Court in which Chief Justice Burger and Justices Powell, Rehnquist, and Stevens joined. Chief Justice Burger and Justices Powell and Rehnquist filed concurring opinions. Justice Blackmum filed an opinion concurring in part and dissenting in part, in which Justices Brennan, White, and Marshall joined.

51. The case developed when a trial judge in Hanover County, Virginia, closed his courtroom to the press and public during the defendant's fourth murder trial. The first trial resulted in a second-degree murder conviction. The Virginia Supreme Court reversed this conviction on the grounds of inadmissible evidence: *Stevenson v. Commonwealth*, 218 Va. 462, 237 S.E. 779 (1977). Both the second and third trials ended in a mistrial. For further discussion of *Richmond Newspapers*, see Lindsey (1984), Kuriyama (1982), Ares (1981), Fenner and Koley (1981), First Amendment Guarantees Public, Press Trial Access (1981), Pequignot (1981), O'Brien (1980a), U.S. Supreme Court Affirms Open Trial Guarantee (1980), U.S. Supreme Court to Rule if Criminal Trials May be Closed to Public and Press (1980).

52. *Richmond Newspapers, Inc., v. Virginia*, 448 U.S. 555 at 572–573 (1980).

53. For further discussion of *Press Enterprise*, see Greenberg (1984, pp. 372–375), Lindsey (1984), Jury Selection Must Be In Public (1984), U.S. Justices Sharply Restrict Secrecy in Selection of Juries (1984), U.S. Supreme Court Takes Jury Selection Case (1983).

54. For further comments, see Ares (1981); Kulwin (1978).

55. See also Ares (1981), Nixon Watergate Tapes Sealed (1978).

56. For further comments, see Ares (1981).

57. For further comments, see Ares (1981), Witt (1981).

58. For further comments, see Ares (1981), Five Abscam Trial Videotapes Aired (1981), Abscam Tape Issue Goes to Supreme Court (1980), Hochberger (1980).

59. *State v. Clifford*, 118 N.E.2d 853 at 855–856 (Ohio Ct. App. 1954) *aff'd* 123 N.E.2d 8 (Ohio Sup. Ct. 1954), *cert. denied* 349 U.S. 929 (1955), cited by Cedarquist (1961, p. 150). See other contempt cases involving cameras in the courtroom: *Ex Parte Sturm*, 152 Md. 121, 136 Atl. 312, 51 A.L.R. 356 (1927); and *Re Seed*, 140 N.Y. Misc. 681, 251 N.Y.S. 615 (1931).

60. *Lyles v. State*, 330 P.2d 734 at 741 (Okla. Crim. App. 1958) cited by Carter (1981a, pp. 8–9).

61. Id., at 741–742, cited by Carter (1981a, p. 9).

62. Id., at 742, cited by Carter (1981a, p. 9).

63. Cited by Carter (1981a, p. 34, fn. 66).
64. For further discussion of this case, see Lindsey (1984), Cohen (1982), Jennings (1982), Kuriyama (1982), Thompson (1982), Ares (1981), Nesson and Koblenz (1981), Pequignot (1982), Tajgman (1981), Wasby (1979), Boyd (1978), Kulwin (1978), Portman (1977), Schmidt (1977), Stanga (1971).
65. *Estes v. Texas,* 381 U.S. 532 at 612 (1965).
66. Id., at 535–536.
67. Id., at 537. While broadcasts of the *trial* "were confined largely to film clips shown on the stations' regularly scheduled news programs," on one occasion the *pretrial* hearings "were rebroadcast in place of the 'late movie'" (Id., at 537–538).
68. Id., at 544–545. See also Id., at 546, where Justice Clark noted that jurors who are televised "would be subjected to the broadest commentary and criticism and perhaps the well-meant advice of friends, relatives and inquiring strangers who recognized them on the streets."
69. Id., at 614–615. Justice William Brennan, writing the final dissenting opinion, also reminded the Court that "today's decision is *not* a blanket constitutional prohibition against the televising of state criminal trials" (Id., at 617).
70. See *Bradley v. Texas,* 470 F.2d 785 (5th Cir. 1972); *Nicholas v. Henderson,* 389 F.2d 990 (6th Cir. 1968), *cert. denied* 393 U.S. 955 (1968); *Bell v. Patterson,* 279 F. Supp. 760 (D.Colo. 1968), *aff'd* 402 F.2d 394 (10th Cir. 1968); *cert. denied,* 403 U.S. 955 (1971); *Gonzales v. People,* 165 Colo. 322, 438 P.2d 686 (1968); *La Blanc v. People,* 161 Colo. 274, 421 P.2d 474 (1966). For further discussion, see Thompson (1982), Roberts and Goodman (1976).
71. For further discussion of this case, see Cohen (1982), Hughes (1982), Pike (1981), Radio, TV and Photo Coverage of Courts Can Be Allowed by States, Justices Rule (1981), Spaniolo and D'Alemberte (1981), States May Allow Cameras in Courtrooms (1981), Winter (1981). For further discussion of the differences between *Chandler* and *Estes,* see Lindsey (1984), Jennings (1982), Kuriyama (1982), Thompson (1982), Ares (1981), Pequignot (1981), Tajgman (1981).
72. In March 1983, 28 organizations, including Associated Press, United Press International, ABC, CBS, NBC, the Public Broadcasting Service, and several major newspapers and professional organizations, presented a petition to the Judicial Conference of the United States asking that video, audio, and still camera coverage be allowed in federal courts. Two principle arguments were presented in the petition: first, that new technology has enabled broadcast and photographic equipment to be totally unobtrusive in the courtroom; and second, that the public should be more fully informed about the workings of the federal judiciary (see Ranii, 1984; Courtroom Cameras Pushing Hard for Access to Trials, 1984; Ashman, 1983; Cameras-in-the-Courtroom Advocates Try for Top, 1983; TV Seeks Access to Federal Courts, 1983). Cameras were barred from federal courts in 1946 under Rule 53 of the Federal Rules of Criminal procedure. However, a recent case involving Florida Judge Alcee L. Hastings—indicted in December 1981 for bribery, conspiracy, and obstruction of justice—re-opened the issue of camera access to federal courtrooms. The judge, who was acquitted, filed an appeal claiming that his Sixth Amendment right to have his trial televised was violated by the Rule 53 prohibition. The news organizations who joined the appeal argued that their First Amendment rights were violated. Both claims were rejected by the Eleventh Circuit, which said Rule 53 is a legitimate "time, place, and manner restriction," and

that the interests of a public trial are adequately served by opening the courtroom to the public and traditional forms of media coverage. See *United States v. Hastings,* 695 F.2d 1278 (11th Cir.), *cert. denied,* 103 S.Ct. 1188 at 1281 (1983). For further discussion of this case, see Lindsey (1984). While cameras are banned from federal courtrooms for news coverage purposes, the videotaping of witness depositions for administrative purposes is not.

73. *Chandler v. Florida,* 449 U.S. 560 at 576 footnote 11 (1981).
74. Id., at 576 footnote 11.
75. Id., at 579 footnote 12.
76. Id., at 570 and 579–580.
77. Id., at 576–577 (1981).
78. Id., at 575.

PART THREE

SUMMARY AND DISCUSSION OF THE COURTROOM CAMERAS RESEARCH

The application of social science research to legal decision making probably began with the Brandeis Briefs in 1908 (Gillmor and Dennis, 1981, p. 334). Later, in the well-known school desegregation case *Brown v. Board of Education* (1954), the U.S. Supreme Court cited empirical literature in a footnote of its opinion, and more recently social science research has been moved from the footnotes into the text of Supreme Court opinions (Tanke and Tanke, 1979, p. 1133).

The legal community has traditionally been skeptical of social science findings. Some have described the scientific approach as a "seduction" of the law away from what should remain a bastion of legal precedent and principled judicial opinion (O'Brien, 1980b). Others have argued justifiably that "information that cannot be properly validated has a high potential for being misinformation and thus worse than no information at all, especially when the conclusions have an aura of scientific respectability and may quite literally affect people's lives" (Konecni and Ebbesen, 1982, p. 258).

Advocates of an interface between empiricism and legal decision making realize that social scientific evidence cannot be used as the sole criterion in adjudication. They emphasize, however, that, while the evidence should be used cautiously, examined thoroughly for reliability, and applied in conjunction legal principles, it is better to take note of scientific findings than to rely on so-called "common knowledge" (Sperlich, 1980a,b,c)

Not every Supreme Court decision, of course, requires an examination of social science literature: many decisions can be justified by thorough review of oral arguments presented to the court, constitutional interpretation, and legal precedent. But cases involving predictions of human behavior and psychological effects, such as *Chandler v. Florida* (1981), deserve more legitimate judgment than judicial perceptions of human nature. In its previous "cameras" decision, *Estes v. Texas* (1965), the Court decided largely on the basis of speculation, supposition, and personal opinion, and, though the body of empirical literature now available does not answer every question—not even, perhaps, the most important ones—it nevertheless adds a significant new dimension to the complex debate.

Judicial concern about the presence of news cameras in courtrooms has been evident for nearly 70 years (Kielbowicz, 1979, p. 15), and legal opinions about the matter have proliferated up to the present day. Empirical interest began to develop in the mid-1970s, when several state courts started to "experiment" with television and photographic coverage of proceedings after several years of denying photographic access to their courtrooms. In *Estes*, the decision which in essence banned courtroom cameras, the Court held that numerous behavioral and psychological dangers are associated with televised trials, (e.g., distracted jurors, inhibited witnesses, grandstanding judges, and flamboyant attorneys) and that these cause irreparable damage to a defendant's case. Some 16 years later, Joel Hirschhorn, counsel for the defendants in *Chandler*, argued that both human nature and scientific research indicate that people behave differently in the presence of cameras, and that "this difference could affect the outcome of trials" (Justices' Questions Suggest Split as Court Weighs Televised Trials, 1980). Explaining that the adverse effects of cameras on trial participants are often "intangible" (Voboril, 1980, p. 12), he placed great store in common sense as the predictor that being televised is different: "We all know that timid people become more timid, and nervous people become more nervous" when cameras are present (Cameras in the Courtroom Issue Goes to Court, 1980).

During oral arguments, however, Justice William Rehnquist doubted the ability of non-social scientists to make such assessments, and asked how the members of the Court, as lay people, could determine that televised trials are inherently prejudicial (Cameras in the Courtroom Issue Goes to Court, 1980; see also Trial Coverage Before Court, 1980). He did not have to look far for an answer to his question. Anticipating the Court's difficulties, the Attorneys General of 17 states submitted an *amicus curiae* brief discussing the courtroom cameras issue from a social scientific as well as legal perspective (Brief and Appendix of the Attorneys General, 1979).[1] The brief and its appendix contained substantial quantities of empirical data on the issue—results and conclusions of nine studies conducted over a period of 5 years. These studies will be examined here, along with ten other pieces of courtroom cameras research that were unavailable at the time of the *Chandler* appeal.[2]

1. COURTROOMS AND COMMUNICATION

In order to place the courtroom cameras studies within the broader context of communications research, it is necessary to briefly review the behavioral and psychological environment of the courtroom *prior* to the introduction of cameras. Specifically, the appellants in the landmark "cameras" cases argued that trial prejudice arises in two ways: (a) as a *direct* result of cameras distracting or supplying prejudicial information to jurors, and (b) as an *indirect* result of cameras causing other trial participants (judges, attorneys, witnesses, and defendants) to behave in ways which, in turn, prejudice the way jurors decide a case. In short, cameras may prejudice trials by distorting (altering) the courtroom atmosphere in such a way that the jury is "persuaded" to reach a verdict it would not have reached, had there been no cameras present. An underlying contention in the following analysis of legal-communications literature is that, if a fair assessment of the impact of cameras in the courtroom is to be made, it is first necessary to establish what factors are operating in the trial environment *before* cameras are introduced. This way, it becomes clear which biases are *inherent* in the trial process, and which may enter it or be exacerbated when cameras are present.

A. Pretrial Stage

Publicity: Prejudice may enter the trial process even before the trial begins. Tans and Chaffee (1966) found that a suspect is not always considered innocent until proven guilty—"the mere fact of questioning or arrest may be prejudicing" (p. 654), and knowledge that a trial has been moved from its original venue may also create juror biases (Miller and Boster, 1977, pp. 21–26). Pretrial and trial publicity has been shown to influence juror *opinions* (Hoiberg and Stires, 1973; Simon and Eimermann, 1971; Simon, 1968; Tans and Chaffee, 1966; Goggin and Hanover, 1965), and in some cases influences jury *verdicts* (Greene and Loftus, 1984; Padawer-Singer, Singer, and Singer, 1977), especially in the absence of judicial instructions to ignore nonevidential information (Kline and Jess, 1966). But the role of the judge should be stressed here, because the verdicts of jurors who comply with judicial instructions to ignore prejudicial publicity are the same as those of jurors who have read nonprejudicial information (Simon, 1968; Kline and Jess, 1966).

Juror Selection: In some states, jury selection procedures may be detrimental to the defendant. While a jury is supposed to represent a cross-section of the community, methods of selection such as the key-man system, and even the use of voter registration lists, city directories, and tax records, have been inherently biased. Until recently they often excluded women, blacks, the poor, and the less educated; hence, the accused may have been tried, not by a group of peers, but by a select group of people whose background and values contrasted completely with those of the defendant (Hood, 1967; Lindquist, 1967; Broeder, 1965a).

Voir Dire: While knowledge of local conditions and contact with trial participants have been shown to contaminate jury verdicts, lawyers and jurors may consciously conceal these facts during *voir dire* (Broeder, 1966, 1965b; Kalven and Zeisel, 1966). Broeder (1965b) also found that some lawyers are reluctant to hold lengthy examinations for fear of irritating the judge and those persons finally chosen as jurors. On the other hand, *voir dire* is the very vehicle which enables lawyers to *introduce* bias into the jury: it is an opportunity to not only weed out prejudiced jurors, but also to select jurors who will favor a particular side of the case. Alice Padawer-Singer, a social psychologist and consultant to New York City courts, has described the selection process as a "blend or art, science, and intuition," an apt description since jurors are chosen on the basis of their "clothing, body language, sex, facial expression, age, occupation, race, nationality, tone of voice, ability to reason, and preference in books, newspapers and magazines" (Grady, 1981, p. 38; see also Diamond and Zeisel, 1974).

B. Trial Stage

Juror Characteristics: The importance of the jury selection process is magnified by the fact that juror characteristics—such as gender, age, race, ethnicity, nationality, educational level, social status, occupational status, individual locus of control, and level of authoritarianism—rather than trial evidence alone, influence verdicts (Mills and Bohannon, 1980; Berg and Vidmar, 1975; Sosis, 1974; Hoiberg and Stires, 1973; Mitchell and Byrne, 1973; Boehm, 1968; Reed, 1965; Broeder, 1965a,b, 1959). For example, authoritarian jurors tend to evaluate a defendant as responsible and guilty; jurors whose ethnic origins are Northern European have been found to reach more guilty verdicts than jurors of Southern European origins; and jurors with high social status are more likely to vote guilty than jurors with low social status. Jurors may also decide cases on the basis of subjective perceptions about the respectability of a victim in a crime (Jones and Aronson, 1973); the character attractiveness of a victim (Landy and Aronson, 1969); similarity of attitudes between the defendant and individual jurors (Mitchell and Byrne, 1973); and the social desirability of traits attributed to the defendant (Edwards, 1953).

Defendant Characteristics: Defendant characteristics that influence jury verdicts include gender (Hoiberg and Stires, 1973; Dion, Berscheid, and Walster, 1972); race (Nemeth and Sosis, 1973; Broeder, 1965a; Bullock, 1961); socioeconomic status (Gleason and Harris, 1976; Landy and Aronson, 1969); occupational status (Reed, 1965); physical attractiveness (Sigall and Ostrove, 1975; Efran, 1974); character attractiveness (Barnett and Field, 1978; Friend and Vinson, 1974; Izzett and Leginski, 1974; Kaplan and Kemmerick, 1974); arrogance (Boone, 1972); previous criminal record (Doob, 1976); and fidgety behavior, poor eye contact, and speech errors (Pryor and Buchanan, 1984). For example, a defendant may be convicted because of race, even though evidence may not support a conviction; arrogant defendants receive more severe sentences, particularly from male jurors; knowledge of a defendant's prior criminal record dramatically affects the likelihood of a guilty verdict; and attractive defendants are likely to receive lighter punishment than unattractive defendants. Kalven and Zeisel (1966) noted two distinct areas of a defendant's characteristics which come to bear on a juror's evaluation: those that affect credibility and those that affect sympathy. Factors affecting sympathy, for example, include handicaps or visible illness, whether the defendant shows remorse or cries, the presence of the defendant's family in court, the defendant's occupation and employment record, and whether or not the defendant is a veteran. Testifying in one's own defense is reacted to negatively by jurors (Frankel and Morris, 1976), but jurors tend to assess a defendant favorably if there is an escaped accomplice involved in the case, or if an accomplice is not indicted with the defendant (DeJong, Hastorf, and Morris, 1976; Broeder, 1965–1966).

Adversary Process: A very basic assumption about the fairness of a trial which may be questioned is that the adversary process is an impartial forum for the discovery of truth. Justice Thomas Clark noted optimistically in *Estes* that "court proceedings are held for the solemn purpose of endeavoring to ascertain the truth which is the *sine qua non* of a fair trial."[3] But Marvin Frankel, who, when commenting on the trial process in 1975, had been a district judge for 9 years, emphasized the apparent inconsistency between the adversary system and the search for truth:

> The business of the advocate, simply stated, is to win if possible without violating the law. . . . His is not the search for truth as such. To put that thought more exactly, the truth and victory are mutually incompatible for some considerable percentage of the attorneys trying cases at any given time (Frankel, 1975, p. 1037).

Mirjan Damaska (1975) has also called attention to some of the shortcomings of the adversary process:

> It may be in the narrow interest of only one party, or in the common interest of both, that some items of information which the witness possesses do not reach the adjudicator—even though their relevancy in the quest for truth is beyond dispute. Evidence unsupportive of one's case has no function in the adversary litigation process, nor do matters which the parties decide to leave out of the disputation. And, as the witness is limited to answering relatively narrow and precise questions, much information may effectively be kept away from the decisionmaker who presumably is responsible for finding the truth within the limits of the charge. Accordingly, the factual basis for the decision may be incomplete (Damaska, 1975, p. 1093).

Presentation of Evidence: A jury's verdict is rarely the result of impartial consideration of witness testimony alone. It is often a function of *how* evidence is presented, rather than *what* evidence is presented. For example, jury verdicts are directly related to the number of arguments presented by either side in the case (Calder, Insko, and Yandell, 1974); the order in which arguments are presented (Walker, Thibault, and Andreoli, 1973; Rosenbaum and Levin, 1968; Weld and Danzig, 1940); the introduction of inadmissable evidence (Sue, Smith, and Caldwell, 1973; Hoffman and Brodley, 1952); and the vividness of the evidence presented (Reyes, Thompson, and Bower, 1980). Moreover, few jurors maintain an attitude of doubt about a defendant until *all* the evidence has been presented (Weld and Danzig, 1940), and jurors tend not to base their evaluations on the preponderance of the evidence but, instead, use this term indiscriminately to support their personal judgments, indicating they neither understand the term or its implications, nor base their judgments solely on the evidence presented (Nagel, 1979).

Behavior of Attorneys: Perhaps the most important influences on the jury are the trial attorneys—their skills often have more impact on a jury's verdict than either the characteristics of the defendant or the facts of the case being tried (Kalven and Zeisel, 1966; Hoffman and Brodley, 1952; Moffat, 1945). Charles Winick (1961) concluded that the key to winning a jury case is a lawyer's successful exploitation of jurors' personalities and emotions. Sometimes even the prestige of a lawyer, on its own, is sufficient to persuade jurors to accept an opinion and maintain it as their own (Weld and Danzig, 1940), and sometimes jurors feel obligated to vote for a lawyer because he is well-known in the local community and has several clients there (Kalven and Zeisel, 1966). The jury measures, not only the attorney's skills of advocacy, but also his appearance and the attractiveness of his personality. Kalven and Zeisel (1966) found that jurors are won over by colorful and amusing lawyers who "play" to the jury, and Hoffman and Brodley (1952) found that jurors tend to describe the most convincing attorney as "a good actor." In one trial, they observed, the lawyers were very obviously "putting on a show for the jury:"

> An atmosphere of heated argument, confusion and histrionics prevailed between the two contending sides, as long as the jury was within the room; but as soon as the jury was dismissed for any reason, the argument would be quickly toned down, the facts clarified and the argument became intelligent off-the-record discussion between judge and counsel rather than a fight to the death (p. 247).

Behavior of Judges: Another significant influence on the jury is the trial judge. A judge's facial expressions, gestures, and eye movements can destroy or enhance a defendant's case by showing the jury belief or disbelief, annoyance, agreement, or disagreement. In fact, smiles, frowns, head-nodding, and head-shaking can have a greater impact on the jury's assessment of evidence than the testimony of witnesses (Conner, 1974). A judge's influence is also expressed through judicial instructions to the jury. However, jurors often do not understand judicial instructions, and do not apply them to the facts of a case, and some jurors ignore the instructions entirely (Pryor, Taylor, Buchanan, and Strawn, 1980; Nagel, 1979; Strawn, Buchanan, Pryor, and Taylor, 1977; Strawn and Buchanan, 1976; Hervey, 1947).

C.   Deliberation Stage

The jury deliberation process is yet another stage in the trial in which factors other than trial testimony determine jurors' opinions and verdicts. Bevan, Albert,

Loiseaux, Mayfield, and Wright (1958) concluded that during deliberations greater respect is shown for the views of high-status people, and that low-status jurors are less active in the deliberation process. Broeder (1965a) has described the racial prejudice that exists in the jury room and determines jury verdicts, and Reed (1965) has pointed out that relatively little of a jury's deliberation time is spent discussing the facts of a case. Instead, jurors discuss topics such as the weather, people on the jury or in the community, the reputation of the parties in the case, the family of the accused, the reputation of the lawyers, and race and racial differences.

After some trials there may not even be a need for deliberations, since jurors may have made up their minds before deliberations begin, or even before all the evidence has been presented (Nagel, 1979; Kline and Jess, 1966; Weld and Danzig, 1940). Broeder (1959) found that, in 90% of the cases he studied as part of the Chicago Jury Project, the majority decision on the first ballot was the verdict, even after deliberations. Finally, jury verdicts may also be affected by the size of the jury (Valenti and Downing, 1975); by whether the jury must reach a unanimous or majority verdict (Padawer-Singer, Singer, and Singer, 1977; Kerr, Atkin, Stasser, Meek, Holt, and Davis, 1976); by whether or not the jury applies the criterion of "beyond reasonable doubt" (Nemeth, 1977); by the need for approval of others in attitude formation (Berger, Levin, and Jacobson, 1977); and by cognitive and memory processes (Calder, Insko, and Yandell, 1974).

2. VIDEO FOR COURT ADMINISTRATION

Another area of research, focusing on various applications of video for judicial administration purposes, has also been linked with the news cameras issue. However, the impact of videotaped witness depositions or testimony on jurors (Kaminski and Miller, 1984; Miller and Fontes, 1979; Juhnke, Vought, Pyszczynski, Dane, Losure, and Wrightsman, 1979; Murray, 1978; Jacoubovitch, Bermant, Crockett, McKinley, and Sanstad, 1977; Smiley, 1977; Ernest H. Short and Associates, 1976; Sims, 1976; Bermant and Jacoubovitch, 1975; Bermant, Chappell, Crockett, Jacoubovitch, and McGuire, 1975; Doret, 1974); the more extensive use of prerecorded videotaped trials and videotaped trial records (McCrystal, 1978, 1977, 1974, 1973; Lieberman, 1976; Brakel, 1975; Kosky, 1975); and the application of video for arraignments (Gilmore, 1980), courthouse information display (MacNeilly, 1976), and legal education (Miller, 1980; Ernest H. Short and Associates, 1976; Salvan, 1975; Kornblum and Rush, 1973) have only limited tangential relevance to the "news cameras" issue. It should be stressed that, while the use of video for judicial administration has been thoroughly explored by important communication and legal scholars, *Chandler* concerned possible prejudice to defendants from televising trials for *broadcast news* purposes, not from showing videotaped testimony to jurors. The following discussion, then, is limited to the more focused empirical research on the impact of news cameras in courtrooms.[4]

3. PREFACE TO THE ANALYSIS

Table 2 lists the empirical research on news cameras in the courtroom compiled in
Florida, Wisconsin, Washington, Nevada, Louisiana, Ohio, California, Connecticut, Massachusetts, Hawaii, and Rhode Island between 1975 and 1983. The various
studies can be divided into three broad categories, ranging from least to most
experimental in methodology (Rogers and Argarwala-Rogers, 1976, p. 152). The
first group consists of eleven judicial reports or *case studies;* seven of these deal with
only one or two trials, contain no quantifiable survey data, but include observational
information compiled during judicial interviews. The other four case studies deal
with one to multiple cases, and include quantifiable questionnaire responses from
trial participants, as well as open-ended interview or written responses. The second
group consists of six *surveys,* utilizing mail, phone, or personal interview questionnaire responses, and yielding quantifiable as well as open-ended data. The third
group consists of an anecdotal experiment and a "quasi-experimental" study; the
former simulating (with several limitations) witness behavior in televised trials, and
the latter employing a multi-tier method, combining experimental, observational,
and survey data.

Any attempt to analyze and synthesize this body of research, which adds up to
nearly 2,000 pages of text and tables, calls for some difficult decisions. Obviously, it
is not possible here to incorporate all data or commentary included in the literature.
Instead, major results and conclusions have been drawn from *across all* the studies
and are highlighted according to specific categories which describe question focus or
trends that were dominant and consistent among the studies. Within each category,
information has been subdivided according to the responses of participant groups—
judges, witnesses, jurors, attorneys, court personnel, and observers/spectators—for
which data is available on a given issue, generally starting with data from case
studies and ending with those from experiments. Note, too, that the responses of a
given participant group about its *own* reaction to a particular issue, e.g., juror
responses about impacts on jurors, are followed by the observations of other participant groups, e.g., attorney responses about juror reactions, judge responses about
juror reactions, court personnel responses about juror reactions, and so forth.

The analysis also poses some significant problems in terms of reaching overall
quantitative as well as qualitative assessments of the data. Most of these difficulties
arise as a consequence of disparities in data collection methods and the superficial
reporting in many studies of both research methods used and the data gathered. For
example, 7 of the 11 judicial reports (case studies) do not contain specific information about the numbers of trial participants who were interviewed or observed, and
rarely quantify the participants' responses or the observers' assessments. Those which
do contain quantified data usually work with group sizes too small to yield meaningful percentages. While information drawn from these types of studies relates to
(and often supports) the results and conclusions of the quantitative studies, it cannot
literally be *combined* with the numerical data from surveys and experiments employing more sophisticated methods.

In an ideal situation, a thorough analysis of results might be accomplished by a scientific meta-analysis (Hunter, Schmidt, and Jackson, 1982). For example, if all raw data could be converted into percentages, a cumulative median response for each participant group could be calculated by combining scores from across all the studies. Variance could then be mearured for each group on similar or identical questions. However, because the research contains a mix of open-ended and numerical data, and because several studies do not adequately report precise questions or responses, many items cannot be matched or incorporated into an overall evaluation.

As a final preface to the ensuing discussion, a word about terminology is in order. Terms such as "camera coverage," "electronic media coverage (EMC)," "media coverage," and "courtroom cameras" have been used in their original context, i.e., if a particular term was used in a specific study, it has been kept here, too. However, unless otherwise stated, these terms generally refer to the same thing: a combination of television and still camera coverage; or a combination of television, photographic, radio, and newspaper coverage. The term "experiment" also needs clarification. Its use as a descriptor for a type of research methodology should not be confused with the general term "experiment," used by many states to describe their pilot programs permitting news camera coverage of courtrooms. Most states initiated what they called "experimental" use of cameras prior to adopting (or rejecting) rules for "permanent" news camera access.

4. DIGNITY, DECORUM, DISRUPTION, AND FAIRNESS

A. Judges

Judicial conclusions about the impact of camera coverage on the trial process were generally positive. Judges usually noted a total absence of added noise or disruption inside the courtroom [2,8,9,10,11] (N.B.: The italic numbers in brackets correspond with the studies listed in Table 2; full citations are in the list of references); cameras simply faded into the background [1]; for all practical purposes, they were just "another piece of furniture" [9]; and they did not detract from the dignity or decorum of proceedings [5,6,7,10,13,19]. In fact, conventional media (newspaper reporters and sketch artists), court personnel, spectators, and people entering and leaving courtrooms were just as, if not more, noticeable than camera equipment and personnel [6,19]. In one case, far from defeating the objective of holding fair trials, camera presence was perceived as making the trial more fair by eliciting "perfection" from all concerned [5].

B. Attorneys

Attorney case study observations were also generally positive: trial fairness was not diluted in any way because of camera coverage [1]; there was no added noise or distraction [8]; and participants were perceived as having performed their functions

Table 2 Empirical Studies on the Presence and Use of Video, Audio, and Still Photography Coverage of Courtroom Proceedings

Study (Names Abbreviated)	Place and year of Research	Type of Research	Quantified Data Included	NUMBER OF INTERVIEW, SURVEY OR EXPERIMENTAL SUBJECTS							
				Jurors	Witnesses	Judges	Attorneys	Defendants	C.P.	Spectators	Others
1. Washington Bench-Bar-Press Committee	Washington 1975	Case Study	No	(11)[a]	(10)	(1)	(5)				(5)[g]
2. Judge Baker's Report re: *State v. Zamora*	Florida 1977	Case Study	No	****	****	(1)	****	(1)			(1)
3. Judge Sholts' Report re: *State v. Herman*	Florida 1978	Case Study	Yes	(11)	****	(1)	(1)			(3)	(2)
4. Judge Mounts' Report re: *State v. Martin*	Florida 1978	Case Study	No	(1)		(1)	(1)				
5. *State v. Solorzano* (Goldman & Larson)	Nevada 1978**	Case Study	No	(1)		(1)	(4)				
6. Judge Guy Humphries' Report	Louisiana 1979	Case Study	No	****	****	(1)	****				
7. Wisconsin Supreme Court Committee	Wisconsin 1979	Case Studies and Survey	Yes	(12)	(11)	(4) 55	(5)	(1)	****	****	(5)[b]
8. Hawaii State Bar Association	Hawaii 1982	Case Studies and Survey	Yes	13/14[b]		(2)	(4)		****	****	****
9. Massachusetts Advisory Committee	Mass. 1982	Case Studies and Survey	Yes	(11)	(39)	***	(2)			(3)	
10. Rhode Island (Weisberger)	R. I. 1982	Case Study	No	(1)		(1)	(2)				
11. Connecticut Chief Court Administrator	Connecticut 1983	Case Studies	No								
12. Florida Conference of Circuit Judges	Florida 1978	Survey	Yes			155					
13. Strawn, Buchanan, Meeske, Pryor Report	Florida 1978	Survey	Yes	(52)	(9)	(2) 247	(10)			(20)	(28)
14. Florida State Courts Administrator	Florida 1978	Survey	Yes	437	654	230[c]	247			150	108

No.	Study	State	Year	Method		Judges	Attorneys	Jurors	Witnesses	Others
15.	Washington State Superior Court Judges	Washington	1978	Survey	Yes	111[d]				258[j]
16.	Kermit Netteburg's Study	Wisconsin	1980	Survey	Yes					
17.	Cleveland Bar Association Study	Ohio	1980	Survey	Yes	34	37	3	14	
18.	James Hoyt's Study		1977	Experiment	Yes	(55)	(56)			36[k]
19.	Ernest H. Short & Associates***	California	1981	Survey and Experiment	Yes	(98) / 464[e] / 225[f]	(48) / 391[e] / 222[f]	(7)		*****[m]

*Data reported in the Sholts study is part of the Strawn et al. (1978) report.

**State v. Solorzano was actually videotaped June 8-12, 1975; Goldman's and Larson's research was not published until 1978.

***Part of the California study involved observer evaluations of participant behavior in experimental versus control conditions; another part of the study gathered data via survey questionnaires.

****The judicial case studies referred to responses from, or observations of, these participants but did not indicate the specific numbers who were interviewed or surveyed.

[a] Figures in parentheses indicate that the subjects were surveyed interviewed, and/or observed either during or directly following a specific trial or series of trials. In the California study, these subjects were in experimental or control trial environments, i.e., with electronic and traditional media coverage, or traditional media coverage only. In the Strawn et al. (1978) study, participants and observers were surveyed directly, following one of a series of five trials where television and still cameras were present. Figures not placed in parentheses indicate responses received from mailed questionnaires, with the exception of the Kermit Netteburg survey, which was conducted by phone.

[b] 13 actual (seated) jurors and 14 prospective (alternate) jurors.

[c] 130 of the judges surveyed by Strawn et al. (1978) were circuit judges. Note that there is probably some duplication between these survey respondents and those surveyed by Judge Arthur J. Franza for the Florida Conference of Circuit Judges. However, the duplication question is hard to answer because Judge Franza received responses from 155 out of 286 circuit judges, while Strawn et al. received 130 responses from 286 mailed questionnaires. The combined total for responses from each survey is 285 (155 plus 130), and it is possible, therefore, that a different set of judges responded to each survey. Neither report clarifies this question of uniqueness versus duplication of responses.

[d] Although 111 judges responded to the survey, only 41 had experienced camera coverage of trials.

[e] Pretest responses.

[f] Post-test responses from the same population.

[g] Media representatives.

[h] Official observers.

[j] General public.

[k] Student subjects.

[m] Observer-evaluators.

even better than usual due to camera presence [5]. The survey responses of attorneys were far more mixed, In two surveys, nearly 85 percent said cameras did not cause serious trial disruptions [13,19]. However, in another survey, nearly half said cameras decreased the dignity of the proceedings, and over half said cameras were disruptive [14]. In a fourth survey, while about three quarters of attorneys said cameras had no effect on the dignity of the proceedings, nearly two thirds said cameras were disruptive [17].

C. Jurors

In the case study literature, jurors responded unanimously that they were only aware of camera presence when entering or leaving the jury box, and that cameras did not affect the flow of the proceedings in any way [8]. In the survey literature, over three quarters of the jurors said cameras were not disruptive; two thirds said cameras had no effect on the dignity of the proceedings, and nearly 20% said cameras actually increased the dignity of trials [14]. In the California study, large numbers of jurors, especially those questioned prior to experiencing camera coverage, said that even the presence of conventional reporters and sketch artists created the potential for disruption, distraction, and participant apprehension [19]. In the Cleveland study, however, about half of the jurors said cameras were disruptive and decreased courtroom dignity [17].

D. Witnesses

Witness attitudes were somewhat more negative than those of other participants, with the exception of attorneys. Only a little over half of the witnesses in two surveys said cameras had no effect on courtroom dignity or disruption; between a quarter and a third said cameras were disruptive and detracted from the dignity of the proceedings [14,17].

E. Court Personnel

Court personnel showed mixed reactions. In the case study literature, they either perceived no added noise or disruption [8], or they regarded still cameras as slightly more disruptive and distracting than television cameras [9]. There was particular concern about over-zealous newspaper photographers who often arrived late and set up their equipment once a trial had begun [9]. Survey responses were generally negative. Between a third to a half of court personnel and court reporters perceived cameras as disruptive and a hinderance to fair and decorous trials [13,14].

5. IMPACTS ON JURORS

A. Jurors

Juror responses reported in the case study literature were very positive. In two studies, jurors unanimously said they were not intimidated or distracted [1,9], and in a third study, 12 of the 13 jurors said they were not distracted; 12 said they would not be reluctant to serve again; all 13 said they had no fears of physical, psychological, reputational, or financial harm; and 11 said camera presence had no impact on their deliberations (two were uncertain) [8]. In other cases, jurors said they were not influenced in any way by camera presence [5]; it did not interfere with their ability to concentrate on witness testimony, counsels' arguments, or the judge's instructions [2]; they placed no greater importance on the trial because of camera coverage, and they were not worried by the fact that a verdict would be announced in front of a television camera [6].

The survey literature revealed more mixed juror perceptions and attitudes. Nearly 50% said cameras made the case seem more important [14,17], and only about 50% felt camera coverage of trials was a desirable practice [13,17]. In two surveys, over 70% of jurors said they were not at all distracted [13,14]; in another survey, 50% said they were distracted [17]. Although about half of all jurors were slightly aware of media presence in the courtroom [14], nearly three quarters said they were not self-conscious, tense, or nervous as a result of camera coverage [13,14,17]. Over 80% said their ability to concentrate on witness testimony was unaffected by camera presence; they were not at all concerned people would try to influence their decision as a consequence of television coverage, and knowing a trial would be televised did not make them unwilling to participate in the case [14]. Just over 60% said they did not fear harm from anyone associated with the case as a result of television coverage, and fear was less for photographic, newspaper, and radio coverage [14]. In the California study, the vast majority of jurors said that conventional newspaper reporters and sketch artists were potentially just as distracting as electronic media, but 25% said they would have preferred no camera coverage [19].

B. *Attorneys*

In two case studies, attorneys said jurors were not distracted [1,5]; in fact, at one trial the presence of cameras increased juror attentiveness, making them more aware and conscientious about listening to witness testimony and judicial instructions [5]. In a third case study, an attorney commented on the fact that jurors objected to close-up frontal photography [9]. The survey literature revealed less positive attitudes: between a third and a half of all attorneys said cameras were distracting to jurors [13,14], although, in the California survey, only 18% of attorneys perceived a negative change in juror behavior due to electronic media coverage [19].

C. *Judges, Witnesses, and Court Personnel*

Judges had very positive perceptions about the impacts of cameras on jurors: they overwhelmingly saw no change in juror behavior [8,9,19], no distraction [5,8,9,12,13], and no influence other than trial evidence on jury decisions [12]. Witnesses, however, perceived jurors as distracted by cameras [9]. About 60% of court personnel said jurors were not distracted by camera presence [13], but some were concerned that information televised during bail hearings would prejudice potential jurors against defendants [9].

6. IMPACTS ON WITNESSES

A. Witnesses

Witnesses had mixed, often negative attitudes toward camera coverage. While some said they were completely unaffected by camera presence [1], others refused to testify for fear of their safety [3,7], and in one case study nearly three quarters said cameras were intimidating, and a third found camera coverage undesirable [9]. In the survey literature, over three quarters of the witnesses said that *still* cameras did not inhibit their testimony, and over two thirds said *television* cameras were not inhibiting [13]. However, only 40% felt *still* camera coverage was fair to witnesses (40% were uncertain) and only 33% felt *television* coverage was fair (33% were uncertain) [13]. One survey found that, while 80% of witnesses were aware of media presence, 61% were not distracted and 71% were either only slightly or somewhat self-conscious due to camera coverage. However, nearly half (47%) the witnesses were nervous [14]. In another survey, 47% of witnesses said cameras made them self-conscious, and 43% said they made them nervous [17].

Witnesses have a tendency to think camera coverage exaggerates the importance of a case: about 59% said it makes a case more important [14,17]. Nevertheless, 83% were not at all concerned people would try to influence their testimony as a result of television coverage (concern was even less for photographic, radio, and newspaper coverage); 71% were not afraid someone might try to harm them as a consequence of television coverage (fear was even less for other media); and 73% were not reluctant to testify in a trial knowing it would receive television coverage (there was even less hesitancy with regard to other media) [14]. However, only about 60% of witnesses were in favor of allowing *still* cameras in courtrooms [14,17], and only 44% felt that *television* coverage was a desirable practice (33% were uncertain) [14].

Although camera coverage seems to make witnesses feel nervous, their ability to communicate effectively does not appear to be impaired by media coverage [19]. Hoyt's (1977) anecdotal experiment showed that subjects who spoke in front of an obtrusive camera included more correct information in their answers, and answered more promptly and more fully than subjects who faced an unobtrusive camera or no camera at all. Far from inhibiting or impairing witness response, this experiment indicates that camera coverage can be a bonus [18].

B. Jurors

Jurors did not generally perceive any distractions or changes in witness behavior due to media coverage [5,8,19], but in one case study 50% were uncertain about inhibiting effects on witness testimony [9], and in one survey jurors tended to perceive cameras as slightly inhibiting and unfair to witnesses [13]. Surprisingly, television coverage was perceived as less inhibiting but also less fair than still camera coverage [13], and 5% of jurors said that camera presence actually helped them to judge the truthfulness of witness testimony [14].

C. Attorneys

Attorneys have a mixed set of perceptions about camera impacts on witnesses. In two case studies, attorneys said the demeanor and responses of witnesses were unaffected by camera presence [1,8]; in the other, attorneys said there was no distraction or inhibition—in fact, there was improved witness articulation [5]. Survey responses showed less positive perceptions about witness behavior; 40–50% of attorneys surveyed immediately following trials said television and still cameras inhibited witness testimony and were unfair to witnesses, and nearly 50% surveyed by mail said *television* cameras adversely affected witness testimony (although 66% said *still* cameras had no adverse effects) [13]. In the California study, however, 78% of attorneys saw no change in witness behavior due to electronic media coverage [19].

D. Judges

Judges tend to have fairly positive views about the impacts of camera coverage on witnesses. In the case study literature, judges reported that witnesses ignored the cameras [1,8]; there were no histrionics [3], no inhibitions [8,9], and camera presence actually encouraged witnesses to carry out their roles to perfection [5]. In one survey, 80% of judges said witnesses were unaffected by camera presence, and 88% said witnesses were not impaired in telling the truth because of camera coverage [12]. In the other survey, about 73% of judges said *television* cameras had no effect on witnesses and 81% said *still* cameras had no effect [13], and in the California study only 12% of judges saw a negative change in witness behavior due to electronic media coverage [19].

7. IMPACTS ON JUDGES

A. Judges

In seven of the case studies, judicial perceptions about the impacts of camera coverage on themselves were entirely positive. One judge said he simply forgot about the cameras and went about his business as usual [1]; another said cameras did not affect his demeanor or attention—in fact, he felt encouraged to carry out his role to perfection [5]; another said cameras were not prejudicial in any way [2]; another said the presence of cameras simply slipped his mind [6]; and, in three other studies, judges saw no adverse impacts on themselves or other trial participants [8,9,10]. In the Connecticut study, 12 of the 13 judges who were questioned said they were not distracted, but two of these respondents added that they were a little self-conscious and apprehensive about camera coverage [11]. Two judicial reports included a series of negative comments about the potential for prejudice and the added administrative burdens involved with camera coverage [3,4]. Several other judges, however, concluded that little extra work was involved when presiding at televised trials [7].

In the survey literature, judicial attitudes were generally neutral to positive. Most judges said that cameras did not distract them [12,13,17]; did not make them feel tense, uncomfortable, or nervous [13,17]; and did not exaggerate the importance of a case [17]. However, only just over half of all judges surveyed wanted camera coverage of trials to continue [13,17]. This lack of enthusiasm was partly due to annoyance about additional supervisory duties, congested hallways, and extra time and taxpayers' money associated with camera coverage [12].

In the California study, however, judges reported little or no increase in their supervisory responsibility (only 10% reported a definite or extreme increase) [19]. Judges were evenly divided in characterizing their experiences with electronic media coverage as either positive or neutral (only 7% reported a negative experience), but about 20% of all judges said they would have preferred no camera coverage at all; 61% strongly disagreed with the removal of party consent requirements as conditions for coverage; and only 54% approved of camera coverage for criminal proceedings (approval was slightly higher for civil and appellate proceedings) [19].

B. Attorneys

In the case study literature, attorneys said judges were not distracted and did not "grandstand" for the cameras [5,8]. In two surveys, attorneys overwhelmingly said judges were not intimidated by the cameras [12,13], but in one survey 84% said *elected* judges may have been influenced by camera coverage [17]. Although only 60% of attorneys said judges were not at all distracted or nervous due to media presence [13], in one survey 27% said judges were more attentive as a result of camera coverage [14]. In the California study, a large majority of attorneys perceived no change in judges' behavior due to electronic media coverage, but 26% of *defense* attorneys perceived a negative change in judges' behavior due to camera presence [19].

C. Jurors, Witnesses, Court Personnel, and Spectators

Juror perceptions about camera impacts on judges were generally very positive. In one case study, jurors unanimously said judges were not affected at all [8]. In one survey, over 90% said judges were not intimidated by the presence of cameras [13], and in the California study only 14% of jurors perceived a negative change in judges' behavior due to electronic media coverage [19]. The vast majority of court personnel, witnesses, and spectators also said that judges were not intimidated by the presence of cameras [*13*].

8. IMPACTS ON ATTORNEYS

A. *Attorneys*

In one case study, five attorneys were interviewed and all reported positive personal experiences; they were able to present their cases without interruption or disturbance, and they did not find cameras distracting [*1*]. In another case study, three of the four attorneys reported that camera presence was conducive to better attorney preparation. The attorney who reported a negative experience said he was aware of the cameras and felt they were an added pressure on attorney performance [*5*]. In four other case studies, attorneys said that cameras were not distracting or disturbing [*1,8*], and they had no influence at all on attorney performance [*6,10*]. In another study, attorneys in 11 out of 13 cases said they had no objections or complaints, while one attorney found the camera pointing at him annoying [*11*].

The survey research revealed mixed and often negative attorney attitudes. Nearly three quarters of all attorneys said they were aware of camera presence (21% were extremely aware) [*14*], and between a quarter and a third were tense and uncomfortable while cameras were present [*13*]. Over a third said media coverage made them slightly self-conscious, but nearly two thirds said they were not nervous [*14*]. Just over a third said they were slightly distracted, and half said media presence made the case seem more important [*14*].

A very interesting trend was that attorneys regarded camera coverage as far more detrimental to their own cases than to their opponents'—opposing counsel were regarded as more flamboyant but less distracted as a result of camera coverage [*14*]. Few attorneys were afraid that someone would try to harm them as a consequence of television coverage, and just over half said they would not hesitate to serve in a trial that was to receive television coverage [*14*]. In one survey, nearly two-thirds of the attorneys said camera coverage extends the length of a trial, over three-quarters said camera presence exaggerates the importance of a trial, and nearly a quarter said trial participants are more flamboyant when cameras are present [*17*]. The California study found that attorneys' ability to communicate effectively was not impaired by electronic media coverage, and only 10–15% of attorneys saw a negative change in their opponents' behavior due to camera presence [*19*]. However, three surveys indicated clear opposition to *continued* camera coverage on the part of attorneys, particularly defense attorneys [*13,14,19*].

Overall, attorney responses about courtroom cameras were more negative than those of other participants, and defenders were clearly the most negative of all attorneys. At the end of California's 1-year experiment, 79% of prosecutors and 90% of defenders strongly disagreed with the removal of party consent requirements for camera coverage of criminal proceedings; 70% of prosecutors and only 30% of defenders approved of appellate camera coverage; 43% of prosecutors and 20% of defenders approved of camera coverage of civil proceedings; and only 47% of prosecutors and 13% of defenders approved of cameras at criminal proceedings [19].

B. Judges

In the case study literature, judges concluded that camera coverage had no effect at all on attorney attention and demeanor, nor did it make them flamboyant [3,5,6,9]. One judge said attorneys showed initial nervousness but this soon dissipated [8], and one judge said that camera presence encouraged attorneys to strive for perfection [5]. Judges who were surveyed said attorneys were generally unaffected by camera coverage, though defense attorneys were more adversely affected than prosecutors or civil attorneys [12]. Although most judges said attorneys were not flamboyant, there was a greater chance of histrionic behavior in front of television rather than still cameras [13], and judges overwhelmingly said that attorneys represented their clients properly during televised trials [12]. In the California study, only about 15% of judges perceived a negative change in attorney behavior due to electronic media coverage [19].

C. Jurors, Court Personnel, and Witnesses

Most jurors said that attorneys were not distracted or flamboyant during televised trials [5,8,9,13], and only 15% of jurors in the California study perceived a negative change in attorney behavior due to camera coverage [19]. About a third of the court personnel who were surveyed said attorneys were slightly distracted and flamboyant because of camera coverage [14], and in one case study 33% of witnesses said television cameras affected attorney behavior [9].

9.   IMPACTS ON DEFENDANTS AND LITIGANTS

Apart from Kermit Netteburg's (1980) anecdotal survey about the influence of televised trials on defendant notoriety [16], few studies have made any meaningful reference to the impacts of camera coverage on defendants or litigants. In one case study, an attorney said he saw no adverse effects from cameras on the defendant [15]; in three other case studies, defense counsel were worried about the effects of biased, edited television coverage on their clients' cases [7,8,10]. Jurors at the Zamora trial were concerned about the impact of television coverage on the defendant's reputation as well as his family [2]; in another case study, all 13 jurors said cameras had no impact on the parties in the trial [8]. One judge perceived some feelings on the part of other trial participants that camera coverage was unfair to defendants [3], and court personnel have expressed concern that pretrial coverage could prejudice identification of the defendant by witnesses [9]. Only one case study (part of the Wisconsin pilot program) actually sought personal reactions to camera coverage from a defendant. In this instance, Pastor Wayne Dillabough said he was not intimidated by the cameras while testifying, but he thought television and radio coverage would result in his receiving more letters and phone calls than if the trial had only been covered by newspaper reporters [7]. In the California study, 29% of defendants said they feared physical, psychological, financial, or reputational harm as a consequence of electronic media coverage of proceedings, but no follow-up was conducted to determine if these fears were warranted [19].

Two surveys included participant perceptions about camera coverage of defendants. Judges overwhelmingly said criminal defendants and civil litigants were unaffected by camera presence [12], and that camera coverage did not cause defendants undue embarrassment or indignities [13]. Attorneys and witnesses, however, had far more negative perceptions: nearly 50% of attorneys said television coverage caused defendants undue embarrassment and indignities, and only about 40% of witnesses said camera coverage was fair to defendants (about a third were uncertain) [13]. Camera coverage was perceived as fair to defendants by only just over 50% of jurors; 60% of spectators, court clerks, and bailiffs; and 20% of court reporters [13].

Netteburg's public opinion survey, concerning a sensational trial involving charges of homicide and attempted arson (see Homicide, Not Murder, 1980), found that the public perceived traditional media reporting of trials as less fair than broadcast coverage. The more critical and more interesting responses concerned public recall of trial issues and participant names. It is important, here, to note the differences between aided and unaided recall responses. The latter responses may reflect a more realistic pattern than the former since people tend to talk with neighbors, friends, and colleagues about news items and would, therefore, recall issues and names in a "prompted" or aided situation. In an unaided recall situation, only 16% of respondents could correctly remember the defendant's name (Jennifer Patri), and 77% could not recall the trial at all. However, when prompted (aided recall), 75% recalled the defendant's name. A clear majority of respondents (61%) also remembered the reason Patri gave for killing her husband (he had beaten her many times). Perhaps more disturbing are results concerning the trial outcome: 59% of respondents believed Patri had been convicted of both homicide and arson; in fact, she was convicted of manslaughter but found not guilty of arson by reason of insanity [16]. It seems that, even when a trial is widely publicized in the media, local residents are unable to recall important details of the case correctly. Whether or not information is recalled more accurately, and by more people, from newspaper reports was not explored in the study.

10. IMPACTS ON COURT PERSONNEL

Few studies documented the attitudes of court personnel about cameras in the courtroom, or the perceptions of other trial participants about the impacts of camera coverage on court personnel. In part, this lack of interest is due to the more "behind the scenes" role played by this group of trial participants. The behavior of court reporters, bailiffs, and clerks has less direct bearing on the conduct or fairness of a trial than the behavior of judges, witnesses, jurors, and attorneys. Nevertheless, court personnel play an important role when media are covering a case. They are often called upon to act as liaisons between media representatives and judges, monitor and supervise media activities, and generally organize daily traffic in and around the courtroom and courthouse. As the interests of broadcasters and photographers in trials grow, so do the duties of court personnel.

In one survey, only just over half of the court personnel were in favor of (or at least not opposed to) cameras in the courtroom [14]. Also, while 85% were not afraid of harm as a consequence of camera coverage, and 80% were not reluctant to participate in a televised trial, between a third and a half were self-conscious, nervous, distracted, and felt media coverage exaggerated the importance of a case [14]. Judges, however, seem relatively unaware of these sentiments: in one survey, 85% of judges said court personnel were unaffected by camera presence [12].

11.   TYPES OF PROCEEDINGS THAT ATTRACTED MEDIA COVERAGE

One of the most disturbing aspects of televised trials, particularly to attorneys and judges, is that broadcasters are generally interested in covering only notorious and sordid types of cases, such as murder, rape, bribary, and corruption [7,9,10,12,19]. A major concern is that, by concentrating on these kinds of issues (in order to maintain high newscast ratings), the viewing public receives a distorted picture of what takes place in the nation's courtrooms on a daily basis. In reality, many proceedings are tedious civil and public interest disputes, domestic cases, summary judgements, and legal arguments in appeals courts.

While these are valid concerns, an analysis of the types of proceedings covered by the electronic media *during state experiments* with news cameras reveals a slightly more optimistic picture. Although over two thirds of the cases selected for coverage were criminal trials, numerous other types of proceedings were covered as well. In Wisconsin, for example, cameras covered sentencings, arraignments, a contested divorce action, an opinion announcement in an affirmative action case, legal arguments concerning pornography, a dispute between state penitentiary guards and the Department of Social and Health Services, an injunction relief, a summary judgment regarding a school issue, an intra-political party dispute, motion calendar arguments, zoning disputes, a traffic violation appeal, and at least two civil trials, as well as a number of criminal trials.

In California, electronic and traditional media covered a total of 203 proceedings: 67 civil cases (including motions as well as trials), 132 criminal cases (including arraignments, motions, preliminary hearings, and sentencings as well as trials), and two appellate and two juvenile proceedings. According to an "importance" rating applied to these proceedings, there was an even distribution between coverage of cases regarded as being of "high importance" and "low importance" (terms which can broadly be applied to sensational versus nonsensational types of cases). Other states for which data is available show that most cases selected for camera coverage were, indeed, criminal trials [8,9,13]. However, it is important to realize that many states purposely chose to experiment with, and report on, camera coverage of criminal trials, because it was the televising of these types of cases, in particular, that drew such heated opposition within legal circles (including legal opinions accompanying Supreme Court decisions).

Perhaps a problem with extended media coverage, even more pressing than the fact that criminal cases are favored over civil cases, is the *amount* and *type* of coverage given to a case. The literature reveals that few trials have been broadcast in any substantial detail, and fewer still have been televised gavel-to-gavel. Most television news stories about cases were little more than snippets of video footage accompanied by a voice-over reporter, and many such stories focused on the defendant or the more exciting opening and closing arguments of counsel. Few judges, and even fewer attorneys, believe that these kinds of excerpted highlights portray the courts or particular cases and trial participants accurately, sympathetically, or informatively [9,10,11]. At least two judicial reports warned that future camera access could be jeopardized unless broadcasters begin to provide more detailed, in-depth coverage of the courts [10,12].

12. CONDUCT OF MEDIA PERSONNEL

Judicial reports also included specific observations about the behavior of media personnel. The majority of comments were positive: *inside the courtroom,* media personnel were generally unobtrusive and cooperative, and they complied with judicial guidelines regarding camera use—e.g., restrictions on the number of cameras allowed in the courtroom and the types of participants who could be photographed or televised. Negative observations were that cameramen, particularly still photographers, were sometimes late in setting up equipment and either delayed the start of trails or disrupted proceedings [1,9]. In one case, media representatives were criticized for "squabbling about camera positions and prerogatives" [15]. Sometimes, there were disruptions or distractions due to equipment function or personnel movement, especially from still photographers [1,9,11]. Often, though, these were clearly accidental, and, as one observer noted, "hardly worthy of mention" [15]. Most reports concluded that media representatives "were beyond reproach" [15] while working inside the courtroom, and one report even commended the media for their "sensitive concern" during coverage of a rape case [9].

However, other observations included in the literature deserve serious consideration and concern the behavior of media personnel *outside* courtrooms. Video camera crews and still photographers were often severely criticized for creating "hallway pandemonium" [12,19]; for intimidating and harassing witnesses, defendants, and jurors as they moved about the courthouse [19]; and for taking pictures of trial participants during proceedings, or in rooms and hallways, that were closed to the press in general [7,9,19]. In Wisconsin, for example, film had to be confiscated from a television reporter who took pictures of prospective jurors from the doorway of the questioning room [7]. In California, a television camera peered through the courtroom door to get footage of a witness's testimony. The operator in question had failed to complete a media coverage request form or obtain the court's consent, but arrived at the courthouse anyway. When the witness noticed the television camera operating through the courtroom door, she became hysterical. In deference to the witness, the still cameraman (who had completed the required application for coverage) was also removed for the remainder of the witness's testimony [19]. These anecdotes reinforce the point that severe problems occur when media representatives abuse the camera coverage guidelines established by courts.

13. JUDICIAL DISCRETION AND GUIDELINES

The case study literature, in particular, included statements from judges that were favorable to the idea and principle of allowing news cameras in courtrooms. In 9 of the 11 case studies, there were specific judicial comments about the give-and-take relationship that can be established between the courts and the media, the main point being that, if media representatives are sensitive to the needs of the court, if they respect judicial authority and reasonable restrictions, then there can continue to be successful camera coverage without disruption, interference, or jeopardy to trial fairness.

Without exception, states permitting camera coverage have instituted comprehensive guidelines which clearly stipulate both the numbers and types of personnel and equipment that can cover a case during any single court session. Such guidelines often require pooling arrangements for interested media, and usually restrict media presence to a single video camera, a single still photographer, and one radio microphone and recorder. Almost all judicial reports also emphasized that absolute discretion rests with judges on decisions about the types of participants who can be photographed or televised. For example, confidential witnesses, undercover agents, children, certain juveniles, the family of the accused, domestic or custody case participants, and victims of physical or sexual abuse should not be required to submit to news camera coverage. Judges are sensitive to the fact that some witnesses and jurors fear retribution from prison inmates or other parties involved in a case, and should therefore not be exposed to unnecessary pressures or dangers.

Many judges seem to agree that, if cameras are allowed in courtrooms on a permanent basis, then they can be carefully monitored by court personnel and judges. Only two judges who wrote individual case study reports were opposed to permanent access to cameras, and in both cases neither judge specified any long-term negative impacts that arose from media coverage of the cases they presided over [3,4]. The other nine judicial studies generally concluded that camera coverage had been successful, and in some cases judges perceived some advantages to the coverage as well. For example, televised trials could be educationally valuable to viewers; they could benefit the courts as well as the public by highlighting some of the real day-to-day problems of administering justice, and the presence of cameras might encourage all participants to perform their very best. One report also stated that the news media can be more objective in reporting court proceedings if permitted to use cameras [6]. Another noted that advantages outweigh disadvantages, and that judges and lawyers will become more positive in their attitudes as their understanding and experience with camera coverage grows [7].

14. NEGATIVE ATTITUDES OF ATTORNEYS AND JUDGES

Six of the 11 judicial case studies included some negative comments from judges or attorneys regarding the impact of cameras on trial participants and the administration of justice in general. These statements were usually speculative, i.e., they were not necessarily based on the actual experiences of the commentator during the case(s) being studied, but instead reflected the participant's personal anxieties about the use of courtroom cameras in general.

In one case study, two of the five attorneys said they were concerned jurors might be pressured by local community attitudes when reaching a decision in the case [1]. Their speculation was that, if friends and neighbors recognize a juror who is televised or photographed during a trial, they may try to influence the juror's decision. Another attorney involved in the same case speculated about how the courtroom atmosphere might be disturbed if unlimited numbers of cameras and media personnel were allowed access [1]. Though understandable, this type of concern was generally found to be unrealistic in view of the guidelines established for media coverage. In another case, one of the defense attorneys made several negative comments about camera coverage [5], though his evaluations were not based on specific experiences during the trial and were not supported by the statements of the other three attorneys who participated in the case. The negative opinions derived from a general sense that cameras simply add one more complication to an already difficult situation faced by an attorney in trying to convince a jury and win the case. Similar views were expressed by a defense attorney in another case who said that extended media coverage adds to the pressures already faced by witnesses and jurors in notorious trials [9]. Other attorneys have expressed negative views about *news* camera coverage but not educational coverage of trails [8].

Two Florida judges also reached negative conclusions about televised trials, although both judges praised the cooperation and conduct of media personnel [3,4]. In one instance, much of the negative attitude stemmed from a series of aggravating administrative problems encountered by the court. Bomb threats and hoax "leads" were telephoned to the courthouse, and one witness, fearing retribution from criminal elements involved in the case, refused to testify for fear of her safety. The judge in this case was also concerned about the financial burden placed on the court in having to sequester jurors, and he suggested that, in future, these costs should be passed on to media organizations seeking access to trials [3]. Massachusetts judges expressed concern about "overcrowding" small courtrooms with camera equipment, and recommended that any renovation of existing structures made to accommodate cables, microphones, or lighting equipment should be paid for by broadcast organizations [9].

In the survey literature, the kinds of negative attitudes expressed by individual judges and attorneys in the case studies surfaced in responses to questions about the principle of allowing cameras in courtrooms, and the desirability of the practice. The reservations and resentments of judges and attorneys became apparent in the dichotomy between their perceptions about the impacts of camera coverage on themselves and other participants, and their general attitudes about continued use of cameras.

While most judges perceived few adverse behavioral or psychological impacts from camera coverage on themselves or on other participants, only a very small majority (just over half) who had actually experienced courtroom cameras wanted the practice to continue, and only a minority of judges without experience found camera coverage a desirable practice [13]. In the California study, only 54% of over 200 judges approved of electronic media coverage for criminal proceedings (percentages were a little higher for civil and appellate proceedings) [19]. Another survey showed that many judges were reluctant to approve of courtroom cameras because they were concerned about criticisms voiced by local bar associations [15].

Attorneys have even more pronounced negative attitudes about the principle of permitting cameras in courtrooms. In one survey, only 48% of those *with* camera coverage experience and 35% of those *without* experience wanted the practice to continue [13]. In the California study, only 47% of prosecutors and 13% of defenders approved of electronic media coverage of criminal proceedings [19].

15. STILL VERSUS VIDEO CAMERAS

The case study literature generally concluded that video cameras were totally inconspicuous, and participants were often surprised at the quietness of their operation [1,2,5,8,10,11]. The "clicking" noise of still cameras was noticeable, as were the photographers who sometimes moved about the courtroom adjusting camera lenses, but both were usually ignored [1,2,5,9]. The survey literature, and one case study, concluded that, while still cameras were a little more distracting than television cameras, they made participants feel less self-conscious or nervous [9,13,14]. Responses of trial participants were similar regarding the fairness of both types of camera coverage to defendants and witnesses, though coverage in general was perceived as less fair to witnesses than to defendants. There was also little difference in attitudes about whether still or television cameras interfered with the overall conduct of a trial, but still camera coverage was regarded as a better public service and a more desirable practice than television coverage [9,13].

16. ATTITUDE CHANGE DUE TO GREATER EXPERIENCE

Several studies showed a clear correlation between more positive attitudes and perceptions about the use of courtroom cameras and experience on the part of participants with camera coverage. Five case studies reported that judges, attorneys, and jurors who were skeptical prior to serving in a televised trial changed their minds after the experience [1,7,8,10,11]. One survey found 13% more attorneys, and 17% more judges, with camera coverage experience than without it were in favor of the practice continuing [13], and another survey of 155 judges concluded that those who had worked with cameras in their courtrooms were less apprehensive about distraction or disruption than those who had no first-hand experience [15].

Perhaps the most systematic and comprehensive analysis of attitude changes over time (with experience) was incorporated in the California survey-experiment. A comparison of pre- and post-test results highlights a positive relationship between electronic media coverage (EMC) experience and the attitudes of jurors, judges, and prosecuting attorneys. Jurors showed the strongest attitude swings in a positive direction. Fewer experienced than nonexperienced jurors felt that EMC would affect sentencing decisions, cause judges to avoid unpopular decisions, lead to disruption of courtroom proceedings, mean a juror's decision would be influenced by friends and acquaintances, affect trial outcomes, cause jurors to have to defend their actions, lead to increased distraction of participants, make people more apprehensive about participating in legal proceedings, affect juror willingness to serve in a case, or cause witnesses to be overly guarded in their testimony. More experienced than nonexperienced jurors said that EMC would *not* affect a juror's ability to decide a case wisely and on its merits, nor a judge's ability to maintain courtroom order. Finally, more experienced than nonexperienced jurors felt that EMC would *increase* juror attentiveness to witness testimony [19].

Judges and prosecutors also responded more positively after camera coverage experience. Sixteen percent more judges, and 8% more prosecutors, became favorable to EMC of *appellate* proceedings; 15% more judges and 10% more prosecutors became favorable to EMC of *civil* proceedings; and 12% more judges and 16% more prosecutors became favorable to EMC of *criminal* proceedings. Only defense attorneys showed a negative swing in attitudes after experiencing camera coverage. Nine percent less were favorable, and 7% more were negative, toward EMC of *appellate* proceedings; 1% less were favorable, and 2% more were negative, toward EMC of *criminal* proceedings; and, while 1% more became favorable to EMC of *civil* proceedings, 5% more became negative [19]. Similarly, a Florida survey found that the attitudes of attorneys, witnesses, jurors, and court personnel about their court service became more negative and undecided after cameras were introduced in the courtroom [*14*].

17. TRANSFERRAL OF IMPACTS

Several studies highlighted an important and interesting phenomenon regarding trial participants' responses about camera impacts. It seems that participants were less likely to report that cameras had an adverse effect on *personal* behavior than to say it affected the behavior of *other* participants. Jurors, for example, were generally adamant that their decisions were not influenced in any way by community pressures; attorneys, in contrast, were fairly sure that there could have been some influence. Judges were convinced that they were not intimidated by cameras (and would never avoid unpopular decisions because of coverage); attorneys, however, said there may have been adverse impacts on judicial behavior (particularly on elected judges). Witnesses often said that camera presence did not inhibit their testimony; attorneys, and to a lesser extent jurors and court personnel, said witness testimony was hampered by media coverage.

Perhaps this "transferral of impacts" trend is most blatantly revealed in attorney responses. For example, attorneys were far more willing to say that their opponents acted flamboyantly in front of cameras than to say the same thing of themselves. Another interesting phenomenon is the amount of agreement between the responses of judges and attorneys, and court personnel and judges. Judges' attitudes tend to support those of attorneys: when attorneys respond negatively on an issue, judges usually respond neutrally-to-negatively. Court personnel seem to place judges on something of a pedestal: their responses match those of judges more closely than any other group of participants, particularly when judicial behavior is in question, such as distraction, intimidation, or grandstanding.

18. DISCUSSION OF THE COURTROOM CAMERAS RESEARCH

In closing this summary of the courtroom cameras research, a few words are in order about the significant contribution which California's study has made to the body of literature as a whole. It was a carefully planned and executed piece of research, gathering a broad spectrum of data from a wide group of legal-proceeding participants over a 12-month period. The study adopted a three-way approach to data collection: (a) case-specific interview responses from participants, (b) evaluator observations to confirm participant interview responses, and (c) general attitudinal survey responses gathered via mail questionnaires. The research also compared shifts in participant attitudes over time, i.e., prior to, during, and after exposure to electronic media coverage, as well as comparing "base-line" (traditional media coverage only) participant behavior with combined electronic and traditional media coverage behavior.

Another noteworthy aspect of this study is that its conclusions support the findings of earlier, less sophisticated research. At first, this might seem a rather contradictory statement. Why would there be anything noteworthy about the results of a study which corroborate weaker research? Perhaps it is merely an unfortunate coincidence or, worse, a case of questionable research following poor research. For the skeptical, this may be an obvious and appropriate attitude to adopt, but for those who would venture a more positive approach, it seems fairly striking that 19 pieces of independent research, conducted in 11 states over a span of 8 years, reached similar conclusions about the relative lack of behavioral prejudice caused by news cameras in courtrooms. It appears that camera coverage of trials (even sensational criminal cases) does not necessarily influence the majority of trial participants to behave in ways that are noticeably different from behavior in nontelevised trials. This is not to say that many trial participants do not have mixed or negative *attitudes* toward camera coverage, only that the bulk of empirical research conducted to date shows little correlation brtween the presence of cameras at trials and perceived prejudicial *behavior* on the part of jurors, witnesses, judges, or attorneys.

While state experiments with news cameras have shown that many of the *Estes* arguments are not borne out in reality, judges, and especially attorneys, have some strong subjective resentments against courtroom cameras which are often unsupported by personal experience or objective observation. The California study, in particular, found that defense attorneys have more negative views about electronic media coverage than any other group of trial participants. Subjective attitudes about courtroom cameras are obviously complex and hard to separate, but various types of anti-camera sentiments were partly explained in the interview and open-ended questionnaire responses included in several judicial reports. Apparently, judges are keen to preserve a decorous courtroom atmosphere and fear losing control over their courtrooms and even courthouses. Administrative concerns such as monitoring the conduct of media personnel and the use of media equipment, and the possibility of an increased need to sequester jurors, add to the lack of enthusiasm on the part of some judges. Attorneys voice objections about the potential impact broadcast trial coverage may have on jury verdicts. They are also concerned about maintaining absolute juror Concentration, and tend to regard the presence of cameras as a nuisance—one more pressure to be dealt with in presenting a case to the jury.

These anxieties are understandable, but they have not been shown to exist in the majority of televised trials. It would seem, then, that there may be some more subtle or hidden agenda reasons for wanting to keep cameras out. Judges may be worried that television exposure will make them more accountable to the public for their rulings and courtroom behavior—elected judges may be particularly concerned. Attorneys may be worried that cameras have a dampening effect on their ability to *sway* the jury and *win* the case, and some attorneys may fear the need for better preparation of cases when appearing in front of cameras.

The picture of courtroom cameras, though, should not be painted in one direction only. The literature clearly shows that problems arise when media representatives circumvent camera coverage guidelines established by courts. In ignoring the rules, whether by failing to follow procedures or by "hounding" sensitive trial participants, a few media representatives have jeopardized the reputations and camera access privileges of all media personnel. As a safeguard, it might be appropriate for courts to appoint more media liaisons and employ more court personnel to monitor media activities, with the cost passed along to media organizations wishing to cover courtroom proceedings.

The courtroom cameras studies also reveal that biased editing of trial footage, and the small amounts and sensational types of coverage given to cases, have diminished positive judicial feelings about courtroom cameras. Judges are well aware that television, as the most widely used news medium, is a crucial source of information to many people who only see courtroom scenes on drama shows, and there is concern that, unless broadcasters devote time to more in-depth and balanced coverage of cases, they will be doing a disservice to viewers as well as to the courts. If, as many judges hope, broadcasters are to take on the role of educators as well as news gatherers, then their responsibility is to inform the public about the trial process in general, the administrative complexities of the justice system, and the daily routine of dealing with often overcrowded court dockets.

Another area of concern for both the courts and the media should be improved communication between court personnel and media representatives. It seems that there are some resentments on the part of bailiffs and court clerks about added administrative and custodial duties associated with broadcast trial coverage, and the behavior of over-zealous broadcast journalists and cameramen have, indeed, warranted criticism. Administrative burdens might be eased if broadcasters were required to apply for media coverage consent well in advance of a case being tried. Custodial duties (monitoring of media equipment and personnel) might be relieved if courtrooms and courthouses were slightly remodelled to accommodate cameras, cables, microphones, and media viewing rooms. And, of course, pooling arrangements should be mandatory to alleviate congested corridors and courtrooms.

Other participants, such as jurors and witnesses, have also expressed skepticism about the appropriateness of televising trials. Often, however, their negative attitudes are speculative, and change once these participants have actually taken part in a proceeding covered by cameras. Since the skepticism stems in part from ignorance, it would perhaps be beneficial to introduce "education sessions" designed to inform prospective jurors and witnesses about their role in a trial, the expectations of the court, trial procedure, and the implications of photographing and televising trials *before* they are subjected to camera coverage. Participants should also be informed of their rights to challenge an application for media coverage.

19. *LIMITATIONS OF THE COURTROOM CAMERAS RESEARCH*

Those who have read at least part of the available courtroom cameras research have, understandably, been quick to criticize it as being unsophisticated and unreliable (Gerbner, 1980; Hirschhorn, 1980a).[5] Indeed, the present analysis shows that complaints might fairly be raised about the lack of well planned, comprehensive survey instruments, the failure to devise studies which would isolate and control the influence of specific variables, the absence of strict control group comparisons, unstructured data collection methods, and superficial reporting of results that were obtained. Another set of criticisms could certainly focus on the fact that almost all of the data which have been collected deal with people's *opinions* about the impacts of camera coverage on trial participants, not with the kinds of behavioral or psychological changes that may *actually occur* as a consequence of such coverage. Indeed, all but two of the courtroom cameras studies are nonexperimental in nature and their conclusions, therefore, cannot support cause and effect relationships. Instead, the research is largely based on attitudinal data—*perceptions* about the impacts of camera presence on trial particpants and the flow of courtroom proceedings in general.

More specifically, the research on courtroom news cameras can be criticized for the following reasons. The observations contained in judicial case study reports may lack validity because they cannot be generalized—these observations relate only to the variables present in a particular trial. The survey results may be inconclusive because they do not prove cause and effect; instead, they document personal reactions and the perceived reactions of others to camera coverage. And the anecdotal studies may be faulted because they do not duplicate the precise variables of a real trial environment, either inside a courtroom or in a local community. However, these weaknesses may not be as severe as they at first appear; they might be countered with the following observations. While the judicial reports describe specific, case-related circumstances, trial proceedings have enough standard features for the observations in one instance to hold true in others. The survey results show relation among variables in each study, and even subjective results have a certain validity when they are repeated from survey to survey or match the findings of other research on the same topic. And, though anecdotal studies may not deal with exact trial or environmental conditions, the results of carefully conducted surveys and simulated experiments may closely predict what might occur during an actual trial. Moreover, on reflection it seems that some of the so-called weaknesses of the courtroom cameras research, i.e., its subjective and predominantly nonexperimental nature, may in part be its strengths. The collection of attitudinal quationnaire responses and personal interview opinions enabled researchers to uncover some of the more revealing and "emotional" attitudes trial participants have toward camera coverage. These sentiments might not have surfaced in strict experimental, objective research.

20. SOME MITIGATING FACTORS

In evaluating the available courtroom cameras literature, readers should also be aware of two very important points which, though they may not entirely excuse the flaws in the research, at least explain some of its inherent weaknesses. The first is that there are some very obvious and extremely compelling reasons why real trials cannot be manipulated as experimental research environments. Any manipulation of standard trial procedures or selection of trial participants, as might be necessary in conducting a laboratory-type study, would be constitutionally reprehensible. The second is the need to remember who the majority of courtroom cameras studies were conducted *by* and *for*. Fourteen of the 19 studies were conducted, that is supervised and reported, by judicial personnel (usually judges and sometimes committees combining judges, lawyers, and court administrators). These "researchers" are not social scientists, they are legal experts, and cannot necessarily be expected to show familiarity with the demands of strict scientific research. Akin to this point is the fact that the intended audience (readers) of these studies were other legal personnel, people often unfamiliar with statistical analysis and therefore unable to interpret complex statistical data.

Moreover, most of the studies were conducted under strict time constraints, i.e., those surrounding the length of specific trials, and had to accommodate not only the schedules of individual trial participants, but also the deadlines set by various state courts for the submission of documentation on the courtroom cameras issue. Taking into consideration the point that many trial participants are no longer in close proximity to the courthouse or its administrative offices once a trial is over, and the fact that many trial participants may have been reluctant to involve themselves in lengthy interviews or large quantities of paperwork, it is understandable why some judicial reports are a little vague in parts. Given these inherent difficulties, the studies accomplished their general evaluative objectives fairly well.

21. SUGGESTIONS FOR NEW RESEARCH

It is also particularly crucial in planning new courtroom cameras research to bear in mind the legal yardstick known as the "qualitative difference test," laid out in two important judicial opinions—*Petition of Post Newsweek Stations* (1979) and *Chandler* (1981). What this test makes clear is that camera impacts on judicial proceedings must be measured against two other types of potentially prejudicial behavioral and psychological impacts: (a) those which may already exist in the trial environment, regardless of *any* type of media coverage; and (b) those which may occur as a result of *traditional* media coverage, e.g., newspaper stories. In other words, camera coverage may only be regarded as detrimental to the well-being of trial participants and the fairness of trials if it poses a threat which is qualitatively *different* from any consequence of the aforementioned variables. In discussing the existing body of research and in designing future studies, then, we must be careful to differentiate between impacts which belong only to cameras, and those which may be inherent in the trial process, or which may *also* belong to coverage which is allowed in the courtroom in any case.

The earlier review of legal-communications literature, though not exhaustive, indicates that a courtroom is not always an impartial forum for the presentation of evidence (see also Miller and Bundens, 1982). It is an environment full of subtle and sometimes obvious biases which influence jurors in reaching a verdict. In essence, a courtroom is simply a microcosm of the society it serves, and jury decisions appear to be functions of individual jurors' backgrounds and personalities, and the verbal and nonverbal behavior of other trial participants. Jurors seem unable to entirely relinquish subjective aspects of judgment about fellow human beings; hence, perceptions about a defendant's guilt or innocence may rarely be based solely on impartial consideration of trial testimony.

The suggestion here is not that conclusions from empirical research remain valid in all circumstances, but that a large quantity of literature indicates, at a minimum, two very important points. First, that many of the prejudicial influences which are said to result from the presence of cameras in courtrooms are, in fact, operative in the courtroom *regardless* of the introduction of cameras (or any other form of media). Second, that many so-called "unfair" aspects of trials are not always, or only, attributable to camera presence, but to the nature of the trial process in general.

It seems, for example, that, whether cameras are present or not, jurors do not always pay close attention to trial testimony; they seldom decide cases on the basis of testimony alone, and they often ignore or misunderstand judicial instructions to consider the preponderance of the evidence. Witness testimony may be inhibited by cross-examination techniques, and by the adversary process in general, which does not necessarily lend itself to a search for the truth. Moreover, judges have been known to grandstand and behave imprudently even when cameras were not present, and attorneys were "playing" to the jury long before cameras entered courtrooms. In fact, abilities to artfully persuade and "perform" flamboyantly for jurors are the very skills which distinguish a lawyer as successful and well-liked. At the very least, it seems that cameras may not measurably alter a courtroom already saturated with subjectivity and partiality, and which, regardless of the presence of cameras, is "a scene of drama, wit, humor and humanity, along with the sorrows and stretches of boredom" (Frankel, 1975, p. 1032).

Following the premise of the qualitative difference test, Slater and Hans (1982) have suggested research which could compensate for some of the deficiencies in the existing courtroom cameras literature, while surmounting some inherent difficulties in manipulating individual trials as part of the research design. They have recommended a field experiment which would compare participant behavior in trials covered only by "traditional" media, with trials covered only by "electronic" media. In order to offset possible contamination of the results by a variety of extraneous variables (which cannot be controlled), they suggest *random* assignment of a sufficiently large number of trials to one of the two experimental conditions.[6] The study proposed by Slater and Hans is, in many respects, a more refined version of the California survey-experiment, though it carefully avoids the internal validity problems associated with shifting from "baseline" to "experimental" coverage within the same trial that afflicted the California study.

Ultimately, however, any kind of experimental study which uses environments as complex and sensitive as real trials faces some potential obstacles. For example, major difficulties could surface if the media, themselves, were unwilling to cooperate in a research project that might preclude them from covering an important (news-worthy) case, i.e., newspaper reporters would be prohibited in the "electronic" setting and photographers and broadcasters would be excluded in the "traditional" setting. Such restrictions might be regarded as an infringement on First Amendment freedoms and would open up the courts to a rash of law suits. Unless the courts could obtain reassurance from interested media organizations that they would participate in such a study under the restraints of the research strategy, the project could hardly get off the ground. While almost all states which now permit camera coverage on a permanent or "experimental" basis have strict guidelines placing ultimate discretion for coverage in the hands of individual judges, these guidelines often make it clear that a judge may not exclude cameras (or traditional media) without cause, and often not without a hearing either. The time-consuming administrative difficulties inher-ent in trying to fairly implement such a system would perhaps be more than a court system could bear. Such an experiment, then, may need to be restricted to only those states in which media cooperation could be guaranteed, or where judicial guidelines still enable a judge to exclude electronic media without cause.

22. *QUESTIONS FOR SOCIAL SCIENTISTS AND THE COURTS*

Apart from methodological deficiencies in the existing courtroom cameras research, there are some inadequacies in terms of research focus—the types of questions being asked and answered. Perhaps the most glaring gap is the lack of data on defendant reactions to being televised. While some researchers asked other trials participants how they believed cameras affected the defendant, very few defendants were asked for their own reactions to the cameras. Defendants are the trial participants most vul-nerable to harm from any type of news coverage, print or broadcast, and future studies should address issues such as defendant embarrassment or humiliation, and defendant concerns about physical, psychological, reputational, and financial harm as a consequence of media trial coverage.

It would also be useful to know whether *viewers* perceive a case differently when it is covered by television rather than by newspaper or magazines. Is greater impor-tance conferred on a crime, or stronger guilt associated with a defendant after watching a televised trial? Does the amount of coverage given a case, i.e., gavel-to-gavel compared with short excerpts, influence viewer perceptions about a defendant or a crime? More generally, there is a need to examine issues of educational versus entertainment (voyeuristic) qualities of televised trials. The following questions have barely been hinted at in existing courtroom cameras studies, and more research is required if broadcasters are to fully understand the implications of their work:

1.   Is the public better informed, or even adequately informed, by electronic versus conventional media coverage of a case?

2. Can gavel-to-gavel broadcasts serve to educate the public about the administration of justice in general?

3. Do time constraints imposed on many broadcast news stories mean that a case is treated either unfairly or inadequately?

4. Does the public get a distorted picture of the judicial system, or a biased view of a particular trial, if stories are edited to highlight sensational testimony, cross examination, or simply the opening and closing arguments of attorneys?

5. How does the public's understanding of the courts and specific cases differ when broadcast versus printed news is the medium of communication?

6. Which type of news coverage has consistently provided the most balanced coverage of legal issues, trial participants, and court administration?

7. What kinds of legal news coverage are "educationally" valuable to the public at large?

8. Do viewers primarily perceive televised trials as a form of entertainment programming?

9. Are televised trials viewed primarily for their voyeuristic (even punitive) value?

10. What kinds of attitudes about defendants and other trial participants are generated by televised trial coverage, and are these attitudes different from those formed by print coverage?

FOOTNOTES

1. Note also that another *amicus curiae* brief was filed in support of courtroom cameras by interested media organizations, but was not mentioned in the Court's majority opinion. See Joint Brief for *Amici Curiae* Radio-Television News Directors Association et al. (1979). For views opposing cameras in the courtroom, see *Amicus Curiae* Brief of the American College of Trial Lawyers (1979), and *Amicus Curiae* Brief of the California State Public Defenders Association, the California Attorneys for Criminal Justice, the Office of the California State Public Defender, the Los Angeles County Public Defenders Association, the Los Angeles Criminal Courts Bar Association, and the Office of the Los Angeles County Public Defender (1979). Reference was also made in the Court's majority opinion to a brief submitted by the American Bar Association. However, according to Coleman Williams, Assistant Clerk to the U.S. Supreme Court, and Ann Johnson, Assistant to the General Counsel for the American Bar Association, Chicago, the ABA did not submit a brief in *Chandler* (telephone conversations, June 2, 1981).

2. Although two of the 10 "new" studies were published in 1980, they were presumably not available in sufficient time prior to the October Term, 1979, to be incorporated in the *amicus* brief of the 17 Attorneys General.

3. *Estes v. Texas,* 381 U.S. 532 at 540 (1965).

4. Other pieces of empirically based literature are available on the courtroom cameras issue, such as opinion polls (see, for example, Law Poll: Cameras in the Courtroom? 1982; Court Coverage by TV, Radio Commands Support of Jurists, 1978, p. A21, also re-

ported in Study Shows State Jurists Favor Cameras in Courts, 1979), and interim reports of court advisory committees (see, for example, Interim Report to the Chief Judge of the New York State Court of Appeals by the Media Advisory Committee, 1980, also discussed in TV-Radio Coverage in Court Endorsed, 1980), but these carry less weight than the research discussed in this chapter.

5.   Hirschhorn (1980a, p. 56) has commented: "Social scientists measure the intelligence of monkeys more effectively than courts have attempted to ascertain the effects of television in the courtroom."

6.   Slater and Hans (1982, p. 380, fn. 2) note that "the number of trials necessary for adequate experimental power . . . depends on the variability of the data. The higher the variability, the more trials one must observe. With an estimate of the variance obtained from a pilot study or from prior work, the researcher may consult a power table."

PART FOUR

FOCUS CHANGES FROM THE COURTROOM TO THE AUDIENCE

After nearly 70 years of courtroom cameras experience, and following 10 years of empirical interest in the question of whether trials should be televised, the crucial issues currently surrounding the courtroom cameras debate appear to focus squarely on the audience. This "audience" approach to the debate juxtaposes proposed *benefits* of televised trials: (a) greater public understanding and awareness of judicial administration; (b) crime deterrent value, and (c) restoration of public confidence in the courts, against several potential *risks:* (a) privacy rights of witnesses, particularly victims of physical and sexual abuse; (b) impacts on the viewing public, particularly children in the audience, and (c) increased prejudicial publicity and public embarrassment of defendants. At the heart of this debate is the premise that accrual of the desired benefits will *inevitably* result in increased risks—at least for defendants, i.e., while trial publicity may serve a crime control function and reassure viewers that justice is being served, this same publicity may encourage negative audience perceptions of criminals and foster prejudice against particular defendants.

1. *THE PROPOSED BENEFITS OF TELEVISED TRIALS*

A. *Education about Judicial Process*

One of the arguments that broadcasters have placed in the forefront of their petitions to televise trials has been the notion of educating the public about the judicial system (see, for example, Joint Brief for *Amici Curiae* Radio Television News Directors Association, et al., 1979, pp. 10–12). Broadcasters have generally reasoned that, since public consumption of *television* news is higher than it is for all other forms of news media, broadcast journalists should be granted full freedoms to use cameras in gathering news about the courts.

Disturbed by the often false messages delivered in fictionalized crime and justice shows (see Dershowitz, 1985; Arons and Katsh, 1977),[1] members of the bench (and to a lesser extent the bar) have quite readily accepted, even promoted, claims about the educational value of televised trials (see Lindsey, 1981; Hanscom, 1978; Weinstein and Zimmerman, 1977). In a 1982 survey of Circuit and Superior Court Judges, ABA Presidents, and prosecuting attorneys, educational value and enhancement of public confidence in the judicial system were ranked highest among a list of seven "pro-access" arguments by all three groups (Stefaniak, 1984). Indeed, when the camera access movement began in earnest in the mid-to-late 1970s, several state Supreme Courts highlighted "education" as an important reason for granting access.[2]

Judges and attorneys, it seems, are not wrong in perceiving a need for public education about the workings of the courts—levels of public understanding about the judicial process have, historically, been far from high. Yankelovich, Skelly, and White (1978) found that 37% of those surveyed thought it is up to the accused to prove his innocence in a criminal trial; 30% thought that a district attorney's job is to defend an accused criminal who cannot afford a lawyer; and 72% thought that every decision made by a state court can be reviewed and reversed by the U.S. Supreme Court. Knowledge about the courts was found to be particularly weak among those with incomes below $10,000 a year, among those with less than high school education, and among Black and Hispanic respondents (pp. 14–15). By 1983, misconceptions had apparently grown worse. A Hearst Corporation public awareness survey showed that 50% thought criminals must prove their innocence, 45% thought district attorneys defend poor criminals, and 77% misunderstood the role of the Supreme Court vis-a-vis state court decisions (pp. 13–15).[3] Perhaps even more worrying, nearly 50% of respondents who said they had served on a jury thought it was up to an accused person tp prove his innocence, and 31% of college graduates gave the same wrong answer to the statement (p. 5).[4] Hans and Slater (1983) found that 70.8% of their survey respondents could not define the legal insanity defense correctly, and that this lack of awareness was partly responsible for negative public opinion surrounding the John Hinckley verdict.

B. A Deterrent to Criminals

Under the rubric of "educational value" it has also been suggested that televised trials may inform people about the consequences of crime, and thus act as a deterrent for those considering criminal activity. Phillips and Hensley (1984) found that, 4 days after media reports of severe punishment of violent crime—life imprisonment, death sentence, or execution for murder—there was a significant decrease in reported homicides. Ellis Rubin, representing 15-year-old Ronny Zamora in the famous "television intoxication" defense, said he received hundreds of letters from adolescents who viewed the televised trial and who said "it gave them second thoughts" about committing crimes (Platte, 1981, p. 17). Similar delinquency deterrent value has also accrued from television exposure of life in the penal system. In the documentary "Scared Straight," incarcerated offenders provided viewers with candid views of the harsh realities of prison life, and proved to be both a popular and successful method of "scaring" juveniles into going "straight" (Heeren and Schichor, 1984).

David Tajgman (1981, p. 511) has also described what he calls the Crime Control function of the press, which he views as working in three ways:

1. "by reporting the system's success in bringing a criminal to justice, the press educates the public as to the efficacy of the criminal justice system, in the end showing that 'crime does not pay.' This, in turn deters criminal activity."
2. "the press makes trial participants [particularly prospective jurors] cognizant of public interest regarding the case. Where public sentiment is against the defendant and is conveyed by the press to trial participants, as in coverage of a trial involving a particularly heinous crime, any influence that coverage has comports with the press' Crime Control function."
3. "Where public sentiment is in favor of the defendant, and is conveyed by the press to trial participants, any influence coverage has on acquittal promotes Crime Control since justice has been done and an innocent man has been freed."

But he simultaneously raises a critical issue: the U.S. Supreme Court's willingness to relegate potential due process risks (associated with pretrial and trial publicity) to a secondary consideration, in favor of media's (particularly television's) potential crime control value. Indeed, Tajgman implies that the Court decided *Chandler* in favor of televised trials, *precisely because* it hoped that the socializing function of television would act as a crime deterrent in a more active and powerful way than traditional newspaper coverage. He points out, however, that "televised coverage may have a Crime Control influence only if viewers' expectations of the criminal justice system are met by what they see" (p. 537). In other words, the hoped-for results of televising trials are dependent upon the types of cases or excerpts of cases that are shown, the substance of the news item or program, and audience perceptions of the prudence of a judicial decision in any given case.

C.   Restoring Confidence in the Courts

Judges and attorneys, as well as media representatives, also believe that broadcast coverage of judicial proceedings could promote greater public awareness of the day-to-day complexities of running the courts, and greater sympathy for the problems of judicial administration. In 1978, a *Washington Post* editorial took up the fight for cameras in the courtroom by arguing these very points: "A televised trial, or even an excerpt from a trial, is likely to do more to advance public understanding of the problem of the administration of justice than all the speeches that have been delivered by judges down through the years" (Television in the Courts, 1978, p. C6).

Lawrence H. Cooke, recently retired Chief Judge of New York, is a well-known advocate of courtroom cameras and has announced his views publicly on several occasions. In 1982, for example, he noted that opening the courts to television would encourage the public to "give greater support to the courts" (N.Y. Chief Judge Supports Television Coverage, 1982, p. 7), and in 1984 he said "today, more than ever, candor and openness are needed to restore public confidence and trust in the legal system" (Widen Use of Cameras in State Courts, 1984, p. 1). Charles Nesson and Andrew Koblenz (1981, p. 409) have argued that the *key rationale* for the Court's *Chandler* decision was to help "shore up the image of the judiciary"—by inviting cameras into the nation's trial courts, the public could *see* (and be assured) that justice was being served. Dallas attorney David Townend has taken the issue a step further by suggesting that "greater public confidence in the judicial branch would alone be a sufficient trade-off for the inconveniences which would be caused by cameras in court" (Townend, 1981, p. 380).

It is clear that increasing judicial concern about public confidence in the courts has not been without reason. A *New York Times*/Channel 2 poll of New York City residents, testing confidence in essential services between 1973 and 1974, found that 57% of those interviewed had no confidence in the justice metered out by the courts (Poll Finds Rise in Hope for Future of New York, 1978). The 1978 Yankelovich, Skelly, and White survey revealed that the general public ranked confidence in state and local courts below that of several other major American institutions, including the medical profession, local police, business, and public schools. Moreover, 62% of respondents with some state court experience, and 52% without experience, said that court efficiency was a serious-to-very-serious social problem in American society (Yankelovich, Skelly, and White, 1978, p. 23, Table 2.1).

Doris Graber's panel-study revealed perceptions of the courts as "remote, forbidding, and unpredictable . . . [and] responsible for returning unreformed criminals to society" (Graber, 1980, pp. 78–79). Forty-two percent evaluated the courts' performance as poor. Reasons given for the poor ratings included overloading of the court system, insufficient numbers of judges, corruption, laziness, excessive judicial leniency, abusive treatment of accused persons, long delays, judgements based on technicalities, inadequate sentencing, and an overly lenient parole system (pp. 80–81). Similar views were reflected in the results of a *Newsweek* poll, published in March 1981, which showed that 59% of those surveyed had very little confidence in the courts to sentence or convict criminals (The Plague of Violent Crime, 1981).

2. *THE POTENTIAL RISKS*

Despite the apparent needs to educate the public about judicial process and to restore public confidence in the courts, many legal professionals seriously doubt that televised news coverage of trials will achieve this objective. The views of those who oppose televised trials range from skepticism to outright mistrust of broadcasters' motives and therefore disapproval. The American College of Trial Lawyers, writing as *amicus curiae* in *Chandler v. Florida* (1981), had this to say about the proposed benefits of televising trials:

> it is highly questionable whether the random televising of trials, by what is essentially a commercial entertainment medium, is at all suited to educating the public in the realities of the law and the judicial process.

The argument that televising dramatic portions of some selected trials will be educational and will show the public what courts do is hardly persuasive to most experienced lawyers and judges (Brief of the American College of Trial Lawyers, 1979, p. 25).

Indeed, during the years since *Chandler* was handed down, televised coverage of sensational trials such as the Claus von Bulow case in Rhode Island and the Big Dan's case in Massachusetts, and *proposed* television coverage of trials such as the Wayne Williams case in Georgia and the McMartin case in California, have fueled and re-fueled the arguments of courtroom cameras opponents. Today's debate, however, presents a new set of arguments from those heard in either *Chandler* or its predecessor *Estes*. What concerns the latest anti-cameras lobbyists are not the potentially prejudicial impacts of camera coverage *inside* the courtroom *during* the trial, but potential negative viewer perceptions of trial participants, and possible adverse effects on the viewing public. Arguments that cameras are physically disruptive, distracting, and detrimental to the dignity and decorum of the courtroom have been laid to rest, as have the rather tenuous arguments that cameras turn witnesses into hysterics, lawyers into flamboyant actors, and judges into political sycophants. In their place has arisen a series of concerns that have less to do with how camera presence affects the behavior of trial participants per se, and much more to do with the quality and quantity of trial footage that is broadcast, and with audience perceptions of the participants and cases that are televised.

3. THE RISKS TO WITNESSES

A. Privacy and Coverage of Sensitive Cases

Legal scholars have been concerned about the right to privacy and its protection under common law for about a hundred years. In his 1888 *Treatise on the Law of Torts*, Thomas Cooley defined privacy as the right "to be let alone" (cited by Warren and Brandeis, 1890, p. 195; see also Pember, 1984, p. 187). Two years later, Samuel Warren and Louis Brandeis published their seminal article, "The Right to Privacy," in which they argued that an individual should not be subjected to "mental pain and distress" as a result of disclosure of information that is of no concern to the public at large (Warren and Brandeis, 1890, p. 196). In 1976, Alfred Hill suggested that a right to privacy should be recognized when the trial record would include "revelations so intimate and unwarranted as to outrage the community's notions of decency" (cited by Ares, 1981, p. 182).

Although in the context of judicial proceedings privacy is considered only an interest and not an absolute right, there are those who stress that in certain sensitive cases judges should close their courtrooms to all media, or certainly to cameras if not to newspapers, in the interests of the participants concerned. The circumstances in which this philosophy becomes compelling, they emphasize, are in cases involving testimony from victims of physical or sexual abuse. In such instances, witness privacy (or at least anonymity) is crucial, not only to protect the victim from further trauma and embarrassment, but also to remove the possibility that other victims of such crimes would be deterred from coming forward because of fears of public humiliation. They further argue that the particular threats to privacy which surface in sensitive cases warrant narrow views of the public's right to know and the media's right to televise trials:

> Traditional methods of trial coverage secure both the media's First Amendment in-
> terests and the defendant's constitutional right to a fair and public trial. *The guarantee of
> freedom of the press should not be confused with freedom to use every available communications
> technology in every setting* (Boone, 1981, p. 26, emphasis added).

At times, then, the issue becomes one of "qualitative difference" between the potentially adverse results of permitting electronic versus traditional news coverage. Specifically, two important questions are raised by this: (a) Are there cases in which privacy interests should override First Amendment freedoms? (b) Should certain witnesses be protected from all forms of media coverage or from broadcast though not newspaper reporting?

B.   *Disclosing Victim Identity: The Big Dan's Rape Case*

Big Dan's is an example of a case where the presiding judge allowed broadcast and newspaper reporters a free rein in covering the trial, but the shocking aftermath of the media coverage has led to some strong self-examination by the courts and the media. Controversy arising from the "on air" naming of the alleged rape victim in the Big Dan's case prompted Senate Judiciary Committee hearings about the privacy rights of certain sensitive witnesses, such as victims of physical and sexual abuse. At the hearings, rape victims described their traumatic ordeals of not only testifying in front of courtroom crowds but also of knowing that their testimony, and perhaps even their faces, would be broadcast locally and maybe nationally. The newspaper as well as broadcast publication of such personal details as their names and places of work resulted in an assortment of crank phone calls, poison pen letters, and even personal insults directed at the victims as well as their families and relatives. So horrific were the hostilities and humiliations resulting from media coverage that, for many victims, they constituted a "second rape."

Without going into excessive detail about the events of the Big Dan's trial, some elements pertaining to media coverage are in order. The case was covered by several newspapers[5] and broadcast media organizations, including Ted Turner's Cable News Network and three other television news enterprises which were hooked up to the courtroom's "pooling" camera for live coverage of the trial. As soon as the rape victim's name was mentioned by the judge and the prosecutors, it was heard throughout America (De Silva, 1984, p. 42; see also When News Becomes Voyeurism, 1984; New Bedford Rape: Rejecting the "Myth," 1984; Rape Trial: "Justice Crucified?" 1984).

Using the argument that any ethical considerations about naming the witness were now moot, three local newspapers and a television station started to include the name in their daily reports of the trial. Gavel-to-gavel coverage by the Providence, Rhode Island, Colony Communications cable system reached 44,000 homes in the New Bedford area where the victim and several defendants were from. Within 48 hours, the Providence *Evening Bulletin, The Providence Journal,* the Fall River *Herald News,* the Portuguese-language paper, *O Journal,* and WLNE-TV, the CBS affiliate in Providence, began using the name in reports. Within four days, U.P.I. distributed wire copy containing the name to its 1,000 subscribers (De Silva, 1984, p. 42).

The result was a barrage of complaints from the public, the legal profession, and even the media. Representatives of media organizations that maintained the policy of withholding the victim's name argued that its publication "adds nothing to the reader's understanding of the story. Furthermore . . . public identification can needlessly add to the pain of the victim and is likely to deter other victims from reporting the crime" (DeSilva, 1984, p. 43). Call-in comments to radio stations and casual comments to the press that the victim "asked for it" and that she "led the men on" prompted Scott Charnos, the victim's lawyer, to point out that public incriminations indicate "it is more odious to be the rape victim than the rapist" (De Silva, 1984, p. 43).

At the close of the trial, Judge William C. Young had some strong words of reprimand for both the broadcast and print media: he told them it was "an abysmal error of judgement" to publish the victim's name; it was a decision for which there was "utterly no reason," and it was a step taken "only for the poorest motives" (De Silva, 1984, p. 44)—prurient commercial ones. Perhaps adding insult to injury, the offending media responded nonchalantly that they were simply broadcasting what the microphone picked up; that they did not realize the name would be mentioned, and that they "could not justify" spending money for a tape delay system to bleep out the name (De Silva, 1984, p. 42).

C. *Witness Protection*

One way to avoid the problem of violating witness privacy is through the adoption and enforcement of guidelines for media trial coverage. Better still would be a commitment on the part of newspapers, television, and radio organizations to withhold the names of victims or other witnesses involved in highly sensitive cases. If the media will not refrain from this of their own volition, the restraints may be applied by the courts.[6]

The issue of protecting sensitive witnesses existed before *Chandler* was handed down, and provision was made for these trial participants in state canons, as well as being mentioned explicitly in the *Chandler* majority opinion. Most of the 43 states which now allow some form of audio-visual coverage of their trial and/or appellate courts have strict guidelines about the types of proceedings and participants who can be recorded, televised, or photographed. These guidelines are sometimes incorporated in a state's Canons of Judicial Ethics, and at other times are simply written as a separate set of rules.

In almost every state, ultimate discretion for camera coverage rests in the hands of individual judges and is dealt with on a case-by-case basis. Many states also require formal written notice to be submitted to a lower court and/or the state Supreme Court for approval: 24 states have made prior consent of the court an absolute precondition to coverage, seven states require that the court receive notice of intent to cover a proceeding *prior* to its commencement, and in 13 states official written consent is not required, although informal notice is pro forma when broadcast media expect to cover trials (see Table 3). The rules of several states emphasize that broadcast coverage will not be permitted when media access is otherwise restricted by law, and a number of states have rules which explicitly prohibit or limit coverage of particular types of cases or specific participants (see Table 4).

Of particular interest to the present discussion are guidelines pertaining to witnesses. In Massachusetts, for example, "[the] judge may limit or temporarily suspend such news media coverage, if it appears that such coverage will create a substantial likelihood of harm to any person or other serious harmful consequences" (Massachusetts Code of Judicial Conduct, Canon 3A(7), revised January 1983). In California, the judge has absolute discretion "to refuse, limit or terminate film or electronic media coverage in the interests of justice, to protect the rights of the parties and the dignity of the court, or to assure the orderly conduct of the proceedings" (California Rules of Court, #980(2b).[7] Other guidelines are even more explicit. In Alabama, Iowa, Maryland, Minnesota, New Mexico, Ohio, Oklahoma, Pennsylvania, Rhode Island, Tennessee, Utah, and Washington, the presiding judge can exclude electronic media coverage during any part of a proceeding at the request of a witness. In Alaska, it is forbidden to broadcast any portion of a trial in which a victim or witness of sexual abuse objects. Even in states where witness consent is not specifically required, judges are advised to prohibit, or at least restrict, camera coverage of police informants, undercover agents, children, certain juveniles, the family of a victim or the accused, custody suits, and victims of sexual crimes (Radio-Television News Directors Association, 1984, pp. B1–B17).

Despite some unsolved problems, the majority of states have managed to deal successfully with the witness protection issue and are adamant that certain witnesses should not be exposed to unnecessary dangers or pressures. In fact, it is generally regarded to be the trial judge's responsibility to inform *all* witnesses that they have the option to request not to be photographed or televised if they can show cause, and some states "permit the court to order that a witness not be filmed *even absent a request*" (Brief and Appendix of the Attorneys General of Alabama et al., 1979, p. 27, emphasis added).

In his *Post-Newsweek* opinion, Justice Alan Sundberg made clear and careful reference to the duties of trial judges when considering whether certain categories of witnesses may be adversely affected by electronic coverage. His ultimate point was that the potential for adverse impacts on some witnesses does not constitute suffi-

Table 3 Consent Requirements

	Court's Consent (All Cases)			Party's Consent (Civil Cases & Criminal Appeals)			Counsel's Consent			Witness's Consent			Juror's Consent			Defendant's Consent			Prosecutor's Consent		
	Prior Consent Absolute Precondition	Prior Notice Absolute Precondition	No Prior Consent/Notice Required	Absolute Precondition	Limited Precondition	Not Required	Absolute Precondition	Limited Precondition	Not Required	Absolute Precondition	Limited Precondition	Not Required	Absolute Precondition	Limited Precondition	Not Required	Absolute Precondition	Limited Precondition	Not Required	Absolute Precondition	Limited Precondition	Not Required
Alabama	x			x			x				x[21]			x							x
Alaska	x				x[3]					x[21]				x		x[43]			x		
Arizona	x					x			x			x			x[27]			x	x		
Arkansas			x	x			x								x[28]			x			x
California	x[1]					x			x						x[29]	x			x		
Colorado	x[5]					x			x			x[22]			x[30]	x[44]		x[45]			x
Connecticut	x					x			x						x[31]			x			x
Delaware		x							x			x									
D.C.																					
Florida	x					x			x			x			x						x
Georgia	x[6]					x[18]			x[18]			x[18]			x[32]	x[18]			x[18]		
Hawaii			x[4]			x[18]			x			x[18]						x			x
Idaho		x[2]				x			x												
Illinois						x			x												
Indiana						x			x												
Iowa	x[7]					x[19]			x		x[21,22]	x[22]			x[33]			x			x
Kansas		x[3]				x			x		x[23]	x			x[34]			x			x
Kentucky	x[8]					x			x						x			x			x
Louisiana			x	x			x								x						
Maine	x[9]					x			x							x			x		
Maryland				x[14,15]					x		x[24,25]	x[24,25]			x[25]						
Massachusetts		x				x			x						x[35]						
Michigan			x[4]																		
Minnesota	x[6]			x					x		x				x[36]			x			x
Mississippi	x[6]																				
Missouri																					
Montana		x				x			x			x			x			x			x
Nebraska	x[1,10]					x			x												
Nevada	x					x			x			x			x[37]			x			x
New Hampshire	x					x			x			x			x[38]			x			x
New Jersey	x					x			x			x			x[39]			x			x

(continued)

Table 3 (*Continued*)

	Court's Consent (All Cases)				Party's Consent (Civil Cases & Criminal Appeals)			Counsel's Consent			Witness's Consent			Juror's Consent			Defendant's Consent			Prosecutor's Consent		
	Prior Consent Absolute Precondition	Prior Notice Absolute Precondition	No Prior Consent/Notice	Required	Absolute Precondition	Limited Precondition	Not Required	Absolute Precondition	Limited Precondition	Not Required	Absolute Precondition	Limited Precondition	Not Required	Absolute Precondition	Limited Precondition	Not Required	Absolute Precondition	Limited Precondition	Not Required	Absolute Precondition	Limited Precondition	Not Required
New Mexico	x[11]																					x
New York	x						x[20]			x[20]			x[26]			x[40]			x			x
North Carolina				x			x			x			x			x[41]			x			x
North Dakota		x					x			x			x									x
Ohio		x[1]					x			x		x				x[42]	x		x			x
Oklahoma						x				x		x			x		x					
Oregon				x			x			x		x										x
Pennsylvania	x					x[16]				x												
Rhode Island				x			x			x		x			x			x				x
South Carolina																						
South Dakota																						
Tennessee				x	x			x				x			x		x		x			
Texas	x[12]						x[12]			x[12]												
Utah				x[13]		x[13]				x[13]		x[13]				x[13]		x[13]				x
Vermont				x			x			x												
Virginia										x												
Washington						x[17]				x		x			x	x		x				x
West Virginia							x			x			x			x		x				x
Wisconsin		x					x			x			x		x				x			x
Wyoming				x			x			x			x									

Consent Requirements (See Radio-Television News Directors Association, 1984, pp. B1–B17):

1. Written approval.
2. Illinois' rules also refer to the notice as a request. The judge or presiding authority, upon receiving written notice, may decide to prohibit coverage prior to the commitment of a proceeding.
3. Trials.
4. Appellate.
5. Approval noted in record.
6. Trial, written approval.
7. For television coverage of appeals.
8. Under Kentucky's rules, requests to cover a proceeding must be made to the court. While there are no specific provisions in the rules concerning the court's response, permission must be obtained for coverage to occur.
9. Maryland's rules require that a request for coverage be submitted. Although the court's consent is not specifically required, the judge must approve the type and location of the equipment to be used prior to the commencement of the proceeding to be covered.

10. Nevada's rules do not state specifically when approval is to be obtained.

11. Written approval, noted in record.

12. Texas permits only audio tapes of appellate proceedings.

13. Utah permits still photography of its courtroom proceedings but forbids broadcasting, televising, or recording of court proceeding.

14. Civil cases.

15. In Maryland a party may move for termination or limitation of coverage in criminal appellate cases. Consent of governmental entities or officials who are parties are not required.

16. Appellate coverage not permitted.

17. It is not entirely clear what would occur in Oklahoma and Washington if a criminal defendant objects to coverage of his appeal. Taken literally, the rules of those States would seem to permit coverage of the proceedings but preclude coverage of the defendant in those circumstances. Since many defendants do not attend their appeal proceedings, the point may be a relatively minor one.

18. Although the general Georgia coverage provisions did not explicitly require the parties' consents, all plans initially approved by the Georgia Supreme Court contained such a requirement. As of July 1, 1982, the coverage provisions were clarified, and the written consent of participants is no longer required in proceedings before the Georgia Supreme Court.

19. In Iowa, consents of parties are not required except in juvenile, dissolution, adoption, child custody, or trade secrets cases.

20. The New York Court of Appeals permitted coverage of its proceedings on a 1-day experimental basis on October 16, 1979 and, on November 21, 1980, issued an order allowing permanent appellate coverage. A 1-year experiment for civil trial proceedings is *contingent* upon amendment or repeal of a New York statute prohibiting coverage of proceedings in which witnesses appear or may appear under subpoena.

21. Victims of sexual offenses only.

22. In Iowa, a victim/witness in a sexual abuse case must consent to coverage of his or her testimony. The objections of certain types of witnesses to coverage of their testimony enjoy a presumption of validity. These include victims/witnesses in other forcible felony prosecutions, police informants, undercover agents, and relocated witnesses.

23. In Kansas, a judge may forbid coverage of a witness if he or she objects; however, when a police informant, undercover agent, relocated witness, juvenile witness or victim/witness objects to being covered, the judge is required to forbid coverage of that person. In addition, when a participant in a proceeding involving divorce, trade secrets, or a motion to suppress evidence objects to coverage, coverage of that participant is forbidden.

24. Victims only.

25. As approved by the Court of Appeals, Maryland's experiment originally encompassed coverage of civil and criminal cases in trial and appellate courts. Subsequently, however, an act barring coverage of criminal trials was passed by the legislature and approved by the Governor. The rule permitting appellate coverage was made permanent in 1982, and the experiment allowing civil trial coverage was continued until permanent rules for such coverage were adopted in 1984.

26. In New Mexico, the judge has sole and plenary discretion to exclude coverage of certain witnesses, including, but not limited to, victims of sex crimes and their families, police informants, undercover agents, relocated witnesses, and juveniles.

27. Arizona does not permit photographing of jurors which allows them to be recognized, and cameras are to be placed so as to avoid photographing the jurors.

28. Arkansas does not permit coverage of the jury.

29. Close-ups of jurors prohibited.

30. Under Colorado's temporary canon, close-up photography of the jury is not permitted.

31. Connecticut does not allow jury coverage, but, if this is unavoidable, coverage must occur in a manner which will not permit recognition of individual jurors.

32. Hawaii does not permit coverage of jurors or prospective jurors.

33. In Iowa, coverage of jury selection and the jury is prohibited, except to the extent that it is unavoidable while covering the remainder of the proceedings. Coverage of the return of the jury's verdict is explicitly permitted.

34. Individual coverage and close-ups of jury prohibited.

35. Frontal close-up shots of jury prohibited.

36. In Minnesota, coverage of the jury, including *voir dire*, is forbidden.

37. Individuals jurors not be to covered deliberately.

38. In criminal cases, prior approval of presiding justice is required.

39. Coverage of jurors in New Jersey is permissable, but it may not be such as to allow actual visual recognition of jurors.

40. New Mexico does not permit filming of the jury in the courtroom or during voir dire.

41. Coverage of jurors is not permitted in North Carolina.

42. Coverage of jurors is not permitted in Ohio.

43. Formerly, Alaska required counsel's consent as an absolute precondition of coverage in all cases. This requirement has since been deleted from the rules for coverage, and now the consent of the defendant must be obtained.

44. Permanent rule.

45. Temporary Canon.

Table 4 Coverage Exemptions for Certain Cases and Participants

	Adoption	Child Custody	Divorce	Juvenile Proceedings	Motions to Suppress	Police Informants	Relocated Witnesses	Sex Crimes	Trade Secrets	Undercover Agents	Probable Cause Proceedings	Witnesses who are Minors	Motions to Dismiss	Voir Dire Hearings	Witnesses in Jeopardy of Serious Bodily Injury
Alabama	x[1]			x											
Alaska	x[1]	x[1]	x[1]	x											
Arizona				x											
Arkansas	x[2]	x[6,2]	x[2]	x[2]		x[2]		x[16,2]		x[2]					
California															
Colorado														x	
Connecticut	x[3]	x[3]	x[3]					x[3]	x[3]						
Delaware															
D.C.															
Florida															
Georgia															
Hawaii					x[14]			x[14]	x[14]			x[14]		x[14]	x[14]
Idaho															
Illinois															
Indiana				x[4]					x[4]						
Iowa	x[4]	x[4]	x[4]												
Kansas															
Kentucky			x												
Louisiana															
Maine															
Maryland	x[5]	x[5]	x[5]	x[5]	x[5]	x[5]	x[5]		x[5]	x[5,12]					
Massachusetts					x						x		x		
Michigan														x	

Minnesota		x	x	x	x	x	x	x	x	x	x		x	x
Mississippi														
Missouri														
Montana														
Nebraska														
Nevada														
New Hampshire														
New Jersey		x[7]	x[7]	x[7]				x[17,7]	x[7]					
New Mexico				x[12]		x[12]	x[12]	x[18,12]		x[12]				x
New York														
North Carolina	x	x	x[11]	x	x	x	x	x[18]	x	x	x	x		
North Dakota														
Ohio														
Oklahoma														
Oregon														
Pennsylvania		x	x											
Rhode Island	x	x[8,9]		x[13]	x[15]								x[19]	x
South Carolina														
South Dakota														
Tennessee														
Texas														
Utah														
Vermont														
Virginia														
Washington														
West Virginia														
Wisconsin		x[10]	x[10]	x[10]	x[10]	x[10]	x[10]	x[10]	x[10]	x[10]				
Wyoming														

(continued)

Table 4 (*Continued*)

Coverage Exemptions for Certain Cases and Participants (See Radio-Television News Directors Association, 1984, pp. B1–B17):

1. Alaska forbids coverage of "family matters," including, but not limited to, matters involving divorce, dissolution of marriage, domestic violence, adoption and paternity, and child support, custody, and visitation.

2. Arkansas prohibits coverage of minors without parental or guardian consent. It totally prohibits coverage of juvenile, adoption, guardianship, or domestic relations proceedings.

3. *Generally*, the Connecticut Superior Court will not permit coverage of these proceedings. The Connecticut Supreme Court forbids coverage of these proceedings and, in addition, prohibits coverage of proceedings held in the jury's absence and sentencing hearings in criminal cases in which the trial was not covered.

4. In these types of cases, Iowa permits coverage if consent of the parties (including the parent or guardian of a minor child) is obtained. In all other cases, Iowa requires no consents of the parties.

5. Maryland provides that the objection of participants are presumed to have validity in cases involving police informants, minors, undercover agents, relocated witnesses, evidentiary suppression hearings, trade secrets, divorce, and custody. Maryland's rules for coverage do not apply to its Orphans' Courts. As approved by the Court of Appeals, Maryland's experiment originally encompassed coverage of civil and criminal cases in trial and appellate courts. Subsequently, however, an act barring coverage of criminal trials was passed by the legislature and approved by the Governor. The rule permitting appellate coverage was made permanent in 1982, and the experiment allowing civil trial coverage was continued until permanent rules for such coverage were adopted in 1984.

6. Guardianship.

7. New Jersey absolutely precludes coverage of these proceedings and uses the broad term "matrimonial disputes."

8. If child is a participant.

9. Rhode Island prohibits coverage in any matters in Family Court in which juveniles are significant participants.

10. Wisconsin requires that objections of participants to coverage in these cases shall be presumed to have validity. Wisconsin's rule extends to the victims of crimes, including sexual crimes.

11. North Carolina forbids coverage of temporary and permanent alimony proceedings as well as divorce proceedings.

12. In New Mexico, the judge has sole and plenary discretion to forbid coverage of these proceedings or individuals. At the court's discretion, photographic coverage of other witnesses may also be forbidden.

13. Rhode Island explicitly forbids coverage in these cases (see also #9 above).

14. Under Hawaii's experiment, a trial judge shall grant requests for coverage unless good cause is found to prohibit coverage. A presumption of good cause exists if: the proceeding is for the purpose of determining the admissability of evidence, testimony regarding trade secrets is being received, child witnesses are testifying, complaining witnesses in sexual offense cases are testifying in a criminal trial, or a witness would be put in substantial jeopardy or serious bodily injury.

15. Rhode Island also forbids coverage of hearings to determine competence or relevance of evidence.

16. Victims.

17. Rape only.

18. Victims and their families.

19. Coverage of motions to dismiss for legal inadequacy of the indictment, information, or complaint (criminal or civil) is not permitted in Rhode Island.

cient grounds for an absolute ban on camera access to all courtrooms. As he explained, problems that may arise with regard to sensitive witnesses are not insurmountable: "What is called for is an articulated standard for the exercise of the presiding judge's discretion in determining whether it is appropriate to prohibit electronic media coverage of a particular participant."[8] Furthermore, Justice Sundberg stressed that it is the duty of the judge to weigh the possible dangers against the principle of open justice, and if necessary to use discretionary authority to bar electronic media coverage of certain participants, *but only if it can be shown that broadcast coverage would have substantially different or more deleterious effects upon that person than traditional newspaper reporting.*[9] This standard is important recognition by the courts that newspapers can just as easily be responsible for disclosing harmful trial related details as broadcast media.

Given the recent heated debate over television coverage of rape and other sexual abuse cases, it might appear that cameras have been permitted in courtrooms without careful consideration by individual judges or collaborative decisions by judicial committees. This is an entirely unrealistic picture. A more appropriate assessment could be reached by asking: (a) whether or not judges use their discretionary powers frequently or strongly enough, and (b) whether or not the media are willing to do a little self-policing "in matters of taste and decency" (Benson, 1984, p. 54).[10] The consequences of headstrong commercial exploitation of trials may be a dangerous path for broadcasters to follow: ultimately, a little self-restraint could protect the First Amendment freedoms of the press as well as the privacy interests of sensitive witnesses. Few would deny that testifying at a trial, even without media coverage, is a highly emotional and perhaps frightening experience for victims as well as their families. There are fears of embarrassment, humiliation, or even retribution from parties involved in the case, or from those who may learn about the case. But while privacy *interests* of witnesses, particularly victims of sexual crimes such as rape or child molestation must be protected, the renewed cry for a ban on all broadcast coverage dismisses the issue with an all too simplistic response. There are rational remedies to situations such as the one caused by media insensitivity in the Big Dan's case; remedies that protect both witnesses and the First Amendment rights of broadcasters.

1. While allowing broadcast coverage of inherently sensational cases, courts must continue to make provisions for restricting coverage of sensitive witnesses.
2. Newspapers as well as broadcast media must be encouraged to police themselves on questions relating to the publication of information which may identify victims or witnesses of sexual crimes.
3. The installation of tape delay systems should be mandatory for media organizations wishing to broadcast "live" coverage of a case.
4. Courts should require prior written notice describing the specifics of intended media coverage, so that participants may be given time to apply for exemptions.
5. The activities of the print as well as broadcast media should be carefully and equally scrutinized by trial judges.

The trial judge plays a crucial role in monitoring who is televised and what kinds of testimony may be broadcast, and while broadcasters may resent judicial authority to limit or refuse camera access, it may be wiser to have restricted coverage than no coverage rights at all. Perhaps the last word on the witness protection issue belongs to Judge Paul Baker, whose affirmative First Amendment stance has often been wisely tempered with some down to earth advice for the media. Referring to the question of whether "unfettered access to news becomes synonymous with unfettered dissemination," he noted that the answer "lies equally between the inherent powers of the Court and the *conscience of the media*" (Baker, 1977, p. 8, emphasis added).

4. THE RISKS TO VIEWERS: THE WAYNE WILLIAMS CASE

Closely related to questions about viewer reactions to trial participants are those concerning potential adverse impacts of televised trials on the public, particularly children in the audience. The argument against permitting a case to be broadcast because of possible adverse impacts on viewers was first used in 1981 as a reason for banning cameras from the Wayne Williams trial in Atlanta, Georgia. Williams was accused of murdering two of Atlanta's missing children. Judge Clarence Cooper, of the Fulton County Superior Court, reached his decision to block cameras after holding a hearing to which he called "expert" witnesses in the fields of sociology, psychology, psychiatry, and mental health. In general, these witnesses testified that televising Williams' trial might adversely affect children and adolescents in the viewing audience, reminding them of the disturbing ordeal that had enveloped Atlanta during the preceding 2 years.

A psychiatrist, for example, noted that live coverage "would tend to aggravate, reopen and reawaken those fears, concerns, and cause more emotional difficulties at a time when we're expending funds and resources to cope with the trauma that has already occurred. A developmental and clinical social psychologist said that the Court should "think more about not only the children here who are in Atlanta, but also children across the nation." A sociologist argued that "social costs" would outweigh the public's right to know. The social costs were defined as "the cost to the families of the murdered and missing children, the cost to the family of the accused, the cost of [sic] the children emotionally . . . ." Finally, a mental health official expressed concern about "what certain segments of the public would do with the information they received from televising the trial." He noted that "in the past some children experienced fears and nightmares after seeing reports of related events" (Cooper, 1981, p. 6).

In his report about the hearing, Judge Cooper concluded: "we must weigh and balance the desire for a televised trial against the potential for harm or danger that might be done to those children and families who were adversely affected by the ordeal" (Cooper, 1981, p. 4). He noted, too, that Georgia's courtroom camera guidelines "do not expressly limit the inquiries which a trial court may make in reaching a decision on whether it will permit broadcast coverage of a trial" (Cooper, 1981, p. 6).

Cameras, of course, were not barred from the Big Dan's case for reasons of audience impact or for any more traditional reasons, but a subsequent event involving a child's imitation of facts mentioned during broadcasts of the trial prompted a rally of anti-cameras sentiments based on arguments similar to those brought forward by Judge Cooper in Atlanta. On April 17, 1984, a 12-year-old boy from Pawtucket, Rhode Island, was arraigned on charges that he sexually assaulted a 10-year-old girl on a pool table while other children watched. The boy had apparently picked up the idea from watching the Big Dan's rape trial on television (Pool Table Sex Assault Charged to Boy, 1984; The Big Dan's Rape: A Copycat Crime? 1984).

From a media effects perspective, few issues have triggered more compelling anti-television arguments or generated more scientific and critical inquiry than those involving children as television viewers. Vast quantities government and private research funding have enabled empirical data on children and television to mushroom over the past 15 or so years.[11] The fact that children may be in the audience presents new negative implications for future televised trials, particularly those broadcast gavel-to-gavel during daytime hours, when children are often viewing without adult supervision. Some might suggest that broadcast trial coverage be regulated along the lines of "indecent" programming. The general argument of the Court in *FCC v. Pacifica Foundation* (1978),[12] better known as the "seven dirty words" case, was that radio and television are "pervasive" media which should be regulated because they are easily accessible to children. Newspapers and magazines, on the other hand, need less restriction and are not regarded as pervasive because the reader must make a conscious decision to purchase printed materials and then to read them. Fewer children, it is thought, are interested in reading than in watching television. Could *Pacifica's* rationale be applied to televised trials if explicitly sexual details or offensive language are broadcast as witness testimony? Though the question is purely conjectural, it invites some interesting speculation, particularly since the issue might become more complicated when a cable system rather than a broadcast station carries a trial.

Perhaps a more fundamental assessment of potential risks to children, such as the Big Dan's-copycat incident, is that fairly isolated examples of media imitation should neither be regarded as the norm nor elevated to a precedent-setting agenda. Even the most sophisticated experimental research has not shown conclusively that television viewing, per se, is to blame for children's delinquent behavior. While, in certain circumstances, children may imitate mediated behavior, research focusing on a cause and effect relationship between a television set and a child can rarely be generalized to everyday settings like a child's home viewing environment. There is usually a concession that other factors, such as socio-economics and family communication patterns, have substantial bearing on how children interpret and relate to what they watch. Ultimately, we may need to ask where the responsibility of parents begins and that of broadcasters ends.[13]

5. THE RISKS TO DEFENDANTS

A. A Form of "Pillory by Publicity"

Of all the risks associated with televised trials, none is more serious than the placing of a defendant's due process rights in jeopardy. After all, a jury's verdict might well mean life imprisonment or even the death penalty for a convicted offender, and any form of media coverage which may prejudice a jury's verdict clearly should be avoided. Defense attorneys are especially concerned about the consequences of television coverage on their clients' cases. They emphasize that showing "clippings" of trial footage on nightly newscasts is far from educational; on the contrary, this type of excerpting is particularly dangerous because it tends to highlight only the prosecution's side of the case, incites public opinion against the defendant, and has serious consequences for the accused in the minds of prospective jurors. Television exposure is also believed to be far more damaging to a defendant's case than traditional newspaper coverage, because it is more widely and speedily disseminated (see Fuoco, 1982; Fahringer, 1981; Tongue and Lintott, 1980; Fretz, 1978a; Kulwin, 1978; Doubles, 1965). One judge has argued, further, that if some cases are selected for coverage and others are not, this "disparate treatment [might] raise an equal protection problem" for the courts (Day, 1981, p. 20).

Other members of the bench and bar are concerned about possible public embarrassment and ridicule of defendants, and claim that cameras pose a severe threat to privacy interests. These views were fully explained in a joint *amicus* brief filed by public defenders in *Chandler*. Arguments centered on the notion that television exposure is a form of punishment—*prior to the proving of guilt or innocence*—leading to permanent stigmatization in the eyes of the public (Amicus Curiae, Brief of the California State Public Defenders Association et al., 1979, p. 3). Public punishments, they emphasized, leave scars on a person's character. and, even if that person is later rehabilitated and reformed, he will be regarded as a pariah (p. 8). The brief also noted that the accused does not lose the right to privacy when charged with a criminal offense:

> Concepts of privacy are not limited to solitary individuals in closed rooms. Privacy is seen as a right to avoid public display. It is obvious that a person charged with a crime loses by necessity, some of his privacy. After all, the traditional trial process requires the accused to be present in the courtroom where others are also present.
>
> The problem arises when a person is displayed to the community for reasons *not necessary* for the court process. The only rights the accused should lose are those *necessary* for the orderly conduct of the court proceedings. Any other loss of rights should only occur as a result of a proper sentencing procedure after a conviction. The presumption of innocence is imbedded in our system (Amicus Curiae Brief of the California State Public Defenders Association et al., 1979, p. 6, original emphasis).[14]

Still others have warned that televised trials are simply offshoots of regular entertainment fare, tailored to fit in with existing fictional crime programs (Gerbner, 1980). Like attorney Joel Hirschhorn, who led the *Chandler* appeal to the U.S. Supreme Court, they claim that broadcasters have only one goal when televising criminal proceedings: "increased ratings and revenue . . . as each television station attempts to feed the American public's almost insatiable desire for the salacious, the sexy, the despair and sorrow of mankind" (Hirschhorn, 1978, p. 4). Given the nature of most trials televised to date, it would appear that such coverage indeed provides greater appeal to voyeuristic instincts, or to a curiosity to witness the shortcomings and punishment of others, than it does any educational service.

B. Hounding Defendants: The Claus von Bulow Case

One highly publicized trial which illustrates these types of privacy and public humiliation concerns is the Claus von Bulow case. Although there is general agreement that the case would have attracted widespread media attention whether or not cameras were allowed in the courtroom, some legal commentators have deplored the insensitive way in which the television camera "hounded" the defendant's every move. Coverage, including close-up shots of the defendant's face and hands while the jury verdict was announced, and later while the judge pronounced sentence, has invited the epithets "immoral" and "inhumane" (Power, 1982, p. 815).

The von Bulow trial, in fact, took on the proportions of an international television drama, with participants who resembled characters in a soap opera. The proceedings began in February 1982, lasted 47 days, and involved testimony from over 60 witnesses.[15] The courtroom was packed to capacity every day with over 100 spectators and 38 reporters from a variety of local, national, and international newspapers, television, and radio stations. Another hundred or so reporters and photographers were housed across the road from the courthouse, in a room set aside for the press (Cameras at Von Bulow Trial, 1982). On certain days (when particular witnesses were on the stand), some 35 extra chairs were squeezed into the courtroom, and one newspaper described how a spectator dragged a chair from the judge's chambers and watched the trial from the courtroom doorway (Showdown Draws Overflow Audience, 1982). The defendant and his famous New York attorney, Herald Price Fahringer, were swarmed by reporters wherever they went, often becoming "trapped" in their hotel lobby, which was crammed with members of the press. WPRI-TV, Rhode Island, produced a 30-minute "special" called "The Von Bulows of Newport" and aired this documentary at the close of the trial. Newspapers carried stories for several days after the trial ended, discussing the lawyers' tactics and rehashing the testimony of key witnesses (see Berreby, 1982; Bruck, 1982).

Between January and April 1982, there was some kind of story on the von Bulow case in almost every local newspaper and television evening news show.[16] During the trial itself, there was live coverage by Cable News Network, and on week nights the three Rhode Island network affiliates reached nearly 300,000 homes with their 30-second to 2-minute stories about the case. Thames Television from London covered the trial for about 4 weeks, and also aired a half-hour special on American "aristocracy" based on the von Bulows of Newport. Rhode Island and Massachusetts newspapers were splattered with headlines and photographs of the trial participants for nearly 15 weeks. Stories varied from the serious to the mundane, the sublime to the ridiculous. Headlines in Boston's *Herald American* favored the latter: "He Won't Have To Do Hard Time," "Drama in Newport," "Their Testimony Was Telling," "The Maid Nailed Claus," "Cool Maid of Steel Did In Von Bulow," and, on March 13, 1982, the *Providence Journal* even found it newsworthy to report the contents of von Bulow's lunch, and to tell its readers the brand of cigarettes he smoked (No Von Bulow Verdict Yet, 1982). Most newspaper stories, however, focused on the testimony of the numerous witnesses and the tactics of the attorneys. The press termed it the "multiple choice" defense, as the lawyers chalked up important facts from key witness testimony on a blackboard in the courtroom.

C. *Publicity about Defendants*

While defendants have few, if any, privacy rights in the context of judicial proceedings, and while it would therefore be difficult to argue that the press (including television cameras) should not have been allowed to cover the von Bulow trial, in this case it was the *type* and *extent* of media reporting—both newspaper as well as television—that invited criticism as being exploitative and in poor taste. Although neither attorney felt that the presence of the single television camera inside the courtroom was detrimental to the fairness of the trial, or in any way detracted from the dignity and decorum of the proceedings, Fahringer expressed concern about the editing of the nightly news footage into "two-minute" stories which were chosen "on the basis of viewability by the audience, rather than on grounds of interest or importance" (Hochberger, 1982). Interestingly, in the aftermath of the trial, little was said about the content of daily newspaper stories, the behavior of newspaper reporters and photographers, or the throngs of spectators who deluged the trial. Attention was riveted, instead, on the television footage:

> Few cases will afford the high drama and popular allure of the von Bulow case: a personable aristocrat who fell from grace. The camera, while now unobtrusive in the courtroom in the wake of improved technology, permitted viewers to see von Bulow's every blink and wrinkle. The camera waits and watches breathlessly, capturing the eternity of suspense the defendant must be enduring. . . . As the axe falls, the audience scrutinizes the face and hands for reaction—a momentary tightening of the fingers, no perceptible change in facial expression, narrated for those viewers who were momentarily distracted at the vital instant or who want their own impressions verified or corrected. Such television reporting may be a substantiation of the premise that Americans are sufficiently committed to voyeurism to prevent a too robust growth of the right to privacy (Power, 1982).

The Big Dan's Rape case also triggered heated debate about the effects of pretrial and trial publicity on defendants. This example, too, emphasizes the particularly intense attention that has been paid to television rather than to other forms of media trial coverage. Those opposed to camera coverage charged that televising the case would only serve to make it highly notorious and prejudice potential jurors. They also claimed that live television broadcasts would incite such negative local community feelings against the defendants that, even if they were later acquitted or granted a retrial, the sentiments would be irreversible.

On closer inspection, though, the first of these two claims is clearly exaggerated. Televising the Big Dan's trial can hardly be blamed for making the case any more notorious than it already was prior to the broadcasts. The case was inherently sensational: it involved a gang rape, and it also questioned the culpability of witnesses who watched the crime and who not only failed to prevent it, but actually "cheered on" the rapists. These facts alone are surely sufficient to attract public attention if not incense a nation. Furthermore, the case drew heated public interest long before cameras entered the courtroom. Only a week after news of the alleged gang rape was first reported in March 1983, some 2,500 people marched through New Bedford protesting violence against women, and similar gatherings took place in other communities around the country. Once the defendants were indicted, the press picked up coverage again, and, for several weeks before the trial began, the print as well as broadcast media carried stories about (though not the name of) the victim, the defendants, the police investigation, and the bar's patrons. No doubt this kind of pretrial coverage added to an already inflammatory jury selection process, but the case presented some inherent administrative problems in any event, such as the issue of jury sequestration—which was compounded by the fact that, with multiple defendants, there would have to be two separate trials, one in the morning and one in the afternoon, because the testimony of some defendants implicated others.

However, while arguments about pretrial and trial notoriety may be fairly easy to refute, challenges to camera coverage based on concerns about defendant reputation are more difficult to parry. Although many concede that personal reputations are at stake in any highly publicized case, whether or not it is televised, several questions specifically relating to television versus print coverage remain unanswered. For example, what happens to a defendant who has been tried and found "not guilty" and who then must return to the community? Are feelings of animosity extended toward this person and, if so, are they exacerbated by television coverage of a case? Would attitudes be the same if the case were only reported in newspapers? Answers to these questions are hard to find, since few "courtroom cameras" studies have made any meaningful reference to the impacts of camera coverage on defendants, either during the trial or after the event. In fact, the lack of convincing empirical research on the psychological effects of televising trials did not go unnoticed by the court in *Chandler*. Worried about possible mental harassment of defendants, both during and after televised trials, the Court emphasized that "particular attention should be paid to this area of concern as the study of televised trials continues."[17]

6. WEIGHING PROPOSED BENEFITS AGAINST POTENTIAL RISKS

Although, to date, no directly applicable empirical research has been conducted to test either the "benefits" or the "risks" hypotheses, a large body of anecdotal media effects research can be applied to the debate. In order to assess the proposed benefits of televised trials, we can review studies concerned with news viewing motivation and attention, and news recall and retention. In order assess potential risks, especially harm to defendants, we can examine studies concerned with television's ability to "cultivate" attitudes, shape perceptions of social reality, and influence public opinion.

A. Learning about Crime, Criminals, and the Courts

Information Sources. Over the past decade, public sources of information about the courts have clearly shifted from more formal educational sources, such as the classroom and books, to less formal sources, such as the news media, entertainment television programs, and interpersonal contacts, such as friends and neighbors (Hearst Corporation, 1983; Graber, 1980; Yankelovich et al., 1978). The latest Roper public opinion survey shows that 64% of adult Americans receive most of their news from television, and 46% rely exclusively on television for their news information (Roper Organization, 1984). Content analyses of local and national newspapers and television news programs show that crime and justice issues are favorite news topics (Skogan and Maxfield, 1981; Gordon and Heath, 1981; Graber, 1980). Their popularity with news producers and editors is due partly to the relative ease and cost-effectiveness of gathering such stories. For audiences, it seems that these stories are particularly popular because they are easy to understand and they provide strong emotional human interest value (Graber, 1984, 1980; Epstein, 1973; Buckalew, 1969–70).

News Viewing Motivation and Attention. Although audiences may be attracted to crime and justice topics, news viewing motivations are diverse (Rubin, 1983, 1981; Gantz, 1978; Katz, Blumler, and Gurevitch, 1973) and information may not always be absorbed because viewing attention is generally superficial and erratic. A large portion of viewers watch news as a way to relax, idle away time, or simply because they happened to catch a news program on any given night, rather than because of an interest in keeping informed (Graber 1980; Katz, Adoni, and Parness, 1977; Neuman, 1976). Even more interesting, when people pay attention to crime and justice news, they are generally interested only in limited aspects of the stories, such as details about the criminal's and victim's past lives, their current lives, their personalities, and the crime (Graber, 1980, pp. 62–63).

News Recall and Retention.   Given the diversity of news viewing motivations, as well as the erratic attention paid to news, it is hardly surprising that, on average, very little news content is actually recalled or recalled accurately. In unaided recall situations, typical viewers recall little more than two out of 15 stories (Katz et al., 1977); when prompted (aided recall) they remember about half of the stories (Neuman, 1976). Even when viewers are specifically asked to pay attention, or when news items are recapped, only between a quarter to half the newscast is recalled correctly (Stauffer, Frost, and Rybolt, 1983; Perloff, Wartella, and Becker, 1982). In fact, while crime and justice system topics are recalled better than other news items, and while negative information is recalled better than positive information, most crime and justice stories are quickly forgotten or ignored (Graber, 1980).

Video Footage May Not Necessarily Help Recall.   Interest in having *televised* coverage of trials stems partly from a belief that, since more people watch news than read it, the chances of people getting information about the justice system will be greater if more court news is televised. In turn, broadcasters have argued that newscasts are enhanced by visual material and that viewers can learn more from actually seeing the courts in action. Usually, however, stories are little more than 30–60 seconds in length, with video footage accompanied by a voice-over reporter, and, while research in this area has been conflicting (Berry, 1983), studies tend to show that video footage may not necessarily enhance or significantly improve viewer understanding or recall of news information (Gunter, Furnham, and Gietson, 1984; Katz et al., 1977; Edwardson, Grooms, and Pringle, 1976; Hazard, 1962–63). Indeed, although there is some evidence that *interesting* video may aid story recall (Edwardson, Grooms, and Proudlove, 1981); film/video footage which does not communicate the facts being reported may actually impede viewer learning (Edwardson et al., 1981; Katz et al., 1977; Neuman, 1976; Edwardson et al., 1976).

Also, contrary to hopes that television news could be an important "knowledge leveler" between the less and the more educated (Tichenor, Donohue, and Olien, 1970), recall is highest among the better educated, especially when stories have video accompaniment (Stauffer, Frost, and Rybolt, 1981; Edwardson et al., 1981; Katz et al., 1977; Newman, 1976; Edwardson et al., 1976). There is also evidence that newspapers are better disseminators of news information than television, due largely to the greater detail in which newspapers report stories (Gunter et al., 1984; Perloff et al., 1982; Stauffer et al., 1981; Graber, 1980; Browne, 1978; McClure and Patterson, 1976), and newspapers are primarily read by better educated, higher income groups (Bogart, 1984).

B.   Potential for Increased Prejudice against Defendants

Television and Perceptions of Social Reality.   Although television audiences appear to recall few of the news items they watch, this does not of course mean that, on a cumulative basis, whatever *is* recalled will not contribute to audience perceptions of people and institutions portrayed in news stories. While the amount of information recalled from television newscasts may be too negligible to serve any serious educational purpose, a residual build-up of details from news items may well serve to shape public attitudes and opinions about crime and criminals.

Media dependency theory suggests that people who have little or no direct experience with certain social phenomena rely more heavily on the media for their picture of reality. Gerbner and others have suggested that, when such people turn to television for this picture, they receive a distorted and often frightening image (Bryant, Carveth, and Brown, 1981; Gerbner, Gross, Morgan, Signorelli, 1980; Gerbner, Gross, Signorielli, Morgan, Jackson-Beeck, 1979; Gerbner, Gross, Jackson-Beeck, Jeffries-Fox, Signorielli, 1978; Gerbner, Gross, Eleey, Jackson-Beeck, Jeffries-Fox, Signorielli, 1977; Gerbner and Gross, 1976a,b). With specific regard to televised trials, Gerbner (1980) has argued that, since an important media function is the reinforcement of existing attitudes, televised trials—which emphasize the lurid and sensational—may simply strengthen existing negative impressions about crime and justice shaped by portrayals in television entertainment programming. Their impact will be particularly powerful among viewers who have had no direct personal experience with the courts.

Media's Influence on Public Opinions.   Allied to television's role in forming perceptions of social reality is the media's function in shaping attitudes and opinions. Research indicates a correspondence between the quantity of crime and justice information available on television and in newspapers, and increased concern about victimization and/or salience of crime as an issue (Einsiedel, Salomone, and Schneider, 1984; Jaehnig, Weaver, and Fico, 1981; Sheley and Ashkins, 1981; Graber, 1980; Roshier, 1973; Davis, 1952). Taking this theory a step further, there is a possibility that increased concern about crime as an issue may lead to negative views of criminals. On the most serious level, exacerbated fears of crime victimization could foster prejudice against defendants, and retributive attitudes about punishment (Barrile, 1984).

Perhaps the largest quantity of literature exploring the media's influence on public opinions has focused on political news (see Nimmo and Sanders, 1981), but while several studies have found a correspondence between public concern for issues and a high incidence of those topics being covered by the news media (Zukin and Snyder, 1984; Cook, Tyler, Goetz, Gordon, Protess, Leff, and Molotch, 1983; MacKuen and Coombs, 1981; Erbring, Goldenberg, and Miller, 1980; McCombs and Shaw, 1972), there is some indication that newspapers have a more powerful effect than television news on public political agendas (McClure and Patterson, 1976). With specific regard to crime news, research has provided mixed evidence of *direct* media influence on public opinions. Concerns about crime have been found to reflect newspaper and television content, but the effects have been limited. For example, in examining public opinions about the causes and remedies of crime,

Graber (1980) found that, while the news media largely blamed the criminal justice system, the public predominantly blamed poverty and economic stress.

Intervening Variables. If the public's image of crime, criminals, and the courts is not coming from the media alone, where is it coming from? McCroskey and Jenson (1975, p. 169) note that one of the most important contributions of media effects research is the knowledge that "what the listener or reader brings to the media situation is a much more important determinant of media impact than anything in the media itself." Re-analysis of Gerbner et al.'s cultivation studies (Hirsch, 1980, 1981a,b; Hughes, 1980), as well as other research on media socialization, have drawn attention to the numerous intervening variables that mediate television's effect on viewers. Paramount among these variables are audience perceptions of media content credibility (O'Keefe, 1984; Slater and Elliott, 1982); audience demographics, socio-economics, and lifestyle (Hawkins and Pingree, 1981a, b; Doob and MacDonald, 1979); and individual viewing motivations (Wakshlag, Bart, Dudley, McCutcheon, and Rolla, 1983; Wakshlag, Vial, and Tamborini, 1983). Other important suggestions are that television's cultivation effects are temporary (Tamborini, Zillman, and Bryant, 1984), and that viewers have a more sophisticated understanding of so-called media reality than many would expect (Sheley and Ashkins, 1981; Roshier, 1973). Even adolescents are aware that social conflicts in reality are considerably more complex and more difficult to solve than is shown in television news (Adoni, Cohen, and Mane, 1984; Cohen, Adoni, and Drori, 1983). This would imply that viewers of televised trials may realize that the complexities of a case are deeper than is shown in the short excerpts of a newscast.

Support for a "transactional" model of media effects has also been expressed by those focusing on agenda-setting functions (Weaver, 1984; Erbring, Goldenberg, and Miller, 1980; Graber, 1980; Zucker, 1978). Basically, this model emphasizes that media impacts are contingent upon *message properties,* e.g., story content, issue immediacy, and message obtrusiveness and duration, and *pre-existing audience sensitivities,* e.g., perceptions of issue salience, personal experience with an issue, political or religious beliefs, media exposure patterns, audience demographics, and conversation with others.

7.   CONCLUSIONS

Several arguments about the detrimental consequences of televising trials are highly compelling, and examples of recently televised trials indicate that certain risks may detract from, if not entirely outweigh, hoped-for educational benefits. While it may be too early to accurately assess the impact of televised trials on defendant reputation or crime deterrence, arguments about the educational benefit of televising excerpts of trials on newscasts appear to be weak. First, the majority of cases selected for coverage are sensational criminal trials, giving viewers a distorted impression of the day-to-day business of the courts. Second, most cases are broadcast in minute part, and this "headline" news format severely restricts recall and understanding of story content. Third, the human interest bias of most trial reports generally precludes any informational value to viewers. Unless broadcasters make radical changes in the quality and quantity of footage that is broadcast, televised excerpts of trials will neither contribute significantly to public education about judicial process, nor correct erroneous images of the courts established by fictional crime and justice programs.

As for helping to restore confidence in the courts, this, again, will depend largely on the type of excerpts that are shown. Major public complaints appear to focus on judicial leniency; if news stories were to concentrate on cases resulting in lengthy sentences or heavy penalties, this particular concern might dissipate. However, televised trials resulting in decisions that are perceived as inappropriate (unjust or lenient) may strengthen existing negative attitudes, particularly among viewers who have little or no real experience with the courts and who perceive television program content as credible. Increased public sympathy for the daily difficulties of administering justice can probably be accomplished only by detailed documentary style programming.

The apparent lack of interest among the electronic media to truly inform and educate the public has certainly not gone unnoticed by opponents of televised trials. It has even been a source of great disappointment to those who support courtroom cameras. As early as 1978, while courtroom camera experiments were in their formative stages, Attorney General Griffin Bell wrote a compelling article for *TV Guide*. Showing a great deal of insight about the kinds of time constraints placed on news reporters, as well as the types of programs that do and do not draw large audiences, he nevertheless urged the networks to use their persuasive and informative powers more constructively and responsibly by providing "solid" coverage of issues facing the justice system. Such coverage, he noted, should not be relegated to unpopular viewing times, but should be promoted to prime-time, and should include documentary and in-depth interview format programs. Topics suggested by the Attorney General included: neighborhood justice centers; the operation and improvement of the justice system in general; inside-exposure of problems associated with overcrowded prisons and jails; disparities in sentences metered out by the courts; and a "start to finish" analysis of a single case, beginning with police response to the commission of a crime, moving through the arrest, arraignment, bail hearing, preparation of cases by the prosecution and defense, plea-bargaining, court delays, and jury selection, to the trial, verdict, and the sentence (Bell, 1978, pp. 2–4). Similar suggestions for improving media coverage of the courts have been made by *Los Angeles Times* reporter David Shaw (1981). Although referring more specifically to newspaper coverage, his concerns about present inadequacies in court reporting apply equally to broadcast media. He emphasizes (p. 19) that there is "an overemphasis on the day-to-day, case-by-case coverage and a concomitant laxity in the coverage of the larger issues confronting the legal system (and, ultimately, society at large).[18]

In its *per curiam* opinion, extending Rhode Island's experiment with camera coverage for a second year between 1983 and 1984, the Rhode Island Supreme Court strongly emphasized its disappointment with the media's poor record of serving public information and education needs, and reminded broadcasters that public education has been the "sole justification for the assumption of additional burdens by trial judges and other participants in the trial process in adjusting to and dealing with the presence of broadcasting, television, and still photography in the courtroom during court proceedings" (*In re Extension of Media Coverage,* 1982, draft copy pp. 2–3). In a distinct warning to the media, the Court said that it would "observe with great interest" their future coverage of Rhode Island's courts, and made it absolutely clear to media representatives that "the burden of proof in the weighing of benefit of media access against its disadvantages has been placed upon them" (*In re Extension of Media Coverage,* 1982, draft copy, p. 3). On March 23, 1984, the Rhode Island Supreme Court further extended the state's experiment with cameras for another year (effective April 1, 1984 to September 30, 1985). In its *per curiam* opinion, the Court repeated verbatim its observations about the responsibility of the media with regard to educating the public about judicial proceedings (from its 1982 opinion), and it registered its concerns even more emphatically as the state embarked on a third year of experimentation with televised trials: "Disregard by the media of its obligation to contribute to public understanding and education during a further experimental period may result in the termination of media access" (*In re Extension of Media Coverage,* March 23, 1984, draft copy pp. 3–5).

Others have also expressed concern about the need for broadcasters to use their new rights more responsibly, warning that there is a need not only to fulfill the promise of public education, but also to show sensitivity in dealing with vulnerable trial participants. In opening Florida's courtrooms to cameras in the 1970s, Judge Paul Baker noted optimistically that there should be a dialogue of give-and-take, a relationship based on "mutual understanding" between the needs of the courts and the goals of the media (Cameras in Courtroom Two-Way Street, 1978). Since then, however, media indifference to the courts (as well as to trial participants) has sharply juxtaposed the interests of those two institutions. The hoped-for dialogue has often turned to feelings of resentment, if not open confrontation. In *Chandler* the Court was quick to point out that "further research may change the picture,"[19] and that broadcasters should therefore proceed cautiously in covering trials. As one commentator has perceptively hinted: "Just how the news media *use* the material they gather in courts with cameras and recorders will be a weighty factor in deciding whether to allow broadcast coverage to continue" (Hughes, 1982, p. 443, emphasis added).

The most crucial yet most difficult questions to answer about televised trials concern their impact on defendants. Available research suggests three possible risks may be involved. First, television's status as the most relied-upon news source, and its ability to disseminate information quickly among a wide audience, implies that large numbers of people will become aware of a defendant whose trial (or pretrial hearing) is televised. Viewers may be selected as jurors, or may be in contact with those eventually chosen as jurors, thus increasing the risk of jury contamination. Second, research suggests that the content of television news and entertainment programming reinforces public perceptions of social reality and public opinions about issue salience. If so, televised trials may exacerbate public concerns about crime—cultivated by large quantities of crime-related entertainment programming and reinforced by exaggerated crime news reporting—and result in stronger negative attitudes toward criminal defendants. Third, there is support for the hypothesis that television viewing is related to retributive attitudes about crime and punishment. Defendants whose cases are televised may become conspicuous and vulnerable targets for general public frustrations about crime and criminals.

These conclusions, however, are only tentative. Ironically, the very reasons why audiences fail to learn from television news viewing—lack of motivation, inattentiveness, and superficial detail in news reports—may also be the reasons why some of the worst fears about its potential harm to defendants could be less severe than has been predicted. Details about cases and defendants who are televised may be ignored or quickly forgotten. Recall of information, however, may be dramatically increased by watching gavel-to-gavel televised trials. Research on news recall has dealt with the typical evening newscast in which stories are given little more than a minute's worth of coverage: results may differ when a trial is broadcast for several hours at a time, or for several hours over several days, almost like a TV mini-series or entertainment drama. The real danger, then, is that, just as greater detail may enhance the educational value of televising trials, it will also increase the potential risks to defendants.

Available "audience effects" research is only anecdotal to the specifics of televised trials, and extrapolation can provide only limited answers. In trying to find more definitive answers, studies must adopt a *comparative* approach and examine impacts of newspaper versus television coverage of trials. Harm may accrue to defendants from newspaper as well as televised trial reporting. It is not within the scope of this book to discuss the merits or abuses of newspaper trial coverage, yet one might briefly consider that a great deal of sensational and damaging reporting has been perpetrated by the print media.[20] Research indicates that newspaper stories are recalled in greater quantity and detail than television news items, and that newspapers may therefore have a stronger influence than television on public opinions. Of course, the suggestion here is *not* that, if newspaper reporting can be damaging, television should be afforded the same "privilege." The point is that both arms of the press should be measured side by side. The "qualitative difference test" has become the key legal yardstick for measuring the potential dangers of televised trial coverage, and any new scientific research must use this measure as well. Some attempt might also be made to ask defendants for their own perceptions about the potential harms of newspaper versus television coverage on their cases and reputations, and follow-up research should be conducted to see if reputation concerns are valid. Serious attention should also be paid to differences, if any, between the consequences of watching gavel-to-gavel trial coverage and excerpts of trials on regular newscasts.

FOOTNOTES

1. A cursory glance at the three commercial networks' prime time listings for the Fall 1985 season shows that just over a third of the programs were devoted to crime-and justice-related topics, whether solved by police officers, private detectives, undercover agents, vice squads, retired judges and investigators, or mystery writers. Outside of prime time, we are still treated to large doses of ever-popular "cops and robbers" reruns, and even situation comedies, the genre traditionally devoted to the tribulations of family life, have been infiltrated by crime and justice themes. Perhaps still more disturbing are the quasi-judicial programs, such as *Miller's Court, People's Court,* and *Divorce Court,* since their "pseudo-judicial" guise may have an even more misleading effect on the audience than the distorted impressions left by other entertainment programs.

2. See, for example, *Petition of Post-Newsweek Stations, Florida, Inc. for Change in Code of Judicial Conduct,* Fla. 370 So. 2d 764 at 780 (1979).

3. These differences may be due to different sampling techniques between the two studies. Yankelovich, Skelly, and White (1978) did not screen out people who were employed by the law enforcement or criminal justice systems, while the Hearst survey did.

4. In fairness, it should be noted that not all results were negative. For example, 81% of respondents knew that convicted persons have the right of appeal; 87% knew the correct definition of a "hung" jury; 79% knew that lawyers have the right to veto prospective jurors.

5. See, for example: A Woman's Defense of a Rape Defendant (1984), Big Dan's Defense Opens for Two (1984), Big Dan's Case Goes to First Jury (1984), Big Dan's Bar Patron Said He Tried to Call the Police (1984), Policeman Testifies on What Two Big Dan's Defendants Said (1984), Rape Trial Testimony Raises ID Questions (1984), Toxicologist Says Woman Had Eight Drinks (1984), Two Convicted in Big Dan's Rape (1984).

6. Concerns over televising sensitive witnesses become even more serious when those witnesses are also children, and when their testimony involves descriptions of child molestation. In May 1984, Cable News Network sparked an uproar when it applied to televise preliminary hearings in the McMartin child molestation case. Seven adults had been indicted on 115 counts of child abuse which allegedly took place at a preschool center in Manhattan Beach, California. Several young children were expected to testify during the proceedings, including victims of the alleged molestation (see Cameras in the Courtroom, 1984; Wilson, 1984).

    Although not an issue of *news cameras* in courtrooms (but of video for court administration purposes), a relatively new approach to protecting the well-being of child witnesses is the use of closed circuit television. This arrangement involves a two-way video link—one bringing the attorneys' questions to the child in a room adjacent to the courtroom, the other relaying the child's testimony back to the jury, judge, and attorneys in the courtroom (see Closed Circuit TV Lauded as Courtroom Aid for Children, 1984; TV Cameras May Calm Young Witnesses, 1984). However, members of the bench and bar have expressed concern that delivering testimony via closed circuit television may be in violation of the defendant's constitutional right to meet his accuser(s) "face-to-face" (Taped Testimony Urged in Abuse Cases, 1984; Safe Testimony: TV Screens for Child Witnesses, 1985).

7. Florida courts have also shown concern for both defendants and witnesses in televised trials. In *State v. Green,* 395 So.2d 532 (Fla. 1981), the Florida Supreme Court held that, if the presence of cameras might cause an unstable defendant to be determined "incompetent," then the trial judge may exclude electronic media after a proper hearing of the facts. In *State v. Palm Beach Newspapers, Inc.,* 395 So.2d 544 (Fla. 1981), the Florida Supreme Court held that prison inmate witnesses could have cameras turned off during their testimony because of fears of reprisal, i.e., a trial judge can legitimately ban cameras when witnesses refuse to testify for fear of their lives.

8. See *Petition of Post-Newsweek Stations, Florida, Inc.,* 370 So.2d 764, at 788 (Fla. 1979).

9. See *Petition of Post-Newsweek Stations, Florida, Inc.,* 370 So.2d 764, at 779, where Justice Sundberg noted that cameras may be excluded only "upon a finding that such coverage will have a substantial effect upon the particular individual which would be qualitatively different from the effect on members of the public in general and such an effect will be qualitatively different from coverage by other types of media." For further discussion of the "qualitative difference test" see Cohen (1982), Pequignot (1981), Tajgman (1981).

10. Benson is citing the *REPORT OF THE CHIEF COURT ADMINISTRATOR ON THE "CAMERAS-IN-THE-COURT" EXPERIMENT OF THE STATE OF CONNECTICUT,* (1983, p. 8): "We would hope the media would police themselves in matters of taste and decency so that it will be unnecessary for the judges to consider more restrictive regulations to remedy such problems."

11. Perhaps the most controversial collection of studies about the impacts of television on children and adolescents was the Report of the Surgeon General's Scientific Advisory Committee on Television and Social Behavior (1972). For further discussion about the impacts of television viewing on children and adolescents see: U.S. Department of Health and Human Services (1982); Comstock, Chaffee, Katzman, McCombs, and Roberts (1978).

12. *FCC v. Pacifica Foundation,* 438 U.S. 726 (1978). But see also *League of Women Voters v. FCC,* 8 Med.L.Rptr. 2081 (1982), in which Pacifica Foundation challenged a Public Broadcasting Act prohibition on editorializing by public television and radio stations that receive federal funds through the Corporation for Public Broadcasting. The California District Court held that funded noncommercial broadcasters have a right to editorialize under full First Amendment protections.

13. Of course, parents may not always be present to monitor their children's viewing activities—many "latch-key kids" watch large quantities of television unsupervised. However, the courts have yet to hold broadcasters responsible for "copy-cat" television crimes. See *Niemi v. NBC,* 74 Cal. App.3d 383 (1977), *cert. denied,* 46 U.S.L.W. 3659 (U.S. April 24, 1978), No. 681-035 (Cal. Super. Ct. Aug. 9, 1978, dismissed), involving an $11-million suit filed against NBC and its local affiliate KRON-TV, San Francisco. The suit resulted from the broadcast of "Born Innocent," which depicted a scene of a girl being raped by other girls using a "plumber's helper." Shortly after the program was aired, 9-year-old Olivia Niemi was raped with a bottle by a gang of three young girls and a boy on a San Francisco beach. The lawsuit alleged that NBC was

negligent in showing a program that might stimulate viewers to imitate its content. The case was finally dismissed because Niemi's lawyer could not show that NBC *intended* to incite the rape. See also NBC Didn't Incite Attack Acquittal Review Denied (1982).

14. The Wisconsin Supreme Court Committee, monitoring the state's progress with courtroom cameras in 1979, also received statements from the Public Defender's Office arguing against continued camera coverage (see *REPORT OF THE WISCONSIN SUPREME COURT COMMITTEE . . .* , 1979, Appendix G). Among the compelling arguments were:

   1. Television coverage is likely to reinforce negative public attitudes toward defendants, particularly those who are minorities or indigents.
   2. Some judges may bend to public opinion by imposing harsher sentences on defendants convicted for "street crimes," and judges will be tempted to use "more colorful and humiliating language" when announcing sentences in front of cameras.
   3. Television has a strong potential to shape public opinion because the audience is so large and passive, because information dissemination is instantaneous and rarely objective, and because information is broadcast very close to the time decisions are made about defendants.
   4. Fair trials will be jeopardized when witnesses refuse to testify and when jurors are swayed by public opinion. It is not a matter of whether witnesses and jurors are *actually* placed in any danger by their public identification, but the fact that they *perceive* public disrespect as a consequence of media coverage.

15. Discussion here relates only to the *first* von Bulow trial in 1982, not his retrial which took place in 1985 and resulted in a "not guilty" verdict.

16. See generally: Mrs. Von Bulow's Doctor Says Her Health Was Good (1982); Doctor Describes His Anguish Over Failure to Tell Mrs. Von Bulow of His Suspicions (1982); Jurors Again Hear Maid's Testimony on First Coma (1982); In von Bulow's Courtroom, Judge Needham is Boss (1982); Von Bulow's Defense Weighing Strategy, (1982); Sunny is Linked to Insulin Shots (1982); Questions About Exercise Teacher Add to Mystery of Von Bulow's Trial (1982); Jury Gets Two Portraits of von Bulow: Anguished Husband, Crafty Villain (1982); Von Bulow Judge Outlines the Law and the Vigil Begins in Newport (1982); Defense Rebuffed in Bid for Mistrial (1982); The Jury Finds the Defendant, Claus von Bulow, Guilty (1982); The Verdict Was Guilty (1982); Jurors Find von Bulow Guilty of Trying Twice to Kill Wife (1982); The Day After: Newport Turns Tranquil Again (1982); Mystery Witness for Von Bulow (1982).

17. Chief Justice Burger in *Chandler v. Florida*, 449 U.S. 560 at 578 (1981), citing Brief of the Attorneys General of Alabama et al., (1979), p. 40. Note that one argument surrounding the defendant reputation issue contends that, since defendants are considered innocent until proven guilty, they must be accorded the same privacy considerations as witnesses or victims. That is, if a trial is closed during a rape victim's testimony, it must also be closed during the defendant's; likewise, if a victim is granted anonymity, the accused should enjoy the same privilege. It should also be noted, however, that some defendants have claimed that their right to a public trial means that public and press (including television) access *must* be allowed, either because they want pressure placed on witnesses, or because they want vindication among a wide public audience. See *United States v. Hastings*, 695 F.2d 1278 (11th. Cir. 1983), *cert. denied*, 103 S.Ct. 1188 (1983); *Cody v. Oklahoma*, 361 P.2d 307 (Okla. Crim. App. 1961);

U.S. ex rel. Latimore v. Sielaff, 561 F.2d 691 (7th Cir. 1977), *cert. denied,* 434 U.S. 1076 (1978).

Publicity may, in fact, lead to positive public opinions about defendants. For example, while extensive publicity may have violated von Bulow's privacy, public response was positive. By the time the trial was over, von Bulow had become a popular local (perhaps even international) hero. On the day jury deliberations began, spectators yelled encouragement to von Bulow as his cab pulled away from the courthouse. A woman wearing a T-shirt imprinted with von Bulow's face, and carrying a bag with "Innocent" written across it, stood outside the courthouse; across the street, a doorway awning displayed the message "Free Claus" (see, for example, Von Bulow Cult Grows, 1982).

18. Similar concerns have been expressed about the lack of in-depth coverage of the U.S. Supreme Court, by both newspaper and television reporters. For general as well as content-analytic discussion of media coverage of the Court see: Cardozo (1985); Tarpley (1984); Katsh (1983); O'Brien (1983); Denniston (1980); Berkson (1978, pp. 57–68); Ericson (1977); Sobel (1970); Grey (1968); Newland (1964).

19. *Chandler v. Florida,* 499 U.S. 560, at 576, footnote 11 (1981).

20. Examples of notorious and potentially damaging newspaper reports include those surrounding the celebrated cases of Hauptmann, Sheppard, Jack Ruby, Sirhan Sirhan, Richard Speck, Charles Manson, and Patty Hearst, to name but a few.

BIBLIOGRAPHY

A Woman's Defense of a Rape Defendant (1984). *BOSTON GLOBE*, March 8, pp. 21 and 24.

ABA Adopts New Cameras Rule (1983). *JUDICATURE*, 66(6), December-January, p. 250.

ABA Ends Opposition to Cameras (1982). *NEWS MEDIA AND THE LAW*, 6(3), September-October, p. 45.

ABA Keeps Courtroom TV Ban (1979). *NEWS MEDIA AND THE LAW*, 3(2), May-June, p. 22.

ABA Makes it Perfectly Clear on Cameras in the Courtroom—It Wants Them Out (1979). *BROADCASTING*, February 19, p. 58.

ABA Tests Cameras in "Court" (1979). *CHRISTIAN SCIENCE MONITOR*, August 15, p. 5.

Abscam Tape Issue Goes to Supreme Court (1980). *BROADCASTING*, October 13, p. 65.

Adoni, H., Cohen, A., and Mane, S. (1984). Social Reality and Television News: Perceptual Dimensions of Social Conflicts in Selected Life Areas. *JOURNAL OF BROADCASTING*, 28(1), 33–49.

Alabama News Photographer Records Courtroom "First" (1976). *WASHINGTON POST*, February 13, p. B12.

American Bar Association Study Opposes Court Secrecy (1978). *NEWS MEDIA AND THE LAW*, 2(1), April, pp. 11–12.

Amicus Curiae Brief of the American College of Trial Lawyers (1979). Filed with the U.S. Supreme Court in *Chandler v. Florida*, October Term.

Amicus Curiae Brief of the California State Public Defenders Association, the California Attorneys for Criminal Justice, the Office of the California State Public Defender, the Los Angeles County Public Defenders Association, the Los Angeles Criminal Courts Bar Association, and the Office of the Los Angeles County Public Defender (1979). Filed with the U.S. Supreme Court in *Chandler v. Florida*, October Term.

Appeal at Trenton (1935). *TIME*, July 1, pp. 11–12.

Appleson, G. (1981). Connecticut Bar, Judges at Odds Over Cameras. *BAR LEADER*, November-December, p. 7.

Appleson, G. (1982). ABA Members, Media Debate Camera Issue. *AMERICAN BAR ASSOCIATION JOURNAL*, 68, March, p. 256.

Ares, C. E. (1981). *Chandler v. Florida:* Television, Criminal Trials, and Due Process. *SUPREME COURT REVIEW*, 6, 157–192.

Arons, S., and Katsh, E. (1977). How TV Cops Flout the Law. *SATURDAY REVIEW*, March 19, pp. 11–18.

Ashman, A. (1983). Cameras in the Courtroom Not Constitutionally Mandated. *AMERICAN BAR ASSOCIATION JOURNAL*, 69, July, p. 970.

At the Observation Post (1935). *LITERARY DIGEST*, January 19, p. 11.

Baker, H. (1984). We're Losing Political and Historical Treasures. *TV GUIDE*, July 21, pp. 32–34.

Baker, Judge P. (1977). *REPORT TO THE SUPREME COURT OF FLORIDA RE. CONDUCT OF AUDIO-VISUAL TRIAL COVERAGE, State v. Zamora*.

Bar Group Moves for TV in Courts (1978). *NEWS MEDIA AND THE LAW*, 2(1), April, p. 22.

Barnett, N. J., and Field, H. S. (1978). Character of the Defendant and Length of Sentence in Rape and Burglary Crimes. *JOURNAL OF SOCIAL PSYCHOLOGY*, 104, 271–277.

Barrile, L. (1984). Television and Attitudes About Crime: Do Heavy Viewers Distort Criminality and Support Retributive Justice. In R. Surrette (Ed.), *JUSTICE AND THE MEDIA: ISSUES AND RESEARCH*. Springfield, IL: Charles C. Thomas Publisher, 141–158.

Bass, M. C. (1981). Television's Day in Court. *NEW YORK TIMES MAGAZINE*, February 15, pp. 36–38, 40, 42, 44, 46, 48, 50, 54.

Bell v. Patterson, 279 F. Supp. 760 (D.Colo. 1968), *aff'd* 402 F.2d 394 (10th Cir. 1968); *cert. denied*, 403 U.S. 955 (1971).

Bell, G. (1978). Questions for Television: Is Justice Fair? What Happens to Victims? Are Jails Effective? *TV GUIDE*, October 21, pp. 2–4.

Belo Broadcasting Corp. v. Clark, 50 U.S.L.W. 2134 (5th Cir., August 28, 1981).

Benson, A. P. (1984). Do Cameras in the Courtroom Hurt the Cause of Justice? *UPDATE*, published by the ABA Special Committee on Youth Education for Citizenship, Spring, 20–54.

Berg, K. S., and Vidmar, N. (1975). Authoritarianism and Recall of Evidence About Criminal Behavior. *JOURNAL OF RESEARCH IN PERSONALITY*, 9(2), 147–157.

Berger, S. E., Levin, P., and Jacobson, L. I. (1977). Gain Approval or Avoid Disapproval: Comparison of Motive Strengths in High Need for Approval Scorers. *JOURNAL OF PERSONALITY*, 45(3), 458–468.

Berkson, L. C. (1978). *THE SUPREME COURT AND ITS PUBLICS*. Lexington, MA: D. C. Heath and Company.

Bermant, G., and Jacoubovitch, M. D. (1975). Fish Out of Water: A Brief Overview of Social and Psychological Concerns about Videotaped Trials. *HASTINGS LAW JOURNAL*, 26, 999–1011.

Bermant, G., Chappell, D., Crockett, G., Jacoubovitch, M. D., and McGuire, M. (1975). Juror Responses to Prerecorded Videotape Trial Presentations in California and Ohio. *HASTINGS LAW JOURNAL*, 26, 975–998.

Berreby, D. (1982). Von Bulow: Examining the Tactics. *NATIONAL LAW JOURNAL*, March 29, p. 1 and p. 11.

Berry, C. (1983). Learning From Television News: A Critique of the Research. *JOURNAL OF BROADCASTING*, 27(4), Fall, 359–370.

Bevan, W., Albert, R., Loiseaux, P., Mayfield, P., and Wright, G. (1958). Jury Behavior as a Function of the Prestige of the Foreman and the Nature of His Leadership. *JOURNAL OF PUBLIC LAW*, 7, 419–449.

Big Dan's Case Goes to First Jury (1984). *BOSTON GLOBE*, March 17, pp. 19–20.

Big Dan's Defense Opens for Two (1984). *BOSTON GLOBE*, March 14, pp. 21–22.

Big Dan's Bar Patron Said He Tried to Call the Police (1984). *BOSTON GLOBE*, March 8, pp. 21 and 24.

Blashfield, A. E. (1962). The Case of the Controversial Canon. *AMERICAN BAR ASSOCIA-TION JOURNAL*, 48, May, pp. 429–434.

Block, I. J. (1978). Cameras and Courtrooms: The Denial of Due Process. *FLORIDA BAR JOURNAL*, 52(6), June, pp. 454–455.

Boehm, V. R. (1968). Mr. Prejudice, Miss Sympathy, and the Authoritarian Personality: An Application of Psychological Measuring Techniques to the Problem of Jury Bias. *WISCONSIN LAW REVIEW*, (3), 734–750.

Bogart, L. (1984). The Public's Use and Perception of Newspapers. *PUBLIC OPINION QUARTERLY*, 48(4), Winter, 709–719.

Boone, J. (1972). The Effects of Race, Arrogance, and Evidence on Simulated Jury Decisions. Ph.D. dissertation, University of Washington.

Boone, K. (1981). TV in the Courtroom: Is Something Being Stolen From Us? *HUMAN RIGHTS*, 9, Summer, 24–27.

Both Guilty (1935). *THE NEW REPUBLIC*, February 27, p. 62.

Boyd, J. A. (1978). Cameras in Court: *Estes v. Texas* and Florida's One Year Pilot Program. *UNIVERSITY OF MIAMI LAW REVIEW*, 32, 815–837.

Bradley v. Texas, 470 F.2d 785 (5th Cir. 1972).

Brakel, S. J. (1975). Videotape in Trial Proceedings: A Technological Obsession? *AMERICAN BAR ASSOCIATION JOURNAL*, 61, 956–959.

Branzburg v. Hayes, 408 U.S. 665 (1972).

Braverman, H. H. (1984). Extended Coverage—Cameras Come to the Courtroom. *ILLINOIS BAR JOURNAL*, 72, March, pp. 334–335.

Brennan, W. J. (1980). Why Protect the Press? *COLUMBIA JOURNALISM REVIEW*, January-February, pp. 59–62.

Bridges v. California, 314 U.S. 252 (1941).

Brief of the American College of Trial Lawyers as *Amicus Curiae* (1979). Submitted to the U.S. Supreme Court in *Chandler v Florida*, October Term, 1979.

Brief and Appendix of the Attorneys General of Alabama, Alaska, Arizona, Iowa, Kentucky, Lousiana, Maryland, Montana, Nevada, New Mexico, New York, Ohio, Rhode Island, Tennessee, Vermont, West Virginia, and Wisconsin as Amici Curiae in Support of Appellee (1979). Submitted to the U.S. Supreme Court in *Chandler v. Florida*, October Term.

Brigner, V. M. (1982). Cameras in the Courtroom: Courts in the Livingroom. *DOCKET CALL*, 16, Winter, 12–16.

Broeder, D. W. (1959). The University of Chicago Jury Project. *NEBRASKA LAW REVIEW*, 38, 744–760.

Broeder, D. W. (1965–1966). The Importance of the Scapegoat in Jury Trial Cases: Some Preliminary Reflections. *DUQUESNE UNIVERSITY LAW REVIEW*, 4, 513–525.

Broeder, D. W. (1965a). The Negro in Court. *DUKE LAW JOURNAL*, 19–31.

Broeder, D. W. (1965b). Voir Dire Examinations: An Empirical Study. *SOUTHERN CALIFORNIA LAW REVIEW*, 38, 503–528.

Broeder, D. W. (1966). The Impact of the Vicinage Requirement: An Empirical Look. *NEBRASKA LAW REVIEW*, 45(1), 99–118.

Broholm, J. R. (1979). Electronic Media in the Courtroom. *MISSOURI BAR JOURNAL*, July-August, pp. 291–297.

Brown v. Board of Education, 347 U.S. 483 (1954).

Browne, Karen (1978). Comparison of Factual Recall from Film and Print Stimuli. *JOURNALISM QUARTERLY*, 55, Summer, 350–353.

Bruck, C. (1982). A Plain-Speaking Prosecutor vs. A Smooth-Talking Defender. *AMERICAN LAWYER* 4, April, pp. 28–32.

Bryant, J., Carveth, R. A., and Brown, D. (1981). Television Viewing and Anxiety: An Experimental Examination. *JOURNAL OF COMMUNICATION,* 31(1), Winter, 106–119.

Buckalew, J. (1969–70). News Elements and Selection of News by Television News Editors. *JOURNAL OF BROADCASTING,* 14(1), Winter, 47–54.

Bullock, H. A. (1961). Significance of the Racial Factor in the Length of Prison Sentences. *JOURNAL OF CRIMINAL LAW,* 52(4), November-December, pp. 411–417.

Burger, W. E. (1975). The Interdependence of Judicial and Journalistic Independence. *NEW YORK STATE BAR JOURNAL,* 47, October, pp. 453–455 and 476–478.

Calder, B. J., Insko, C. A., and Yandell, B. (1974). The Relation of Cognitive and Memorial Processes to Persuasion in a Simulated Jury Trial. *JOURNAL OF APPLIED SOCIAL PSYCHOLOGY,* 4(1), 62–93.

Camera Ban Pleases Judges, Keeps Journalists Plugging (1981). *ST. LOUIS POST-DISPATCH,* May 7, p. 9.

Cameras Allowed in 37 States' Courts (1983). *NEWS MEDIA AND THE LAW,* 7(1), March-April, pp. 42–43.

Cameras and Mikes Allowed in Massachusetts Courts (1980). *BROADCASTING,* March 17, p. 85.

Cameras at von Bulow Trial (1982). *NEW YORK LAW JOURNAL,* March 18, p. 2, col. 3.

Cameras in Court: Justices' Prejudice Caps Lenses (1983). *MICHIGAN BAR JOURNAL,* 62, September, pp. 733–734.

Cameras in Courtroom Two-Way Street (1978). *NEWS PHOTOGRAPHER,* 33(9), September, p. 11.

Cameras in the Courtroom (1984). *CALIFORNIA LAWYER,* September, p. 36.

Cameras in the Courtroom Issue Goes to Court (1980). *BROADCASTING,* November 17, p. 65.

Cameras in the Courtroom: Florida's Bundy Case Tests the Fairness of Televising Trials (1979). *TIME,* July 23, p. 76.

Cameras Out of Courtrooms? Editorial (1979). *AMERICAN BAR ASSOCIATION JOURNAL,* 65, March, p. 304.

Cameras-in-the-Courtroom Advocates Try for the Top (1983). *BROADCASTING,* March 14, pp. 172–174.

Cardozo, M. (1985). PREVIEW Helps Reporters Cover the Supreme Court. *JUDICATURE,* 68(7–8), February-March, pp. 297–299.

Carter, C. A. (1981a). *MEDIA IN THE COURTS.* Williamsburg, VA: National Center for State Courts.

Carter, C. A. (1981b). Television in the Courts. *STATE COURT JOURNAL,* 6(15), Winter, 6–10.

Carter, C. A., and Ito, J. A. (1982). Media Coverage and the State Courts: An Update. *STATE COURT JOURNAL,* 6, Winter, 26–31.

CBS v. Democratic National Committee, 412 U.S. 94 (1973).

Cedarquist, W. B. (1961). Televising Court Proceedings, A Plea for Order in the Court. *NOTRE DAME LAWYER,* 36, 147–157.

Chandler v. Florida, 449 U.S. 560 (January 26, 1981).

Chandler v. State, 376 So.2d 1157 (Fla. 1979).

Chandler v. State, 366 So.2d 64 (D.C.A. Fla. 1978).

Clark v. Community For Creative Non-Violence et al., 104 S.Ct. 3065 (1984).

Closed Circuit TV Lauded As Courtroom Aid For Children (1984). *LOS ANGELES DAILY NEWS,* May 31.

Cody v. Oklahoma, 361 P.2d 307 (Okla. Crim. App. 1961).

Cohen, Akiba, Adoni, H., and Drori, G. (1983). Adolescents' Perceptions of Social Conflicts in Television News and Social Reality. *HUMAN COMMUNICATION RESEARCH,* 10(2), Winter, 203–225.

Cohen, J. (1982). Cameras in the Courtroom and Due Process: A Proposal for a Qualitative Difference Test. *WASHINGTON LAW REVIEW,* 57, 277–291.

Comstock, G., Chaffee, S., Katzman, N., McCombs, M., and Roberts, D. (1980). *TELEVISION AND HUMAN BEHAVIOR,* New York: Columbia University Press.

Conner, L. L. (1974). The Trial Judge's Demeanor: Its Impact on the Jury. *THE JUDGE'S JOURNAL,* 13, 2–4.

Cook, F. L., Tyler, T., Goetz, E., Gordon, M., Protess, D., Leff, D., and Molotch, H. (1983). Media and Agenda Setting: Effects on the Public, Interest Group Leaders, Policy Makers, and Policy. *PUBLIC OPINION QUARTERLY,* 47(1), Spring, 16–35.

Cooke, L. H. (1982). Television in Courtroom: New Generation of Progress. *NEW YORK LAW JOURNAL,* May 3, p. 25.

Cooper, Judge C. (1981). *IN RE: PETITION FOR EXTENDED NEWS COVERAGE,* Fulton County Superior Court, Georgia, August 25.

Court Coverage by TV, Radio Commands Support of Jurists (1978). *WASHINGTON POST,* July 16, p. A21.

Court TV in 14 States (1978). *NEWS MEDIA AND THE LAW,* October, p. 30.

Court Watch Summary (1980). *NEWS MEDIA AND THE LAW,* 4(3), August-September, pp. 4–5.

Courtroom Cameras Pushing Hard for Access to Trials. (1984). *CHRISTIAN SCIENCE MONITOR,* May 24, pp. 1 and 28.

Cox Broadcasting Corp. v. Cohn, 420 U.S. 469 (1975).

Craig v. Harney, 331 U.S. 367 (1947).

Craig, R. S. (1979). Cameras in Courtrooms in Florida. *JOURNALISM QUARTERLY,* 56(4), Winter, 703–710.

D'Alemberte, T. (1980). Cameras in the Courtroom: Yes. *BARRISTER,* 7, Spring, 6, 8, 38–39.

D'Alemberte, T. (1982). Cameras in the Courtroom. *LITIGATION,* 9, Fall, 20–23.

Damaska, M. (1975). Presentation of Evidence and Factfinding Precision. *UNIVERSITY OF PENNSYLVANIA LAW REVIEW,* 123(5), 1083–1106.

Davis, F. J. (1952). Crime News in Colorado Newspapers. *AMERICAN JOURNAL OF SOCIOLOGY,* 50, June, pp. 325–330.

Davis, N. (1980). Television in Our Courts: The Proven Advantages, the Unproven Dangers. *JUDICATURE,* 64(2), August, pp. 85–92.

Davis, N. (1981). Courtroom Television on Trial: It's Here, It Works. *TELEVISION QUARTERLY,* 18(3), Fall, 7–27.

Day, J. G. (1981). The Case Against Cameras in the Courtroom. *JUDGES JOURNAL,* 20, Winter, 18–21 and 51.

De Silva, B. (1984). The Gang-Rape Story. *COLUMBIA JOURNALISM REVIEW,* May-June, pp. 42–44.

Defense Rebuffed in Bid for Mistrial (1982). *PROVIDENCE JOURNAL,* March 15, p. A1 and A18.

DeJong, W., Hastorf, A. H., and Morris, W. N. (1976). Effect of An Escaped Accomplice on the Punishment Assigned to a Criminal Defendant. *JOURNAL OF PERSONALITY AND SOCIAL PSYCHOLOGY,* 33(2), 192–198.

Denniston, L. (1980). *THE REPORTER AND THE LAW.* New York: Hastings House.

Dershowitz, A. (1985). These Cops Are All Guilty. *TV GUIDE,* May 25, pp. 4–7.

Diamond, S., and Zeisel, H. (1974). A Courtroom Experiment on Juror Selection and Decision-Making. *PERSONALITY AND SOCIAL PSYCHOLOGY BULLETIN,* 1(1), 276–277.

Did TV Make Him Do It? (1977). *TIME,* October 10, p. 87.

Dion, K., Berscheid, E., and Walster, E. (1972). What is Beautiful is Good. *JOURNAL OF PERSONALITY AND SOCIAL PSYCHOLOGY,* 24(3), 285–290.

Doctor Describes His Anguish Over Failure to Tell Mrs. Von Bulow of His Suspicions (1982). *PROVIDENCE JOURNAL,* February 23, p. A1 and A10.

Doe v. Sarasota-Bradenton Television, 436 So.2d 328 (Fla. App., 1983).

Doob, A. N. (1976). Evidence, Procedure, and Psychological Research. In G. Bermant, C. Nemeth, and N. Vidmar (Eds.), *PSYCHOLOGY AND THE LAW.* Lexington, MA: Lexington Books, 135–147.

Doob, A. N., and MacDonald, G. E. (1979). Television Viewing and Fear of Victimization: Is the Relationship Causal? *JOURNAL OF PERSONALITY AND SOCIAL PSYCHOLOGY,* 37(2), 170–179.

Doret, D. M. (1974). Trial by Videotape: Can Justice Be Seen to Be Done? *TEMPLE LAW QUARTERLY,* 47, 228–268.

Dorfman v. Meiszner, 430 F.2d 558 (7th Cir. 1974).

Doubles, M. R. (1965). A Camera in the Courtroom. *WASHINGTON AND LEE LAW REVIEW,* 22(1), Spring, 1–16.

Douglas, W. O. (1960). The Public Trial and the Free Press. *AMERICAN BAR ASSOCIATION JOURNAL,* 46, August, pp. 840–844.

Douglass, P. (1982). Media Technology, Fair Trial, and the Citizen's Right to Know. *NEW YORK STATE BAR JOURNAL,* 54, October, pp. 364–369.

Driver, T. (1981). Cameras in the Courtroom: Committee Reviews Proposed Guidelines. *TEXAS BAR JOURNAL,* 44, April, pp. 393–397.

Edwards, A. L. (1953). The Relationship Between the Judged Desirability of a Trait and the Probability That the Trait Will Be Endorsed. *JOURNAL OF APPLIED PSYCHOLOGY,* 37(2), 90–93.

Edwardson, M., Grooms, D., and Pringle, P. (1976). Visualization and TV News Information Gain. *JOURNAL OF BROADCASTING,* 20(3), Summer, 373–380.

Edwardson, M., Grooms, D., and Proudlove, S. (1981). Television News Information Gain from Interesting Video vs. Talking Heads. *JOURNAL OF BROADCASTING,* 25(1), Winter, 15–24.

Efran, M. (1974). The Effect of Physical Appearance on the Judgment of Guilt, Interpersonal Attraction, and Severity of Recommended Punishment in a Simulated Jury Task. *JOURNAL OF RESEARCH IN PERSONALITY,* 8(1), 45–54.

Einsiedel, E. F., Salomone, K. L. and Schneider, F. (1984). Crime: Effects of Media Exposure and Personal Experience on Issue Salience. *JOURNALISM QUARTERLY,* 61(1), Spring, 131–136.

Eisenstadt v. Baird, 405 U.S. 438 (1972).

Epstein, E. J. (1973). *NEWS FROM NOWHERE.* New York: Random House.

Erbring, L., Goldenberg, E. N., and Miller, A. H. (1980). Front Page News and Real World Cues: A Look at Agenda-Setting by the Media. *AMERICAN JOURNAL OF POLITICAL SCIENCE,* 24(1), February, pp. 16–49.

Ericson, D. (1977). Newspaper Coverage of the Supreme Court: A Case Study. *JOURNALISM QUARTERLY,* 54(3), 605–607.

Ernest H. Short and Associates, Inc. (1976). *A REPORT TO THE JUDICIAL COUNCIL ON VIDEOTAPE RECORDING IN THE CALIFORNIA CRIMINAL JUSTICE SYSTEM.* Second Year Findings and Recommendations. 1976.

Ernest H. Short and Associates, Inc., (1981). *EVALUATION OF CALIFORNIA'S EXPERIMENT WITH EXTENDED MEDIA COVERAGE OF COURTS.* Submitted to the Administrative Office for the Courts; the Chief Justice's Special Committee on the Courts and the Media, and the California Judicial Council.

Estelle v. Williams, 425 U.S. 501 (1976).

Estes v. Texas, 381 U.S. 532 (1965).

Evans, H. B. (1982). Opening of Trial Courts to Broadcast Media Urged. *NEW YORK LAW JOURNAL,* May 3, pp. 25 and 27.

Ex Parte Sturm, 152 Md. 114, 136 A. 312 (Ct. App. 1927).

Fahringer, H. P. (1981). Cameras in the Courtroom. *TRIAL,* January, pp. 18–20 and 61.

Fanfare for the First Amendment (1980). *BROADCASTING,* March 24, p. 30.

FCC v. Pacifica Foundation, 438 U.S. 726 (1978).

Fenner, G. M., and Koley, J. L. (1981). Access to Judicial Proceedings: To *Richmond Newspapers* and Beyond. *HARVARD CIVIL RIGHTS-CIVIL LIBERTIES LAW REVIEW,* 16, 415–459.

Final Report of the Hawaii State Bar Association Committee on "Cameras in the Courtroom" (1982). *HAWAII BAR JOURNAL,* 17(1), Winter, pp. 3–39.

Finley, R. C. (1969). Free Press and Fair Trial: A Commonsense Accommodation. *NEW YORK STATE BAR JOURNAL,* 41, January, pp. 9–20.

First Amendment Guarantees Public, Press Trial Access. (1981). *NEWS MEDIA AND THE LAW,* 5(2), February-March, pp. 9–10.

Five Abscam Trial Videotapes Aired: Lower Courts Mull Public Release (1981). *NEWS MEDIA AND THE LAW,* 5(2), February-March, pp. 7–8.

Flemington Aftermath (1935). *THE CHRISTIAN CENTURY,* February 27, pp. 264–266.

Florida Conference of Circuit Judges (1978). *REPORT IN RE: PETITION OF POST-NEWSWEEK STATIONS, FLORIDA, INC., FOR CHANGE IN CODE OF JUDICIAL CONDUCT.*

Fox, M. (1980). U.S. Supreme Court to Review Issue of Cameras in Courts. *NEW YORK LAW JOURNAL,* 183, April 22, p. 1.

Frankel, A., and Morris, W. N. (1976). Testifying In One's Own Defense: The Ingratiator's Dilemma. *JOURNAL OF PERSONALITY AND SOCIAL PSYCHOLOGY,* 34(3), 475–480.

Frankel, M. (1975). The Search for Truth: An Umpireal View. *UNIVERSITY OF PENNSYLVANIA LAW REVIEW,* 123(5), 1031–1059.

Free Press-Fair Trial Proposed Revised Guidelines of the Judicial Conference of the United States—1980: A Recommendation Relating to Information by Attorneys in Criminal Cases. 91 *F.R.D.* 289 (1981).

Freedman, E. (1980). Cooke's Panel Favors Cameras at all Appellate Proceedings. *NEW YORK LAW JOURNAL,* 183(108), June 4, p. 1, Col. 3.

Fretz, D. (1978a). Cameras in the Courtroom: No, or at Least a Cautious "Only If." *AMERICAN BAR ASSOCIATION JOURNAL,* 64, April, pp. 549–550.

Fretz, D. R. (1978b). Cameras in the Courtroom. *TRIAL,* 14(9), September, pp. 28–29 and 47.

Friend, R. M., and Vinson, M. (1974). Leaning Over Backwards: Jurors' Responses of Defendants' Attractiveness. *JOURNAL OF COMMUNICATION,* 24(3), 124–129.

Fuoco, R. J. (1982). The Prejudicial Effects of Cameras in the Courtroom. *UNIVERSITY OF RICHMOND LAW REVIEW,* 16, 867–883.

Gannett Co. v. DePasquale, 443 U.S. 368 (1979).

Gantz, W. (1978). How Uses and Gratifications Affect Recall of Television News. *JOURNALISM QUARTERLY,* 55(4), 664–672, and 681.

Garay, R. (1978). Television and the 1951 Senate Crime Committee Hearings. *JOURNAL OF BROADCASTING,* 22(4), 469–490.

Geis, G. (1957). A Lively Public Issue: Canon 35 in the Light of Recent Events. *AMERICAN BAR ASSOCIATION JOURNAL,* 43, May, pp. 419–422 and 475.

Gerbner, G. (1980). Trial by Television: Are We at the Point of No Return? *JUDICATURE,* 63(9), April, pp. 416–426.

Gerbner, G., and Gross, L. (1976a). Living With Television: The Violence Profile, *JOURNAL OF COMMUNICATION,* 26(2), 173–199.

Gerbner, G., and Gross, L. (1976b). The Scary World of TV's Heavy Viewer. *PSYCHOLOGY TODAY,* April, pp. 41–44, 89.

Gerbner, G., Gross, L., Eleey, M. F., Jackson-Beeck, M., Jeffries-Fox, S., and Signorielli, N. (1977). TV Violence Profile No. 8: The Highlights. *JOURNAL OF COMMUNICATION,* 27(2), Spring, 171–180.

Gerbner, G., Gross, L., Eleey, M. F., Jackson-Beeck, M., Jeffries-Fox, S., and Signorielli, N. (1978). Cultural Indicators: Violence Profile No. 9. *JOURNAL OF COMMUNICATION,* 28(3), Summer, 176–207.

Gerbner, G., Gross, L., Signorielli, N., Morgan, M., and Jackson-Beeck, M. (1979). The Demonstration of Power: Violence Profile No. 10. *JOURNAL OF COMMUNICATION,* 29(3), Summer, 177–196.

Gerbner, G., Gross, L., Morgan, M., and Signorielli, N. (1980). The "Mainstreaming" of America: Violence Profile No. 11. *JOURNAL OF COMMUNICATION,* 30(3), Summer, 10–29.

Gertz v. Robert Welch, Inc., 481 U.S. 323 (1974).

Gertz Wins $400,000 in Damages Following 14-year Court Battle. (1982). *NEWS MEDIA AND THE LAW,* 6(3), September-October, p. 21.

Gillmor, D., and Barron, J. (1974). *MASS COMMUNICATION LAW,* 2nd ed., St. Paul, Minn.: West Publishing.

Gillmor, D. M., and Dennis, E. E. (1981). Legal Research in Mass Communication. In G. H. Stempel and B. H. Westley (Eds.), *RESEARCH METHODS IN MASS COMMUNICATION.* Englewood Cliffs, N.J.: Prentice-Hall, Inc.

Gilmore, W. H. (1980). Arraignment By Television: A New Way to Bring Defendants to the Courtroom. *JUDICATURE,* 63(8), 396–401.

Giving Cameras a Day in Court (1981). *NEWSWEEK,* February 9, p. 102.

Gleason, J. M., and Harris, V. (1976). Group Discussion and Defendant's Socio-Economic

Status and Determinants of Judgments by Simulated Jurors. *JOURNAL OF APPLIED SOCIAL PSYCHOLOGY*, 6(2), 186–191.

Globe Newspaper Co. v. Superior Court, 401 N.E. 2d 360 (Mass. 1980).

Globe Newspaper Co. v. Superior Court, 457 U.S. 596 (1982).

Goggin, T. P., and Hanover, G. M. (1965). Fair Trial v. Free Press: The Psychological Effect of Pretrial Publicity on the Juror's Ability To Be Impartial; A Plea For Reform. *SOUTHERN CALIFORNIA LAW REVIEW*, 38, 672–688.

Goldman, P. S., and Larson, R. S. (1978). News Cameras in the Courtroom During *State v. Solorzano:* End to the *Estes* Mandate? *SOUTHWESTERN UNIVERSITY LAW REVIEW*, 10, 2001–2067.

Gonzales v. People, 165 Colo. 322, 438 P.2d 686 (1968).

Goodale, J. C. (1979). Open Justice: The Threat of Gannett. *COMMUNICATIONS AND THE LAW*, 1(1), Winter, 3–13.

Goodwin, A. T. (1979). A Report on the Latest Rounds in the Battle Over Cameras in the Courts. *JUDICATURE*, 63(2), August, pp. 74–77.

Gordon, M., and Heath, L. (1981). The News Business, Crime and Fear. In D. Lewis (Ed.), *REACTIONS TO CRIME*. Beverly Hills, CA: Sage.

Graber, D. A. (1980). *CRIME NEWS AND THE PUBLIC*. New York: Praeger.

Graber, D. A. (1984). *PROCESSING THE NEWS*. New York: Longman Inc.

Grady, D. (1981). Picking a Jury. *DISCOVER*, 2(1), January, pp. 38–41.

Graham, F. (1978). Cameras in the Courtroom: Yes, Bring Them In. *AMERICAN BAR ASSOCIATION JOURNAL*, 64, April, pp. 545–548.

Graves, D. (1979). Cameras in the Courts: The Situation Today. *JUDICATURE*, 63(1), June-July, pp. 24–27.

Greenberg, S. L. (1984). Spotlight on the Jury: Trial Publicity and Juror Privacy. *COMM/ENT*, 6(2), 369–389.

Greene, E., and Loftus E. (1984). What's New in the News? The Influence of Well-Publicized News Events on Psychological Research and Courtroom Trials. *BASIC AND APPLIED SOCIAL PSYCHOLOGY*, 5(3), September, pp. 211–221.

Grey, D. L. (1968). *THE SUPREME COURT AND THE NEWS MEDIA*. Evanston, IL: Norwestern University Press.

Griswold v. Connecticut, 381 U.S. 479 (1965).

Gunter, B., Furnham, A., and Gietson, G. (1984). Memory for the News as a Function of the Channel of Communication. *HUMAN LEARNING*, 3(4), October-December, pp. 265–271.

Hall, F. H. (1962). Colorado's Six Years' Experience Without Judicial Canon 35. *AMERICAN BAR ASSOCIATION JOURNAL*, 48, December, pp. 1120–1122.

Hallam, O. (1940). Some Object Lessons on Publicity in Criminal Trials. *MINNESOTA LAW REVIEW*, 24(4), 453–508.

Hans, V. P., and Slater, D. (1983). John Hinckley, Jr. and the Insanity Defense: The Public's Verdict. *PUBLIC OPINION QUARTERLY*, 47(2), Summer, 202–212.

Hanscom, R. J. (1978). Cameras in the Courtroom: A Challenge for California. *CALIFORNIA STATE BAR JOURNAL*, July-August, pp. 226–228.

Hauptmann v. New Jersey, 115 N.J.L. 412; *cert. denied*, 296 U.S. 649 (1935).

Hawkins, R. P., and Pingree, S. (1981a). Uniform Messages and Habitual Viewing: Unnecessary Assumptions in Social Reality Effects. *HUMAN COMMUNICATION RESEARCH*, 7, 291–301.

Hawkins, R. P., and Pingree, S. (1981b). Using Television to Construct Social Reality. *JOURNAL OF BROADCASTING*, 25, 347–364.

Hazard, W. R. (1962–63). On the Impact of Television's Pictured News. *JOURNAL OF BROADCASTING*, 7, Winter, 43–51.

Hearings Closed (1978). *NEWS MEDIA AND THE LAW*, 2(1), April, p. 6.

Hearst Corporation (1983). *THE AMERICAN PUBLIC, THE MEDIA AND THE JUDICIAL SYSTEM: A NATIONAL SURVEY ON PUBLIC AWARENESS AND PERSONAL EXPERIENCE.*

Heeren, J., and Schichor D. (1984). Mass Media and Delinquency Prevention: The Case of "Scared Straight." *DEVIANT BEHAVIOR*, 5(4), 375–386.

Heflin, H. T. (1977). Fair Trial v. Free Press: Time for a Rehearing. *JUDICATURE*, 61(4), October, pp. 154–155.

Hervey, J. G. (1947). The Jurors Look At Our Judges. *OKLAHOMA BAR ASSOCIATION JOURNAL*, 18, 1508–1513.

High Court Bars Trial Held in Secret. (1980). *BROADCASTING*, July 7, p. 27.

High Court to Review Pretrial Secrecy (1978). *NEWS MEDIA AND THE LAW*, 2(2), July, p. 16.

Hirsch, P. M. (1980). The "Scary World" of the Nonviewer and Other Anomalies: A Reanalysis of Gerbner et al.'s Finding on Cultivation Analysis. Part 1. *COMMUNICATION RESEARCH*, 7, 403–456.

Hirsch, P. M. (1981a). Distinguishing Good Speculation From Bad Theory: Rejoinder to Gerbner et al. *COMMUNICATION RESEARCH*, 8, 73–95.

Hirsch, P. M. (1981b). On Not Learning From One's Own Mistakes: A Reanalysis of Gerbner et al.'s Findings on Cultivation Analysis. Part 2. *COMMUNICATION RESEARCH*, 8, 3–37.

Hirschhorn, J. (1978). *AMICUS CURIAE BRIEF IN OPPOSITION TO PETITION OF POST-NEWSWEEK STATIONS, FLORIDA, INC. FOR CHANGE IN CODE OF JUDICIAL CONDUCT.* (Submitted to the Florida Supreme Court *In Re: Petition of Post-Newsweek Stations, Florida, Inc.*, 1979).

Hirschhorn, J. (1980a). Cameras in the Courtroom? No. *BARRISTER*, 7(3), pp. 7, 9 and 56.

Hirschhorn, J. (1980b). Does Television Make a Fair Trial Impossible?—A Debate. *JUDICATURE*, 64(3), September, pp. 145–146.

Hochberger, R. (1980). U.S. Supreme Court Frees Abscam Films for Broadcast. *NEW YORK LAW JOURNAL*, October 15, p. 1, col. 2 and p. 2, col. 3.

Hochberger, R. (1982). Von Bulow's Lawyer No Fan of Cameras in Courtroom. *NEW YORK LAW JOURNAL*, March 18, p. 1 col. 2 and p. 2 col. 3.

Hoffman, H. M., and Brodley, J. (1952). Jurors on Trial. *MISSOURI LAW REVIEW*, 17(3), 235–251.

Hoiberg, B. C., and Stires, L. K. (1973). The Effect of Several Types of Pretrial Publicity On the Guilt Attributions of Simulated Jurors. *JOURNAL OF APPLIED PSYCHOLOGY*, 3(3), 267–275.

Holt v. U.S., 218 U.S. 245 (1910).

Homicide, Not Murder (1980). *JUDICATURE*, 64(2), August, p. 57.

Hood, J. T. (1967). Recent Developments: Trial By Jury. *ALABAMA LAW REVIEW*, 20, 76–88.

Houchins v. KQED, Inc., 483 U.S. 1 (1978).

House Begins TV Coverage (1979). *NEWS MEDIA AND THE LAW*, 3(2), May-June, p. 24.

Hoyt, J. (1977). Courtroom Coverage: The Effects of Being Televised. *JOURNAL OF BROADCASTING,* 12(4), Fall, 487–495.

Hoyt, J. (1978). Cameras in the Courtroom: Another Chance. *PUBLIC TELECOMMUNICATIONS REVIEW,* 6(3), May-June, pp. 28–34.

Hoyt, J. (1980). Prohibiting Courtroom Photography: It's Up to the Judge in Florida and Wisconsin. *JUDICATURE,* 63(6), December-January, pp. 290–295.

Hughes, M. (1980). The Fruits of Cultivation Analysis: A Reexamination of Some Effects of Television Watching. *PUBLIC OPINION QUARTERLY,* 44(3), 287–302.

Hughes, R. L. (1982). *Chandler v. Florida:* Cameras Get Probation in Courtrooms. *JOURNAL OF BROADCASTING,* 26(1), Winter, 431–444.

Humphries, Judge G. E., Jr. (1979). *REPORT ON PILOT PROJECT ON THE PRESENCE OF CAMERAS AND ELECTRONIC EQUIPMENT IN THE COURTROOM.* (Louisiana).

Hunter, J. E., Schmidt, F. L., and Jackson, G. B. (1982). *META-ANALYSIS: CUMULATING RESEARCH FINDINGS ACROSS STUDIES* Beverly Hills: Sage.

In re Application of National Broadcasting Co., Inc., (Jenrette) 653 F.2d 609 (D.C. Cir. 1981).

In re Application of National Broadcasting Co., Inc., (Myers) 635 F.2d 945 (2d Cir. 1980).

In re Extension of Media Coverage for a Further Experimental Period. Per Curiam Opinion (1982). Rhode Island Supreme Court, draft copy, December 31.

In re Extension of Media Coverage for a Further Experimental Period. Per Curiam Opinion (1984). Rhode Island Supreme Court, draft copy, March 23.

In re Murchison, 349 U.S. 133 (1955).

In re Oliver, 333 U.S. 257 (1948).

In von Bulow's Courtroom, Judge Needham is Boss (1982). *PROVIDENCE JOURNAL,* March 1, p. A1 and A18.

Interim Report to the Chief Judge of the New York State Court of Appeals by the Media Advisory Committee (May 30, 1980).

Irvin v. Dowd 366 U.S. 717 (1961).

Izzett, R., and Leginski, W. (1974). Group Discussion and the Influence of Defendant Characteristics in a Simulated Jury Setting. *JOURNAL OF SOCIAL PSYCHOLOGY,* 93, 271–279.

Jacobs, T. (1980). The Chilling Effect in Press Cases: Judicial Thumb on the Scales. *HARVARD CIVIL RIGHTS-CIVIL LIBERTIES LAW REVIEW,* 15, 685–712.

Jacoubovitch, M.D., Bermant, G., Crockett, G., McKinley, W., and Sanstad, A. (1977). Juror Responses to Direct and Mediated Presentations of Expert Testimony. *JOURNAL OF APPLIED SOCIAL PSYCHOLOGY,* 7(3), 227–238.

Jaehnig, W. B., Weaver, D. H., and Fico, F. (1981). Reporting Crime and Fearing Crime in Three Communities. *JOURNAL OF COMMUNICATION,* 31, Winter, 88–96.

Jennings, J. M. (1982). Is *Chandler* a Final Rewrite of *Estes? JOURNALISM QUARTERLY,* 59(1), Spring, 66–73.

Jersey to Test TV in a Courtroom (1978). *NEW YORK TIMES,* November 26, p. 42, Col. 3.

Jersey's High Court Admits Cameras and TV as a Test (1978). *NEW YORK TIMES,* December 13, p. 4, Col. 1.

Joint Brief for *Amici Curiae* Radio Television News Directors Association, et al. (1979). Filed with the U.S. Supreme Court in *Chandler v. Florida,* October Term.

Jones, C., and Aronson, E. (1973). Attribution of Fault to a Rape Victim As a Function of

Respectability of the Victim. *JOURNAL OF PERSONALITY AND SOCIAL PSYCHOLOGY*, 26(3), 415–419.

Judicial Planning and Coordination Unit, Office of the State Courts Administrator, (1978). *A SAMPLE SURVEY OF THE ATTITUDES OF INDIVIDUALS ASSOCIATED WITH TRIALS INVOLVING ELECTRONIC MEDIA AND STILL PHOTOGRAPHY COVERAGE IN SELECTED FLORIDA COURTS BETWEEN JULY 5, 1977, AND JUNE 30, 1978.*

Juhnke, R., Vought, C., Pyszczynski, T., Dane, F., Losure, B., and Wrightsman, L. (1979). Effects of Presentation Mode Upon Mock Jurors' Reactions to a Trial. *PERSONALITY AND SOCIAL PSYCHOLOGY BULLETIN*, 5(1), 36–39.

Jurors Again Hear Maid's Testimony On First Coma (1982). *BOSTON GLOBE*, March 13, pp. 13–14.

Jurors Find Von Bulow Guilty of Trying Twice to Kill Wife (1982). *NEW YORK TIMES*, March 17, p. A1 and A18.

Jury Gets Two Portraits of Von Bulow: Anguished Husband, Crafty Villain (1982). *PROVIDENCE JOURNAL*, March 11, p. A1 and A12.

Jury Selection Must Be In Public (1984). *NEWS MEDIA AND THE LAW*, 8(1), January-February, p. 21.

Justices to Decide TV Trial Coverage (1980). *NEWS MEDIA AND THE LAW*, June-July, pp. 2–6.

Justices' Questions Suggest Split As Court Weighs Televised Trial (1980). *NEW YORK TIMES*, November 13, p. A24.

Kalven, H., and Zeisel, H. (1966). *THE AMERICAN JURY*. Boston: Little Brown and Company.

Kaminski, E. P., and Miller, G. R. (1984). How Jurors Respond to Video-Taped Witnesses. *JOURNAL OF COMMUNICATION*, 34(1), 88–102.

Kaplan, M. F., and Kemmerick, G. D. (1974). Juror Judgment as Information Integration: Combining Evidential and Nonevidential Information. *JOURNAL OF PERSONALITY AND SOCIAL PSYCHOLOGY*, 30(4), 493–499.

Katsh, E. (1983). The Supreme Court Beat: How Television Covers the U.S. Supreme Court. *JUDICATURE*, 67(1), June-July, pp. 6–12.

Katz, E., Adoni, H., and Parness, P. (1977). Remembering the News: What the Picture Adds to Recall. *JOURNALISM QUARTERLY*, 54, Summer, 231–239.

Katz, E., Blumler, J., and Gurevitch, M. (1973). Uses and Gratifications Research. *PUBLIC OPINION QUARTERLY*, 37, 509–523.

Kerr, N. L., Atkin, R., Stasser, G., Meek, D., Holt, R., Davis, J. (1976). Guilt Beyond a Reasonable Doubt: Effects of Concept Definition and Assigned Decision Rule on the Judgment of Mock Jurors. *JOURNAL OF PERSONALITY AND SOCIAL PSYCHOLOGY*, 34(2), 282–294.

Kielbowicz, R. B. (1979). The Story Behind the Adoption of the Ban on Courtroom Cameras. *JUDICATURE*, 63(1), June-July, pp. 14–23.

King v. State, 390 So.2d 315 (Fla. 1980).

Kline, G. F., and Jess, P. H. (1966). Prejudicial Publicity: Its Effect On Law School Mock Juries. *JOURNALISM QUARTERLY*, 43, 113–116.

Knight, R. A. (1936). Trial by Fury. *THE FORUM*, January, pp. 8–10.

Konecni, V. J., and Ebbesen, E. B. (1982). *THE CRIMINAL JUSTICE SYSTEM: A SOCIAL-PSYCHOLOGICAL ANALYSIS*. San Francisco: W. H. Freeman and Company.

Kornblum, G. O., and Rush, P. E. (1973). Television in the Courtroom and Classroom. *AMERICAN BAR ASSOCIATION JOURNAL,* 59, 273–276.

Kosky, I. (1975). Videotape in Ohio. *JUDICATURE,* 59(5), 230–238.

Krasno, M. (1983). Judicial Improvement: What's Going On in the States? *JUDICATURE,* 67(3), September, pp. 149–151.

Kulwin, S. B. (1978). Televised Trials: Constitutional Constraints, Practical Implications, and State Experimentation. *LOYOLA UNIVERSITY LAW JOURNAL,* 9, 910–934.

Kuriyama, D. N. (1982). The "Right of Information Triangle": A First Amendment Basis for Televising Judicial Proceedings. *UNIVERSITY OF HAWAII LAW REVIEW,* 4, 85–138.

La Blanc v. People, 161 Colo. 274, 421 P.2d 474 (1966).

Landau, J. C. (1976). Fair Trial and Free Press: A Due Process Proposal—The Challenge of the Communications Media. *AMERICAN BAR ASSOCIATION JOURNAL,* 62, January, pp. 55–60.

Landmark Communications, Inc., v. Virginia, 435 U.S. 829 (1978).

Landy, D., and Aronson, E. (1969). The Influence of the Character of the Criminal and His Victim on the Decision of Simulated Jurors. *JOURNAL OF EXPERIMENTAL SOCIAL PSYCHOLOGY,* 5(2), 141–152.

Law Poll (Cameras in the Courtroom)? (1982). *AMERICAN BAR ASSOCIATION JOURNAL,* 68, April, pp. 416–417.

Lawyers Defer Action on TV Trial Proposal (1978). *NEWS MEDIA AND THE LAW,* 2(3), October, p. 29.

League of Women Voters v. FCC, 8 Med.L.Rptr. 2081 (1982).

Legality of Secret Sex Trials Approved if Victim Under Eighteen (1980). *NEWS MEDIA AND THE LAW,* 4(3), August-September, pp. 5–6.

Lewis, D. A. (1981). *REACTIONS TO CRIME.* Beverly Hills, CA: Sage.

Lieberman, J. K. (1976). Will Courts Meet the Challenge of Technology. *JUDICATURE,* 60(2), 84–91.

Linde, H. (1977). Fair Trials and Press Freedom—Two Rights Against the State. WILLAMETTE LAW JOURNAL, 13(2), Spring, 211–220.

Lindquist, C. A. (1967). An Analysis of Juror Selection Procedures in United States District Courts. *TEMPLE LAW QUARTERLY,* 41, 32–50.

Lindsey, R. (1981). After 5 Years, Judges and Lawyers See Courts Adjusting to the Camera's Eye. *NEW YORK TIMES,* February 7, p. 6N.

Lindsey, R. P. (1984). Cameras in Court: An Assessment of the Use in State and Federal Courts. *GEORGIA LAW REVIEW,* 18, Winter, 389–424.

Lyles v. State, 330 P.2d 734 (Okla. Crim. App. 1958).

MacKuen, M. B., and Coombs, S. L. (1981). *MORE THAN NEWS: MEDIA POWER IN PUBLIC AFFAIRS.* Beverly Hill: Sage.

MacNeilly, M. D. (1976). The Electronic Courthouse. *JUDICATURE,* 60(4), 188–190.

Marshall, M. (1935). The Biggest Show on Earth. *THE NATION,* 140, January 23, pp. 93–94.

Martin, S. (1978). Cameras in the Courtroom: A Denial of Due Process? *BAYLOR LAW REVIEW,* 30, 853–864.

Maryland Experiment Begins Jan. 1 (1980). *NEWS PHOTOGRAPHER,* 35(13), December, p. 10.

Maryland v. Baltimore Radio Show, 338 U.S. 912 (1950).

McCall, A. V. (1956). Courtroom Television. *TEXAS BAR JOURNAL* 19(2), February, pp. 73–74, 106–110.

McClure, R. D., and Patterson, T. E. (1976). Print v. Network News. *JOURNAL OF COMMUNICATION,* 26(2), Spring, 23–28.

McCombs, M. E., and Shaw, D. L. (1972). The Agenda-Setting Function of Mass Media. *PUBLIC OPINION QUARTERLY,* 36(2), Summer, 176–187.

McCroskey, J. C., and Jensen, T. A. (1975). Image of Mass Media News Sources. *JOURNAL OF BROADCASTING,* 19(2), Spring, 169–180.

McCrystal, J. L. (1973). Videotape Trials: Relief for Our Congested Courts. *DENVER LAW JOURNAL,* 49, 463–488.

McCrystal, J. L. (1974). The Videotape Trial Comes of Age. *JUDICATURE,* 57(10), 446–449.

McCrystal, J. L. (1977). The Promise of Prerecorded Videotape Trials. *AMERICAN BAR ASSOCIATION JOURNAL,* 63, 977–979.

McCrystal, J. L. (1978). Videotaped Trials: A Primer. *JUDICATURE,* 61(6), 250–256.

Merry, G. B. (1981). More States Clear Way for TV to Record Trial Proceedings. *CHRISTIAN SCIENCE MONITOR,* May 27, p. 5.

Middleton, M. (1982). Delegates Broaden Rules on Cameras in Court. *AMERICAN BAR ASSOCIATION JOURNAL,* 68, October, pp. 1199–1200.

Miller, G. R., and Boster, F. J. (1977). Three Images of the Trial: Their Implications for Psychological Research. In D. B. Sales (Ed.), *PSYCHOLOGY IN THE LEGAL PROCESS.* New York: Spectrum Publications, Inc.

Miller, E. J. (1980). In Video Veritas. *BOSTON BAR JOURNAL,* 24, 21–25.

Miller, G. R., and Bundens, R. W. (1982). Juries and Communication. In B. Dervin and M. J. Voigt (Eds.), *PROGRESS IN COMMUNICATION SCIENCES,* Vol. 3. Norwood, N J: Ablex Publishing Corporation.

Miller, G. R., and Fontes, N. E. (1979). *VIDEOTAPE ON TRIAL: A VIEW FROM THE JURY BOX.* Beverly Hills, CA: Sage.

Mills, C. J., and Bohannon, W. E. (1980). Juror Characteristics: To What Extent Are They Related to Jury Verdicts? *JUDICATURE,* 64(1), 22–31.

Mirror of Opinion: Courtroom Cameras (1979). *CHRISTIAN SCIENCE MONITOR,* May 8, p. 19.

Mitchell, H. E., and Byrne, D. (1973). The Defendant's Dilemma: Effects of Jurors' Attitudes and Authoritarianism on Judicial Decisions. *JOURNAL OF PERSONALITY AND SOCIAL PSYCHOLOGY,* 25(1), 123–129.

Moffat, D. W. (1945). As Jurors See a Lawsuit. *OREGON LAW REVIEW,* 24, 199–207.

Morrow, B. (1980). Judicial Council Could Cancel or Delay Cameras in California's Courtrooms. *LOS ANGELES DAILY JOURNAL,* 93, April 25, pp. 1 and 23.

Mounts, Judge M., Jr. (1978). *REPORT TO THE SUPREME COURT OF FLORIDA CONCERNING AUDIO-VISUAL TRIAL COVERAGE, State v. Martin.*

Mrs. Von Bulow's Doctor Says Her Health Was Good (1982). *PROVIDENCE JOURNAL,* February 20, p. A1 and A18.

Mundt, W. R. (1980). One Step Forward, Two Steps Back: An Update on Cameras in Louisiana Courtrooms. *LSU RESEARCH BULLETIN,* 3(1), (LSU School of Journalism).

Murray, T. J. (1972). First Videotape Trial: Experiment in Ohio. *DEFENSE LAW JOURNAL,* 21(3), 276–279.

Murray, T. J. (1978). Videotaped Depositions: The Ohio Experience. *JUDICATURE*, 61(6), 258–261.

Mystery Witness for von Bulow (1982). *BOSTON GLOBE*, March 18, p. 24.

N.Y. Chief Judge Supports Television Coverage (1982). *NEW JERSEY LAW JOURNAL*, June 24, p. 7.

Nagel, S. (1979). Bringing the Values of Jurors in Line With the Law. *JUDICATURE*, 63(4), 189–195.

NBC Didn't Incite Attack Acquittal Review Denied (1982). *NEWS MEDIA AND THE LAW*, 6(3), September-October, p. 49.

Nebraska Press Association v. Stuart, 427 U.S. 539 (1976).

Nemeth, C. (1977). Interaction Between Jurors as a Function of Majority vs. Unanimity Decision Rules. *JOURNAL OF APPLIED SOCIAL PSYCHOLOGY*, 7(1), 38–56.

Nemeth, C., and Sosis, R. (1973). A Simulated Jury: Characteristics of the Defendant and Jurors. *JOURNAL OF SOCIAL PSYCHOLOGY*, 90, 221–229.

Nesson, C. R., and Koblenz, A. D. (1981). The Image of Justice: Chandler v. Florida. *HARVARD CIVIL RIGHTS-CIVIL LIBERTIES LAW REVIEW*, 16, Fall, 405–413.

Netteburg, K. (1980). Does Research Support the Estes Ban on Cameras in the Courtroom? *JUDICATURE*, 63(10), May, pp. 467–475.

Neuman, W. R. (1976). Patterns of Recall Among Television News Viewers. *PUBLIC OPINION QUARTERLY*, 40, 115–123.

New Bedford Rape: Rejecting "the Myth" (1984). *NEWSWEEK*, March 26, p. 39.

New State Ice Co. v. Liebmann, 285 U.S. 262 (1932).

New York Times v. Sullivan, 376 U.S. 254 (1964).

Newland, C. A. (1964). Press Coverage of the United States Supreme Court. *WESTERN POLITICAL QUARTERLY*, 17, 15–36.

News Media Hoping for Turnaround in Gannett Case (1979). *BROADCASTING*, December 17, p. 72.

Nicholas v. Henderson, 389 F.2d 990 (6th Cir. 1968), *cert. denied* 393 U.S. 955 (1968).

Niemi v. NBC, 74 Cal. App.3d 383 (1977), *cert. denied*, 46 U.S.L.W. 3659 (U.S. April 24, 1978), No. 681-035 (Cal. Super. Ct. Aug. 9, 1978, dismissed).

Nimmo, D., and Sanders, K., Eds. (1981). *HANDBOOK OF POLITICAL COMMUNICATION*. Beverly, CA: Sage.

Nixon v. Warner Communications, 435 U.S. 589 (1978); 551 F.2d 1252 (D.C. Cir. 1976).

Nixon Watergate Tapes Sealed (1978). *NEWS MEDIA AND THE LAW*, 2(2), July, pp. 19–20.

No von Bulow Verdict Yet (1982). *PROVIDENCE JOURNAL*, March 13, p. A1 and A18.

Nye v. United States, 313 U.S. 33 (1941).

O'Brien, D. M. (1980a). Reassessing the First Amendment and the Public's Right to Know in Constitutional Adjudication. *VILLANOVA LAW REVIEW*, 26(1), November, pp. 1–62.

O'Brien, D. M. (1980b). The Seduction of the Judiciary: Social Science and the Courts. *JUDICATURE*, 64(1), 8–21.

O'Brien, T. (1983). Yes, but . . ." (a response to Ethan Katsh, "The Supreme Court Beat. . ."). *JUDICATURE*, 67(1), June–July, pp. 12–15.

O'Keefe, G. J. (1984). Public Views on Crime: Television Exposure and Media Credibility.

In R. N. Bostrom (ed.), *COMMUNICATION YEARBOOK 8*. Beverly Hills, CA: Sage, 514–535.

Ohio Court Nears Decision to Permit TV Coverage of Trials (1978). *NEW YORK TIMES*, December 10, p. 101, Col. 2.

Olson, E. (1980). U.S. High Court to Rule on T.V. Airing of Criminal Trials. *NEW JERSEY LAW JOURNAL*, 105, May 8, p. 5.

Open and Shut Cases (1979). *NEWSWEEK*, August 27, p. 69.

Owles, D. (1980). U.S. Legal News: Cameras in Court. *NEW LAW JOURNAL*, 130, December 4, p. 1136.

Owles, D. (1982). Annual Meeting of the American Bar Association (Cameras in the Courtroom). *NEW LAW JOURNAL*, 132, October 21, pp. 985–986.

Padawer-Singer, A. M., Singer, A. N., and Singer, R. (1977). Legal and Social-Psychological Research in the Effects of Pre-Trial Publicity on Juries, Numerical Make-Up of Juries, Non-Unanimous Verdict Requirements. *LAW AND PSYCHOLOGY REVIEW*, 3, 71–79.

Paul v. Davis, 424 U.S. 693 (1976).

Paul, D., and Kamp, S. (1982). Access in Florida: The Sunshine State of Mind. *FLORIDA BAR JOURNAL*, 56, March, pp. 233–238.

Pember, D. R. (1984). *MASS MEDIA LAW*, 3d. Dubuque, IA: Wm. C. Brown.

Pennekamp v. Florida, 328 U.S. 331 (1946).

People v. Jelke, 123 N.E.2d 769 (1954).

People v. Latimore, 33 Ill. App. 3rd 812, 342 N.E. 2d 209 (1975).

People v. Munday, 280 Ill. 32; 117 N.E. 286 (1917).

Pequignot, M. (1981). From *Estes* to *Chandler:* Shifting the Constitutional Burden of Courtroom Cameras to the States. *FLORIDA STATE UNIVERSITY LAW REVIEW*, 9, 315–350.

Perloff, R. M., Wartella, E. A., and Becker, L. B. (1982). Increasing Learning from TV News. *JOURNALISM QUARTERLY*, 59, Spring, 83–86.

Petition of Post-Newsweek Stations, Florida, Inc. for Change in Code of Judicial Conduct, 370 So.2d 764 (Fla., April 12, 1979).

Petition of Post-Newsweek Stations, Florida, Inc., Fla. 347 So.2d 404 (1977).

Phillips, D., and Hensley, J. (1984). When Violence is Rewarded or Punished: the Impact of Mass Media Stories on Homicide. *JOURNAL OF COMMUNICATION*, 34(3), Summer, pp. 101–116.

Pike, D. F. (1981). Victory for Cameras in Courtroom: Justices See No Constitutional Bar. *NATIONAL LAW JOURNAL*, February 9, p. 5.

Platte, M. K. (1981). TV in the Courtroom: Right of Access? *COMMUNICATIONS AND THE LAW*, 3(1), Winter, pp. 11–29.

Policeman Testifies On What Two Big Dan's Defendants Said. (1984). *BOSTON GLOBE*, March 5, pp. 13–16.

Poll Finds Rise in Hope For Future of New York (1978). *NEW YORK TIMES*, January 3, p. 1 and p. 25.

Pool Table Sex Assault Charged to Boy, Twelve (1984). *NEW YORK TIMES*, April 18, p. A14.

Portman, S. (1977). The Defense of Fair Trial from *Sheppard* to *Nebraska Press Association:* Benign Neglect to Affirmative Action and Beyond. *STANFORD LAW REVIEW*, 29, February, pp. 393–410.

Power, R. W. Television in the Courtroom: Von Bulow and *The Jazz Singer* (1982). *SAINT LOUIS UNIVERSITY LAW JOURNAL, 25, 813–820.*

Press Enterprise Co. v. Superior Court, 52 U.S.L.W. 4113 (1984).

Pressman, S. (1980). Consent to Cameras Seen as Malpractice Violation. *LOS ANGELES DAILY JOURNAL, 93,* May 14, p. 1, col. 6.

Prosser, W. L. (1961). The Lindbergh Case Revisited: George Waller's "Kidnap." *MINNESOTA LAW REVIEW, 46, 383–391.*

Pryor, B., and Buchanan, R. (1984). The Effects of a Defendant's Demeanor on Juror Perceptions of Credibility and Guilt. *JOURNAL OF COMMUNICATION, 34(3),* Summer, pp. 92–99.

Pryor, B., Strawn, D., Buchanan, R., and Meeske, M. (1979). The Florida Experiment: An Analysis of On-the-Scene Responses to Cameras in the Courtroom. *SOUTHERN SPEECH COMMUNICATION JOURNAL, 45,* Fall, 12–26.

Pryor, B., Taylor, K. P., Buchanan, R., and Strawn, D. (1980). An Affective-Cognitive Consistency Explanation for Comprehension of Standard Jury Instructions. *COMMUNICATION MONOGRAPHS, 47(1), 68–76.*

Questions About Exercise Teacher Add to Mystery of Von Bulow's Trial (1982). *PROVIDENCE JOURNAL,* March 8, p. A16.

Quiat, M. (1960). The Freedom of Pressure and the Explosive Canon 35. *ROCKY MOUNTAIN LAW REVIEW, 33,* 10–22.

Radio, TV and Photo Coverage of Courts Can Be Allowed by States, Justices Rule (1981). *WALL STREET JOURNAL,* January 27, p. 4.

Radio, TV Coverage of Senate Floor Proceedings Begins Soon (1986). *NEWS MEDIA AND THE LAW,* 10(1), Spring, pp. 3–4.

Radio-TV News Directors Association (1984). News Media Coverage of Judicial Proceedings With Cameras and Microphones: A Survey of the States, July 1.

Ranii, D. (1984). Cameras Come to Court: Rapid Acceptance Follows Tryouts. *NATIONAL LAW JOURNAL,* January 30, pp. 1, 8 and 10.

Rape Trial Tape Privileged (1984). *NEWS MEDIA AND THE LAW,* 8(1), January-February, p. 43.

Rape Trial Testimony Raises ID Questions (1984). *BOSTON GLOBE,* March 7, pp. 17 and 20.

Rape Trial: Justice Crucified? (1984). *NEWSWEEK,* April 2, p. 39.

Re Seed, 140 N.Y. Misc. 681, 251 N.Y.S. 615 (1931).

Reaves, L. (1983). "Cameras in Court: Colorado Test Pleases Judge. *AMERICAN BAR ASSOCIATION JOURNAL, 69,* September, p. 1213.

Red Lion Broadcasting Co. v. FCC, 395 U.S. 367 (1969).

Reed, D. (1967). Canon 35: Flemington Revisited. *FREEDOM OF INFORMATION CENTER REPORT,* No. 177, March, pp. 1–5.

Reed, J. P. (1965). Jury Deliberations, Voting, and Verdict Trends. *THE SOUTHWESTERN SOCIAL SCIENCE QUARTERLY, 45,* 361–370.

Regan v. Time, Inc., 104 S.Ct. 3262 (1984).

REPORT AND RECOMMENDATIONS OF THE AD HOC COMMITTEE OF THE BAR ASSOCIATION OF GREATER CLEVELAND ON THE EFFECT OF CAMERAS IN THE COURTROOM ON THE PARTICIPANTS IN SUCH A TRIAL (1980).

REPORT OF THE ADVISORY COMMITTEE TO OVERSEE THE EXPERIMENTAL USE OF CAMERAS AND RECORDING EQUIPMENT IN COURTROOMS TO THE SUPREME JUDICIAL COURT OF MASSACHUSETTS (July 16, 1982).

REPORT OF THE CHIEF COURT ADMINISTRATOR ON THE "CAMERAS-IN-THE-COURT" EXPERIMENT OF THE STATE OF CONNECTICUT (May 1, 1983).

REPORT OF THE PRESIDENT'S COMMISSION ON THE ASSASSINATION OF PRESIDENT JOHN F. KENNEDY (1964).

Report of the Special Committee on Cooperation Between Press, Radio and Bar as to Publicity Interfering with Fair Trial of Judicial and Quasi-Judicial Proceedings. (1937). *AMERICAN BAR ASSOCIATION REPORTS,* 62, 1134–1135.

Report of the Surgeon General's Scientific Advisory Committee on Television and Social Behavior (1972). Television and Growing Up: the Impact of Televised Violence.

REPORT OF THE WISCONSIN SUPREME COURT COMMITTEE TO MONITOR AND EVALUATE THE USE OF AUDIO AND VISUAL EQUIPMENT IN THE COURTROOM (April 1, 1979).

Revised Report of the Judicial Conference Committee on the Operation of the Jury System on the 'Free Press-Fair Trial' Issue, 87 F.R.D. 518 (approved by the U.S. Judicial Conference, September 25, 1980).

Reyes, R., Thompson, W., and Bower, G. (1980). Judgmental Biases Resulting From Differing Availabilities of Arguments. *JOURNAL OF PERSONALITY AND SOCIAL PSYCHOLOGY,* 39(1), 2–12.

Reynolds v. U.S., 98 U.S. 145 (1878).

Richmond Newspapers, Inc. v. Commonwealth of Virginia, 448 U.S. 555 (1980).

Rideau v. Louisiana, 373 U.S. 723 (1963).

Roberts, M. L., and Goodman, W. R. (1976). The Televised Trial: A Perspective. *CUMBERLAND LAW REVIEW,* 7, 323–342.

Rogers, E. M., and Argarwala-Rogers, R. (1976). *COMMUNICATION IN ORGANIZATIONS.* New York: Free Press.

Roney, P. H. (1976). Fair Trial and Free Press: A Due Process Proposal—The Bar Answers the Challenge. *AMERICAN BAR ASSOCIATION JOURNAL,* 62, January, pp. 60–64.

Roper Organization, Inc. (1984). *PUBLIC ATTITUDES TOWARD TELEVISION AND OTHER MEDIA IN A TIME OF CHANGE.* New York: Television Information Office of the National Association of Broadcasters.

Rosenbaum, M., and Levin, I. (1968). Impression Formation as a Function of Source Credibility and Order of Presentation of Contradictory Information. *JOURNAL OF PERSONALITY AND SOCIAL PSYCHOLOGY,* 10(2), 167–174.

Roshier, Bob (1973). The Selection of Crime News By the Press. In Stanley Cohen and Jock Young (Eds.), *THE MANUFACTURE OF NEWS.* Beverly Hills, CA: Sage, 28–39.

Rubin, A. M. (1981). An Examination of Television Viewing Motivations. *COMMUNICATION RESEARCH,* 8, April, pp. 141–165.

Rubin, A. M. (1983). Television Uses and Gratifications: The Interaction of Viewing Patterns and Motivations. *JOURNAL OF BROADCASTING,* 27(1), Winter, 37–51.

Safe Testimony: TV Screens for Child Witnesses (1985). *TIME,* July 3, p. 64.

Salvan, S. A. (1975). Videotape for the Legal Community. *JUDICATURE,* 59(5), 222–229.

Sanford, B. W. (1980). Richmond Newspapers: End of a Zigzag Trail? *COLUMBIA JOURNALISM REVIEW,* September-October, pp. 46–47.

Schmidt, B. C. (1977). *Nebraska Press Association:* An Expansion of Freedom and Contraction of Theory. *STANFORD LAW REVIEW,* 29, February, pp. 431–476.

Secret Court Watch (1979). *NEWS MEDIA AND THE LAW,* 3(4), November-December, pp. 17–23.

Secret Pretrial Proceedings Upheld (1979). *NEWS MEDIA AND THE LAW,* 3(3), August-September, pp. 2–4.

Senate's Turn for "TV or not TV" (1981). *BROADCASTING,* April 13, pp. 29–30.

Settle, M. L. (1972). *THE SCOPES TRIAL.* New York: Franklin Watts, Inc.

Shaw, D. (1981). Media Coverage of the Courts: Improving But Still Not Adequate. *JUDICATURE,* 65(1), June-July, pp. 18–24.

Sheley, J. F., and Ashkins, C. D. (1981). Crime, Crime News and Crime Views. *PUBLIC OPINION QUARTERLY,* 45, 492–506.

Sheppard v. Maxwell, 384 U.S. 333 (1966).

Sheppard v. State, 135 N.E. 2d 340 (1955).

Sholts, Judge T. E. (1978). *REPORT TO THE SUPREME COURT OF FLORIDA RE: AUDIO-VISUAL TRIAL COVERAGE, State v. Herman.*

Showdown Draws Overflow Audience (1982). *PROVIDENCE JOURNAL,* March 11, p. A12, 1.

Sigall, H., and Ostrove, N. (1975). Beautiful But Dangerous: Effects of Offender Attractiveness and Nature of the Crime On Juridic Judgment. *JOURNAL OF PERSONALITY AND SOCIAL PSYCHOLOGY,* 31(3), 410–414.

Simon, R. (1968). The Effects of Newspapers on the Verdicts of Potential Jurors. In R. Simon (Ed.), *THE SOCIOLOGY OF THE LAW.* San Francisco: Chandler Publishing Company, 617–627.

Simon, R., and Eimermann, T. (1971). The Jury Finds Not Guilty: Another Look at Media Influence on the Jury. *JOURNALISM QUARTERLY,* 48, 343–344.

Sims, T. E. (1976). Teletest. *JUDICATURE,* 59(9), 434–437.

Skogan, W. G., and Maxfield, M. E. (1981). *COPING WITH CRIME: VICTIMIZATION, FEAR AND REACTIONS TO CRIME IN THREE AMERICAN CITIES.* Beverly Hills, CA: Sage.

Slater, D., and Elliott, W. R. (1982). Television's Influence on Social Reality. *QUARTERLY JOURNAL OF SPEECH,* 68, 69–79.

Slater, D., and Hans, V. P. (1982). Methodological Issues in the Evaluation of "Experiments" With Cameras in the Courts. *COMMUNICATION QUARTERLY,* 39(4), 376–380.

Smiley, R. (1977). Use of Videotape in Aviation Accident Liability Trials. *ABA-FORUM,* 13(1), 191–205.

Smith v. Daily Mail Publishing Co., 443 U.S. 97 (1979).

Sobel, L. S. (1970). News Coverage of the Supreme Court. *AMERICAN BAR ASSOCIATION JOURNAL,* 56, June, pp. 547–550.

Sosis, R. H. (1974). Internal-External Control and the Perception of Responsibility of Another for an Accident. *JOURNAL OF PERSONALITY AND SOCIAL PSYCHOLOGY,* 30(3), 393–399.

Spain, T. B., Fuqua, W., Shobe, B., and Venters, E. (1981). Closing Criminal Trials: A Report of the Kentucky Circuit Judges' Association's Committee. *KENTUCKY BENCH AND BAR,* 45(2), January, pp. 20 and 41.

Spaniolo, J. D., and D'Alemberte, T. (1981). Despite "Cameras" Ruling, Some Questions Persist. *PRESSTIME,* March, pp. 16–17.

Sperlich, P. W. (1980a). And Then There Were Six: The Decline of the American Jury. *JUDICATURE,* 63(6), 262–279.

Sperlich, P. W. (1980b). Postrealism: Should Ignorance be Elevated to a Principle of Adjudication?" *JUDICATURE,* 64(2), 93–98.

Sperlich, P. W. (1980c). Social Science Evidence and the Courts: Reaching Beyond the Adversary Process. *JUDICATURE*, 63(6), 280–289.

Spies v. Illinois, 123 U.S. 131 (1887).

Stanga, J. E., Jr., (1971). Judicial Protection of the Criminal Defendant Against Adverse Press Coverage. *WILLIAM AND MARY LAW REVIEW*, 13, (1), Fall, 1–74.

State ex rel. Grinnell Communications Corp. v. Love, 62 Ohio St. 2d 399, 406 N.E. 2d 809 (1980).

State ex. rel. Miami Valley Broadcasting Corp. v. Kessler, 64 Ohio St. 2d 165, 413 N.E. 2d 1203 (1980).

State v. Clifford, 118 N.E.2d 853 (Ohio Ct. App. 1954) *aff'd* 123 N.E.2d 8 (Ohio Sup. Ct. 1954), *cert. denied* 349 U.S. 929 (1955).

State v. Green, 395 So.2d 532 (Fla. 1981).

State v. Hauptmann, 115 N.J.L. 412, 180 A. 809 (1935).

State v. Palm Beach Newspapers, Inc., 395 So.2d 544 (Fla. 1981).

States May Allow Cameras in Courtrooms (1981). *NEWS MEDIA AND THE LAW*, 5(2), February-March, pp. 5–6.

Stauffer, J., Frost, R., and Rybolt W. (1983). The Attention Factor in Recalling Network Television News. *JOURNAL OF COMMUNICATION*, 33(1), Winter, 29–37.

Stauffer, J., Frost, R., and Rybolt, W. (1981). Recall and Learning from Broadcast News: Is Print Better? *JOURNAL OF BROADCASTING*, 25(3), Summer, 253–262.

Stefaniak, G. (1984). Indiana Legal Leaders' Perceptions of Camera Trial Access Arguments. *JOURNALISM QUARTERLY*, 61(2), Summer, 399–403.

Stern, C. (1976). Free Press/Fair Trial: The Role of the News Media in Developing and Advancing Constitutional Process. *OKLAHOMA LAW REVIEW*, 29, 349–360.

Stevenson v. Commonwealth, 218 Va. 462, 237 S.E. 779 (1977).

Stone, W., and Edlin, S. (1978). T.V. or Not T.V.: Televised and Photographic Coverage of Trials. *MERCER LAW REVIEW*, 29, 1119–1135.

Strawn, D., and Buchanan, R. (1976). Jury Confusion: A Threat to Justice. *JUDICATURE*, 59(10), 478–483.

Strawn, D., Buchanan, R., Meeske, M., and Pryor, B. (1978). *REPORT TO THE FLORIDA SUPREME COURT IN RE: PETITION OF POST-NEWSWEEK STATIONS, FLORIDA, INC., FOR CHANGE IN CODE OF JUDICIAL CONDUCT.*

Strawn, D., Buchanan, R., Pryor, B., and Taylor, K. P. (1977). Reaching a Verdict, Step by Step. *JUDICATURE*, 60(8), 383–389.

Stroble v. California, 343 U.S. 181 (1952).

Study Shows State Jurists Favor Cameras in Courts (1979). *NEWS MEDIA AND THE LAW*, 3(2), May-June, pp. 20–21.

Sue, S., Smith, R. E., and Caldwell, C. (1973). Effects of Inadmissiable Evidence On the Decisions of Simulated Jurors: A Moral Dilemma. *JOURNAL OF APPLIED SOCIAL PSYCHOLOGY*, 3, 345–353.

SUMMARY OF CAMERAS IN STATE COURTS (January 15, 1985). Compiled by the Research and Information Service, National Center for State Courts, Williamsburg, VA.

Sunny is Linked to Insulin Shots (1982). *BOSTON HERALD AMERICAN*, March 4, p. 5.

Tajgman, D. (1981). From *Estes* to *Chandler:* The Distinction Between Television and Newspaper Trial Coverage. *COMM/ENT*, 3(3), 503–541.

Tamborini, R., Zillman, D., and Bryant, J. (1984). Fear and Victimization: Exposure to

Television and Perceptions of Crime and Fear. In R. N. Bostrom (Ed.) *COMMUNICA-TION YEARBOOK 8.* Beverly Hills, CA: Sage, 492–513.

Tanke, E. D., and Tanke, T. J. (1979). Getting Off a Slippery Slope. *AMERICAN PSYCHOLOGIST,* 34(12), 1130–1138.

Tans, M., and Chaffee, S. (1966). Pretrial Publicity and Juror Prejudice. *JOURNALISM QUARTERLY,* 43, 647–654.

Taped Testimony Urged In Abuse Cases (1984). *BOSTON GLOBE,* November 17, p. 25.

Tarpley, J. (1984). American Newsmagazine Coverage of the Supreme Court. *JOURNALISM QUARTERLY,* 61(4), Winter, pp. 801–804.

Television Coverage in the State Courts: An Update (1983). *STATE COURT JOURNAL,* 7, Spring, 13–15.

Television in the Courtroom—Limited Benefits, Vital Risks? (1981). *COMMUNICATIONS AND THE LAW,* 3(1), Winter, 35–50.

Television in the Courts (1978). *WASHINGTON POST,* February 19, p. C6, col. 1.

Tello, S. (1977). Photojournalism Stands Trial With Ronny Zamora in Florida. *NEWS PHOTOGRAPHER,* 32(11), November, pp. 10–12.

The Big Dan's Rape: A Copycat Crime (1984). *NEWSWEEK,* April 30, p. 25.

The Day After: Newport Turns Tranquil Again (1982). *BOSTON GLOBE,* March 18, p. 24.

The Greatest Show on Earth? (1982). *NEWS MEDIA AND THE LAW,* 6(2), June-July, p. 41.

The Jury Finds the Defendant, Claus von Bulow, Guilty (1982). *BOSTON GLOBE,* March 17, pp. 1, 24 and 28.

The Plague of Violent Crime (1981). *NEWSWEEK,* March 23, pp. 46–54.

The Verdict Was Guilty (1982). *BOSTON HERALD AMERICAN,* March 17, pp. 1, 4–5, and 26–27.

Thompson, S. G. (1982). Electronic Media in the Courtroom: Some Observations on Federalism and State Experimentation. *OHIO NORTHERN UNIVERSITY LAW REVIEW,* 9(3), 349–368.

Tichenor, P. J., Donohue, G. A., Olien, C. N. (1970). Mass Media Flow and Differential Growth in Knowledge. *PUBLIC OPINION QUARTERLY,* 34(2), Summer, 159–170.

Toledo Newspaper Company v. United States, 247 U.S. 402 (1918).

Tongue, T., and Lintott, R. (1980). The Case Against Television in the Courtroom. *WILLAMETTE LAW REVIEW,* 16, 777–801.

Townend, D. W. (1981). Cameras in the Courtroom: Let's Give Them Another Try. *TEXAS BAR JOURNAL,* April, pp. 374–380.

Toxicologist Says Woman Had Eight Drinks (1984). *BOSTON GLOBE,* March 16, pp. 21 and 24.

Trial Coverage Before Court (1980). *NEWS PHOTOGRAPHER,* 35(13), December, pp. 8–10.

Tumey v. Ohio 273 U.S. 510 (1927).

Turner v. Louisiana, 379 U.S. 466 (1965).

TV Cameras May Calm Young Witnesses (1984). *LOS ANGELES DAILY JOURNAL,* June 1.

TV in Senate Debated (1983). *NEWS MEDIA AND THE LAW,* 7(2), September-October, p. 53.

TV ON TRIAL (1978). A transcript of the program "TV On Trial" broadcast by PBS station WPBT, Miami, Florida, May 23, 1978. Kent, OH: PTV Publications.

TV Seeks Access to Federal Courts (1983). *NEWS MEDIA AND THE LAW,* 7(2), September-October, p. 51.

TV to Start in Congress, But Probably With House Control of News Content (1977). *NEWS MEDIA AND THE LAW,* 1(2), December, pp. 27–28.

TV-Radio Coverage in Court Endorsed (1980). *NEW YORK TIMES,* January 26, p. 1, col. 1 and p. 24, col 1.

Two Convicted in Big Dan's Rape (1984). *BOSTON GLOBE,* March 18, pp. 1 and 26.

U.S. Department of Health and Human Services (1982). *TELEVISION AND BEHAVIOR: TEN YEARS OF SCIENTIFIC PROGRESS AND IMPLICATIONS FOR THE EIGHTIES.* Washington, D.C.

U.S. Justices Sharply Restrict Secrecy in Selection of Juries (1984). *NEW YORK TIMES,* January 19, p. A1, col. 1.

U.S. Supreme Court Affirms Open Trial Guarantee (1980). *NEWS MEDIA AND THE LAW,* 4(3), August-September, pp. 2-4.

U.S. Supreme Court Rules that Courts and Judges are Public Issues (1979). *NEWS MEDIA AND THE LAW,* 3(3), January, p. 10.

U.S. Supreme Court Takes Jury Selection Case (1983). *NEWS MEDIA AND THE LAW,* 7(1), March-April, p. 6.

U.S. Supreme Court to Rule if Criminal Trials May Be Closed to Public and Press (1980). *NEWS MEDIA AND THE LAW,* 4(2), March-April, pp. 4–5.

U.S. Supreme Court Upholds Broad Pretrial Secrecy (1980). *NEWS MEDIA AND THE LAW,* 4(2), March-April, pp. 7–8.

U.S. v. Dickinson, 465 F.2d 496 (5th Cir. 1972) *cert. denied,* 414 U.S. 797 (1973).

United Press Association v. Valente, 308 N.Y. 71, 123 N.E.2d 777 (1954).

United States ex rel. Latimore v. Sielaff, 561 F.2d 691 (7th Cir. 1977), *cert. denied,* 434 U.S. 1076 (1978).

United States v. CBS, 497 F.2d 102 (5th Cir. 1974).

United States v. Criden 501 F. Supp. 854 (F.D. Pa. 1980); 648 F.2d 814 (3d Cir. 1981).

United States v. Haldeman, 559 F.2d 31 (D.C. Cir. 1976).

United States v. Hastings, 695 F.2d 1278 (11th Cir.), *cert. denied,* 103 S.Ct. 1188 (1983).

United States v. Mitchell, 551 F.2d 1252 (D.C. Cir. 1976).

Valenti, A. C., and Downing, L. L. (1975). Differential Effects of Jury Size On Verdicts Following Deliberation As a Function of the Apparent Guilt of a Defendant. *JOURNAL OF PERSONALITY AND SOCIAL PSYCHOLOGY,* 32(4), 655–663.

Voboril, M. (1980). Cameras On Trial. *COLUMBIA JOURNALISM REVIEW,* September-October, p. 12.

Von Bulow Cult Grows (1982). *BOSTON HERALD AMERICAN,* March 18, pp. 4–5.

Von Bulow Judge Outlines the Law and the Vigil Begins in Newport (1982). *PROVIDENCE JOURNAL,* March 12, p. A1 and A16.

Von Bulow's Defense Weighing Strategy (1982). *PROVIDENCE JOURNAL,* March 2, p. A1 and A14.

Wakshlag, J., Bart, L., Dudley, J., McCutcheon, J., and Rolla, C. (1983a). Viewer Apprehension About Victimization and the Appreciation of Crime Drama Programs. *COMMUNICATION RESEARCH,* 10(2), 195–217.

Wakshlag, J., Vial, V., and Tamborini, R. (1983b). Selecting Crime Drama and Apprehension About Crime. *HUMAN COMMUNICATION RESEARCH,* 10(2), Winter, 227–242.

Walker, L., Thibault, J., and Andreoli, V. (1972). Order of Presentation At Trial. *YALE LAW JOURNAL*, 82, 216–226.

Waller v. Georgia, 10 Med.L.Rptr. 1714 (1984).

Warren, S., and Brandeis, L. (1890). The Right to Privacy. *HARVARD LAW REVIEW*, 4(5), December, pp. 193–220.

Wasby, S. L. (1979). Laying *Estes* to Rest: A Case Note. *JUSTICE SYSTEM JOURNAL*, 5, 58–69.

WASHINGTON BENCH-BAR-PRESS COMMITTEE, SUBCOMMITTEE ON CANON 35, REPORT (April 5, 1975).

Washington State Superior Court Judges' Association Committee on Courts and Community, (1978). *CAMERAS IN THE COURTROOM—A TWO YEAR REVIEW IN THE STATE OF WASHINGTON*.

Weaver, D. (1984). Media Agenda-Setting and Public Opinion: Is There a Link? In R. N. Bostrom (ed.) *COMMUNICATION YEARBOOK 8*. Beverly Hills, CA: Sage, 680–691.

Weingarten, G. (1980). Riot Puts TV Court Coverage on Trial. *NATIONAL LAW JOURNAL*, 2, June 2, p. 10.

Weinstein, J. B., and Zimmerman, D. L. (1977). Let the People Observe Their Courts. *JUDICATURE*, 61(4), October, pp. 156–165.

Weisberger, J. R. (1983). Cameras in the Courtroom: The Rhode Island Experience. *SUFFOLK UNIVERSITY LAW REVIEW*, 17(2), 299–311.

Weld, H., and Danzig, E. (1940). A Study of the Way in Which a Verdict Is Reached By a Jury. *AMERICAN JOURNAL OF PSYCHOLOGY*, 53, 518–536.

Wesolowski, J. W. (1975). Before Canon 35: WGN Broadcasts the Monkey Trial. *JOURNALISM HISTORY*, 2(76), 76–87.

Whalen v. Roe, 429 U.S. 589 (1977).

When News Becomes Voyeurism (1984). *TIME*, March 26, p. 64.

Whisenand, J. D. (1978a). Cameras and Courtrooms: Fair Trial-Free Press Standards. *FLORIDA BAR JOURNAL*, 52(6), June, pp. 456–459.

Whisenand, J. D. (1978b). Florida's Experience With Cameras in the Courtroom. *AMERICAN BAR ASSOCIATION JOURNAL*, 64, December, pp. 1860–1864.

White, F. W. (1979). Cameras in the Courtroom: A U.S. Survey. *JOURNALISM MONOGRAPHS*, 60, April, pp. 1–41.

Widen Use of Cameras in State Courts (1984). *NEW YORK LAW JOURNAL*, June 18, p. 1, col. 2.

Wilson, D. B. (1984). A Trial Not Fit for TV Screens. *BOSTON GLOBE*, May 29.

Wilson, J. (1974). Justice in Living Color: The Case for Courtroom Television. *AMERICAN BAR ASSOCIATION*, 60, March, pp. 294–297.

Winick, C. (1961). The Psychology of Juries. In H. Toch (Ed.), *LEGAL AND CRIMINAL PSYCHOLOGY*. New York: Holt, Rinehart and Winston.

Winter, B. (1981). Cameras in the Courtroom: What Next After *Chandler?* *AMERICAN BAR ASSOCIATION JOURNAL*, 67, March, pp. 277–279.

Witt, E. (1981). Television in the Courtroom. *EDITORIAL RESEARCH REPORTS*, 1(2), January 16, pp. 18–36.

Wood v. Georgia, 370 U.S. 375 (1962).

Wright, J.S. (1964). A Judge's View: The News Media and Criminal Justice. *AMERICAN BAR ASSOCIATION JOURNAL*, 50, December, pp. 1125–1129.

Yankelovich, Skelly and White, Inc. (1978). The Public Image of Courts: Highlights of a National Survey of the General Public, Judges, Lawyers, and Community Leaders. In T. J. Fetter (Ed.), *STATE COURTS: A BLUEPRINT FOR THE FUTURE.* Williamsburg, VA: National Center for State Courts.

Younger, E. E. (1977). The *Sheppard* Mandate Today: A Trial Judge's Perspective. *NEBRASKA LAW REVIEW,* 56(1), 1–22.

Younger, E. J. (1970). Fair Trial, Free Press and the Man in the Middle. *AMERICAN BAR ASSOCIATION JOURNAL,* 56, February, pp. 127–130.

Zucker, H. G. (1978). The Variable Nature of News Media Influence. In D. Ruben (Ed.), *COMMUNICATION YEARBOOK 2.* New Brunswick, NJ: Transaction Books.

Zukin, C., and Synder, R. (1984). Passive Learning: When the Media Environment Is the Message. *PUBLIC OPINION QUARTERLY,* 48(3), Fall, 629–638.

Author Index

A

Adoni, H., 116, 117, 119, 127, 131, 138
Albert, R., 66, 128
Andreoli, V., 65, 149
Appleson, G., 19, 28, 127
Ares, C.E., 33, 56, 57, 59, 99, 127
Argarwala-Rogers, R., 68, 144
Arons, S., 95, 127
Aronson, E., 64, 137, 139
Ashkins, C.D., 118, 119, 145
Ashman, A., 59, 127
Atkin, R., 67, 138

B

Baker, H., 128
Baker, P., 21, 23, 128
Barnett, N.J., 64, 128
Barron, J., 9, 41, 134
Barrile, L., 118, 128
Bart, L., 119, 148
Bass, M.C., 24, 32, 128
Becker, L.B., 117, 142
Bell, G., 120, 128
Benson, A.P., 128
Berg, K.S., 64, 128
Berger, S.E., 28, 67, 128
Berkson, L.C., 126, 128
Bermant, G., 67, 128, 137
Berreby, D., 113, 128
Berry, C., 117, 128
Berscheid, E., 132
Bevan, W., 66, 128
Blashfield, A.E., 9, 11, 12, 27, 129
Block, I.J., 37, 47, 129
Blumler, J., 116, 138

Boehm, V.R., 64, 129
Bogart, L., 117, 129
Bohannon, W.E., 64, 140
Boone, J., 64, 129
Boone, K., 37, 100, 129
Boster, F.J., 63, 140
Bower, G., 65, 144
Boyd, J.A., 29, 56, 57, 59, 129
Brakel, S.J., 67, 129
Brandeis, L., 99, 149
Braverman, H.H., 28, 129
Brennan, W.J., 35, 58, 59, 129
Brigner, V.M., 38, 129
Brodley, J., 65, 66, 136
Broeder, D.W., 63–65, 67, 129
Broholm, J.R., 9, 38, 129
Brown, D., 118, 130
Browne, K., 117, 129
Bruck, C., 113, 130
Bryant, J., 118, 119, 129, 146
Buchanan, R., 23, 64, 66, 71, 143, 146
Buckalew, J., 116, 130
Bullock, H.A., 64, 130
Bundens, R.W., 91, 140
Burger, W.E., 28, 35, 43, 44, 51, 52, 55, 58, 130
Byrne, D., 64, 140

C

Calder, B.J., 65, 67, 130
Caldwell, C., 65, 146
Cardozo, M., 126, 130
Carter, C.A., 9, 28, 58, 59, 130
Carveth, R.A., 118, 130
Cedarquist, W.B., 58, 130

Chaffee, S., 63, 124, 131, 147
Chandler, N., 22, 53, 54, 59, 61
Chappell, D., 67, 128
Cohen, A., 119, 127, 131
Cohen, J., 59, 124, 131
Comstock, G., 124, 131
Conner, L.L., 66, 131
Cook, F.L., 118, 131
Cooke, L.H., 32, 131
Coombs, S.L., 118, 139
Cooper, C., 110, 111, 131
Craig, R.S., 21, 22, 131
Crockett, G., 67, 128, 137

D
D'Alemberte, T., 37, 38, 59, 131, 145
Damaska, M., 65, 131
Dane, F., 67, 138
Danzig, E., 65–67, 149
Davis, F.J., 67, 118, 131, 138
Davis, N., 24, 25, 131
Day, J.G., 112, 131
DeJong, W., 65, 132
Dennis, E.E., 61, 134
Denniston, L., 126, 132
Dershowitz, A., 95, 132
De Silva, B., 100, 101, 131
Diamond, S., 64, 132
Dion, K., 132
Donohue, G.A., 117, 147
Doob, A.N., 64, 119, 132
Doret, D.M., 67, 132
Doubles, M.R., 36, 37, 47, 112, 132
Douglas, W.O., 28, 132
Douglass, P., 16, 19, 27, 132
Downing, L.L., 67, 148
Driver, T., 28, 132
Drori, G., 119, 131
Dudley, J., 119, 148

E
Ebbesen, E.B., 61, 138
Edlin, S., 32, 37, 146
Edwards, A.L., 64, 132
Edwardson, M., 117, 132
Efran, M., 64, 132

Eimermann, T., 63, 145
Einsiedel, E.F., 118, 132
Eleey, M.F., 118, 134
Elliott, W.R., 119, 145
Epstein, E.J., 116, 133
Erbring, L., 118, 119, 133
Ericson, D., 126, 133
Ernest, H.S., 133
Evans, H.B., 32, 133

F
Fahringer, H.P., 112, 133
Fenner, G.M., 55–58, 133
Fico, F., 118, 137
Field, H.S., 64, 128
Finley, R.C., 43, 133
Fontes, N.E., 67, 140
Fox, M., 22, 133
Frankel, A., 65, 133
Frankel, M., 65, 91, 133
Freedman, E., 28, 134
Fretz, D.R., 37, 47, 112, 134
Friend, R.M., 64, 134
Frost, R., 117, 146
Fuqua, W., 28, 145
Fuoco, R.J., 36, 47, 112, 134
Furnham, A., 117, 135

G
Gantz, W., 116, 134
Garay, R., 32, 134
Geis, G., 11, 12, 13, 134
Gerbner, G., 88, 113, 118, 134
Gietson, G., 117, 135
Gillmor, D., 41, 61, 134
Gilmore, W.H., 9, 67, 134
Gleason, J.M., 64, 134
Goetz, E., 118, 131
Goggin, T.P., 63, 135
Goldenberg, E.N., 118, 119, 133
Goldman, P.S., 2, 9, 27, 135
Goodale, J.C., 58, 135
Goodman, W.R., 9, 33, 57, 59, 144
Goodwin, A.T., 16, 17, 135
Gordon, M., 116, 118, 131, 135
Graber, D.A., 98, 116–119, 135

Grady, D., 64, 135
Graham, F., 135
Graves, D., 16, 135
Greenberg, S.L., 135
Greene, E., 63, 135
Grey, D.L., 126, 135
Grooms, D., 117, 132
Gross, L., 118, 134
Gunter, B., 117, 135
Gurevitch, M., 116, 138

H
Hall, F.H., 14, 135
Hallam, O., 3–6, 8, 9, 27, 135
Hanover, G.M., 63, 135
Hans, V.P., 91, 94, 96, 135, 145
Hanscom, R.J., 9, 32, 95, 135
Harris, V., 64, 134
Hastorf, A.H., 65, 132
Hauptmann, B.R., 2, 126
Hawkins, R.P., 119, 135, 136
Hazard, W.R., 117, 136
Hearst, P., 126
Heath, L., 116, 135
Heeren, J., 96, 136
Heflin, H.T., 136
Hensley, J., 96, 142
Hervey, J.G., 66, 136
Hirsch, P.M., 119, 136
Hirschhorn, J., 21, 29, 37, 47, 62, 88,
    94, 113, 136
Hochberger, R., 58, 114, 136
Hoffman, H.M., 65, 66, 136
Hoiberg, B.C., 64, 136
Holt, R., 67, 138
Hood, J.T., 63, 136
Hoyt, J., 3, 4, 24, 74, 137
Hughes, M., 119, 137
Hughes, R.L., 59, 121, 137
Humphries, G.E., 137
Hunter, J.E., 69, 137

I
Insko, C.A., 65, 67, 130
Ito, J.A., 28, 130
Izzett, R., 64, 137

J
Jackson, G.B., 69, 137
Jackson-Beeck, M., 118, 134
Jacobs, T., 55, 57, 137
Jacobson, L.I., 128
Jacoubovitch, M.D., 67, 128, 137
Jaehnig, W.B., 118, 137
Jeffries-Fox, S., 118, 134
Jennings, J.M., 59, 137
Jensen, T.A., 119, 140
Jess, P.H., 63, 67, 138
Jones, C., 64, 137
Juhnke, R., 67, 138

K
Kalven, H., 63, 64, 66, 138
Kaminski, E.P., 67, 138
Kamp, S., 32, 142
Kaplan, M.F., 64, 138
Katsh, E., 95, 126, 127, 138
Katz, E., 116, 117, 138
Katzman, N., 124, 131
Kemmerick, G.D., 64, 138
Kerr, N.L., 67, 138
Kielbowicz, R.B., 1–4, 7, 9, 27, 62, 138
Kline, G.F., 63, 67, 138
Koblenz, A.D., 53, 59, 98, 141
Knight, R.A., 5, 7, 138
Koley, J.L., 55–58, 133
Konecni, V.J., 61, 138
Kornblum, G.O., 67, 139
Kosky, I., 67, 139
Krasno, M., 28, 139
Kulwin, S.B., 33, 47, 56, 59, 112, 139
Kuriyama, D.N., 33, 55–57, 59, 139

L
Landau, J.C., 41, 139
Landy, D., 64, 139
Larson, R.S., 2, 9, 27, 135
Leff, D., 118, 131
Leginski, W., 64, 137
Levin, I., 144
Levin, P., 65, 67, 128
Lewis, D.A., 139

Lieberman, J.K., 67, 139
Linde, H., 55, 139
Lindquist, C.A., 63, 139
Lindsey, R.P., 35, 56, 58–60, 95, 139
Lintott, R., 36, 47, 112, 147
Loftus, E., 63, 135
Loiseaux, P., 67, 128
Losure, B., 67, 138

M

MacDonald, G.E., 119, 132
MacKuen, M.B., 118, 139
MacNeilly, M.D., 67, 139
Mane, S., 119, 127
Marshall, M., 4, 7, 27, 58, 139
Martin, S., 5, 9, 11, 139
Maxfield, M.E., 116, 145
Mayfield, P., 67, 128
McCall, A.V., 11, 12, 140
McClure, R.D., 117, 118, 140
McCombs, M., 118, 124, 131, 140
McCroskey, J.C., 119, 140
McCrystal, J.L., 67, 140
McCutcheon, J., 119, 148
McGuire, M., 67, 128
McKinley, W., 67, 137
Meek, D., 67, 138
Meeske, M., 23, 71, 143, 146
Merry, G.B., 28, 140
Middleton, M., 19, 140
Miller, A.H., 67, 133
Miller, E.J., 67, 91, 118, 119, 140
Miller, G.R., 63, 138, 140
Mills, C.J., 64, 140
Mitchell, H.E., 64, 140
Moffat, D.W., 66, 140
Molotch, H., 118, 131
Morgan, M., 118, 134
Morris, W.N., 65, 132, 133
Morrow, B., 28, 140
Mounts, M., 23, 140
Mundt, W.R., 28, 140
Murray, T.J., 67, 140, 141

N

Nagel, S., 66, 67, 141
Nemeth, C., 64, 67, 141
Nesson, C.R., 53, 59, 98, 141

Netteburg, K., 78, 79, 141
Neuman, W.R., 116, 117, 141
Newland, C.A., 126, 141
Nimmo, D., 118, 141

O

O'Brien, D.M., 55, 57, 58, 61, 141
O'Brien, T., 126, 141
O'Keefe, G.J., 119, 141
Olien, C.N., 117, 147
Olson, E., 22, 142
Ostrove, N., 64, 145
Owles, D., 19, 29, 142

P

Padawer-Singer, A.M., 63, 64, 67, 142
Parness, P., 116, 117, 138
Patterson, T.E., 117, 118, 140
Paul, D., 32, 142
Pember, D.R., 58, 99, 142
Pequignot, M., 55–57, 59, 124, 142
Perloff, R.M., 117, 142
Phillips, D., 96, 142
Pike, D. F., 59, 142
Pingree, S., 119, 135, 136
Platte, M.K., 3, 96, 142
Portman, S., 57, 59, 142
Power, R.W., 113, 114, 143
Pressman, S., 29, 143
Prosser, W.L., 27, 143
Protess, D., 118, 131
Proudlove, S., 132
Pryor, B., 23, 64, 66, 71, 143, 146
Pyszczynski, T., 138

Q

Quiat, M., 13, 14, 28, 143

R

Ranii, D., 59, 143
Reaves, L., 28, 143
Reed, D., 3, 4, 7, 27, 143
Reed, J.P., 64, 67, 143
Reyes, R., 65, 144
Roberts, D., 131
Roberts, M.L., 9, 33, 57, 59, 124, 144
Rogers, E.M., 68, 144
Rolla, C., 119, 148

Roney, P.H., 42, 144
Rosenbaum, M., 65, 144
Roshier, B., 118, 119, 144
Rubin, A.M., 144
Rush, P.E., 67, 139
Rybolt, W., 117, 146

S
Salomone, K.L., 118, 132
Salvan, S.A., 67, 144
Sanders, K., 118, 141
Sanford, B.W., 45, 144
Sanstad, A., 67, 137
Schichor, D., 86, 136
Schmidt, B.C., 41, 56, 57, 59, 144
Schmidt, F.L., 69, 137
Schneider, F., 118, 132
Settle, M.L., 2, 145
Shaw, D.L., 118, 120, 140, 145
Sheley, J.F., 118, 119, 145
Shobe, B., 28, 145
Sholts, T.E., 22, 23, 71, 145
Sigall, H., 64, 145
Signorielli, N., 118, 134
Simon, R., 63, 145
Sims, T.E., 67, 145
Singer, A.N., 63, 67, 142
Singer, R., 63, 67, 142
Skogan, W.G., 116, 145
Slater, D., 91, 94, 96, 119, 135, 145
Smiley, R., 67, 145
Smith, R.E., 65, 146
Snyder, R., 118, 150
Sobel, L.S., 126, 145
Sosis, R.H., 64, 141, 145
Spain, T.B., 28, 145
Spainolo, J.D., 59, 145
Sperlich, P.W., 61, 145, 146
Stanga, J.E., 56, 57, 59, 146
Stasser, G., 67, 138
Stauffer, J., 117, 146
Stefaniak, G., 146
Stern, C., 32, 146
Stires, L.K., 64, 136
Stone, W., 32, 37, 146
Strawn, D., 23, 66, 71, 143, 146
Sue, S., 65, 146

T
Tajgman, D., 54, 59, 97, 124, 146
Tamborini, R., 119, 146, 148
Tanke, E.D., 61, 147
Tanke, T.J., 61, 147
Tans, M., 63, 147
Tarpley, J., 126, 147
Taylor, K.P., 66, 71, 143, 146
Tello, S., 21, 147
Thibault, J., 65, 149
Thompson, S.G., 59, 147
Thompson, W., 59, 65, 143
Tichenor, P.J., 117, 147
Tongue, T., 36, 47, 112, 147
Townend, D.W., 98, 147
Tyler, T., 118, 131

V
Valenti, A.C., 67, 148
Venters, E., 28, 145
Vial, V., 119, 148
Vidmar, N., 64, 128
Vinson, M., 64, 134
Voboril, M., 22, 62, 148
Vought, C., 138

W
Wakshlag, J., 119, 148
Walker, L., 65, 149
Walster, E., 64, 132
Warren, S., 41, 99, 149
Wartella, E.A., 117, 142
Wasby, S.L., 59, 149
Weaver, D.H., 118, 119, 137, 149
Weingarten, G., 25, 149
Weinstein, J.B., 32, 95, 149
Weisberger, J.R., 149
Weld, H., 65–67, 149
Wesolowski, J.W., 1, 2, 149
Whisenand, J.D., 9, 29, 149
White, F.W., 9–11, 55, 58, 149
Wilson, D.B., 123, 149
Wilson, J., 37, 149
Winick, C., 66, 149
Winter, B., 59, 149
Witt, E., 9, 22, 24, 58, 149
Wright, G., 128

Wright, J.S., 38, 41, 67, 149
Wrightsman, L., 67, 138

Y
Yandell, B., 65, 67, 130
Younger, E.E., 41, 57, 150
Younger, E.J., 42, 150

Z
Zeisel, H., 63, 64, 66, 132, 138
Zillman, D., 119, 146
Zimmerman, D.L., 32, 96, 149
Zucker, H.G., 119, 150
Zukin, C., 118, 150

SUBJECT INDEX

Access to judicial proceedings, 44–46
Adversary process, 65
American Bar Association discussion of
    courtroom cameras, 7–10, 14–17,
    19–20, 22
  Canon 35, 7, 9, 10, 14, 15
  Canon 3A(7), 15, 17, 19, 20, 22
  Committee on Cooperation Between
    Press, Radio and Bar, 9
  Committee on Ethics and Professional
    Responsibility, 19
  Committee on Fair Trial and Free Press,
    16
  Committee on Professional Ethics and
    Grievances, 9
  Committee on Standards for Criminal
    Trials, 19
  lifting of the news camera ban, 19–20
  proposed revisions to Canon 3A(7), 15–
    17
  re-examination of Canon 35, 14–20
  Special Committee on Publicity in Crim-
    inal Trials, 8
  state adoption of new camera rules, 17–
    19
Army-McCarthy hearings, 32
Attitude changes toward camera coverage,
    85–86
Attorney behavior in non-televised trials,
    66
Audience perceptions of criminals, 112
Audience perceptions of justice system,
    52–54
  crime control, 54
  judicial image, 53

Baker Committee report, 8–9
Baker, Judge Paul, 20–21
Bell, Griffin, 120
Benefits of televised trials, 95–98
  crime deterrence, 96–97
  education about judicial process, 95–96
  restoring confidence in the courts, 97–
    98
Belo Broadcasting Corporation v. Clark, 46
Big Dan's rape trial coverage, 100–102,
    109, 111, 114–115
  adverse publicity about defendants, 114–
    115
  disclosure of victim identity, 100–101
  potential impacts on young viewers, 111
  protection of sensitive witnesses, 101–
    102, 109
Bridges v. California, 43
Broadcasting audio-taped evidence, 46
Brown v. Board of Education, 61
Burger, Chief Justice Warren E., 35

Camera access to courtrooms, 46–52
Camera access guidelines, 82–83
Camera impacts on courtroom dignity and
    decorum, 69, 72
Camera impacts on trial participants, 69–
    80
  on attorneys, 77–78
  on court personnel, 79–80
  on defendants and litigants, 78–79
  on judges, 75–77
  on jurors, 72–74
  on witnesses, 74–75
Chandler v. Florida, 17, 21–22, 31, 36,

Chandler v. Florida, cont.
      61–62, 52–54, 97–98, 101, 112,
      115
   interpretations of the decision, 52–54
Cody v. Oklahoma, 47
Conduct of media personnel, 81–82
Contempt of court, 41, 43–44
Cooke, Lawrence H., 97
Cooper, Judge Clarence, 110–111
Courtroom cameras research, *see also* Cam-
      era impacts on trial participants
   discussion, 86–88
   limitations, 88–89
   mitigating factors, 89–90
   new research suggestions, 90–92
Courtroom environment, 36–37
   dignity and decorum, 36
   physical disruption, 36
   psychological dangers, 37
Cowart, Judge Edward, 24
Cox Broadcasting v. Cohn, 34
Craig v. Harney, 43
Crime news, 116
   public interest in, 116
   public recall of, 117

Dangers of televising trials, 48–50, *see also
      Estes v. Texas*
Defendant characteristics, 64–65
Doe v. Sarasota-Bradenton Television, 34
Dorfman v. Meiszner, 43

Early coverage after passage of Canon 35,
      10–14
   Colorado, 12–14
   Oklahoma and Kansas, 10–11
   Waco murder trial, 11–12
Estelle v. Williams, 39
Estes v. Texas, 14, 31, 39, 47–50, 53–54,
      61
   interpretations of the decision, 52–54
Ex Parte Sturm, 2

Fahringer, Herald Price, 113
FCC v. Pacifica Foundation, 111
Federal rules of criminal procedure, Rule
      53, 9

Florida's experience with courtroom cam-
      eras, 20–27
   Arthur McDuffie case, 24–25
   Mark Herman case, 22–24
   Noel Chandler and Robert Granger case,
      21–22
   Post-Newsweek Opinion, 25–27
   Ronny Zamora case, 20–21
   Theodore Bundy case, 24

Gannett v. DePasquale, 44
Globe Newspaper v. Superior Court, 34–36
Goodwin, Judge Alfred T., 17
Graham, John Gilbert, 12–14

Hall, Justice Frank H., 14
Hallam, report of Oscar, 8–9
Hauptmann, trial of Bruno Richard
   confusion in the courtroom, 5–6
   crowds outside the courtroom, 6–7
   newspaper reports, 4–5
Holt v. United States, 38
Hirschhorn, Joel, 21–22, 61

Impacts of still versus video cameras, 84–
      85
*In re Application of National Broadcasting
      Co., Inc.* (Jenrette), 46
*In re Application of National Broadcasting
      Co., Inc.* (Myers), 46
In re Extension of Media Coverage (Rhode
      Island, 1982 and 1984), 121
Irwin v. Dowd, 39

Judicial behavior in non-televised trials, 66
Judicial discretion regarding camera cover-
      age, 82–83
Juror characteristics, 64
Juror impartiality, *see* Publicity and juror
      impartiality
Juror selection, 63
Jury deliberation, 66–67

Kefauver Committee hearings, 32
King v. State, 50

Landmark Communications, Inc. v. Virginia, 43

Learning about crime and the courts, 116–117
  information sources, 116
  news recall and attention, 117
  news viewing motivation, 116
  video footage and news recall, 117

Legal decision-making, 61
  social science approach, 61

Lyles v. State, 47

Media personnel, *see* Conduct of media personnel

Moore, Justice Otto, 12–13

Nebraska Press Association v. Stuart, 43

Negative attitudes toward camera coverage, 83–84

New courtroom cameras research questions, 92–93

Nixon v. Warner communications, 46

Nye v. U.S., 43

Pennekamp v. Florida, 43

People v. Jelke, 34

People v. Munday, 1

Petition of Post-Newsweek Stations, Florida, Inc., 21–22, 25–27, 34, 102, 109

Potential for increased prejudice in televised trials, 117–119

Prejudicial publicity, 38–44, *see also* Reardon Report and Warren Report
  Sheppard mandate, 41–42
  stemming publicity, 43–44
  Supreme Court views, 38–40

Presentation of evidence, 65–66

Press Enterprise Co. v. Superior Court, 45

Presumption of openness, 31–33
  access to meetings, places, institutions, 32
  scrutiny of public officials, 32–33

Prior restraint, 43–44

Privacy considerations, 33–34, 99–100
  defendant claims, 112–114
  humiliation of defendants, 33
  public figure status, 33

  safeguarding public morals, 34
  scrutiny of the courts, 34
  victims of physical and sexual abuse, 34–36, 101–102, 109

Proceedings that attract media coverage, 80–81

Proposed advantages of televised trials, *see* Benefits of televised trials

Public pillory atmosphere in televised trials, 112

Publicity and juror impartiality, 37–44

Qualitative difference test, 90, 109, 122

Reactions to camera coverage, *see* Camera impacts on trial participants *and* Courtroom cameras research

Reardon Report, 40–41

Reynolds v. United States, 38

Richmond Newspapers v. Virginia, 44

Rideau v. Louisiana, 39

Risks involved in televised trials, 99–116
  to defendants, 112–116
  to victims, 99–101
  to viewers, 110–111

Rubin, Ellis, 96

Scopes "monkey" trial, 1–2

Sheppard v. Maxwell, 14, 15, 39, 41, 43

Sholts, Judge Thomas, 22–23

Spies v. Illinois, 38

State v. Clifford, 46–47

State ex rel. Grinnell Communications Corp. v. Love, 50

State ex rel. Miami Valley Broadcasting Corp. v. Kessler, 50

Stroble v. California, 38

Sundberg, Justice Alan, 25–27, 102, 109

Television and audience effects, 117–119
  influence on public opinions, 118–119
  intervening variables, 119
  shaping perceptions of social reality, 117–118

Toledo Newspaper Co. v. United States, 43

Transferral of camera impacts to other trial participants, 86

Trenchard, Judge Thomas, 3–5
Tumey v. Ohio, 38
Turner v. Louisiana, 39

United States v. CBS, 43
United States v. Criden, 46
United States v. Haldeman, 46
United States v. Mitchell, 46

Verbal and non-verbal courtroom commu-
    nication, 62–67
  deliberation stage, 66–67

pretrial stage, 63–64
trial stage, 64–66
Video for court administration, 67
Voir dire examination, 63
Von Bulow, Claus, 113–114

Waller v. Georgia, 34
Warren Report, 40–41
Williams, Wayne, 110–111
Wood v. Georgia, 43

Zamora, Ronny, 20, 96

DATE DUE

261-2500

Printed in USA